Personal Terms

Also by Frederic Raphael from Carcanet

The Necessity of Anti-Semitism

Frederic Raphael

Personal Terms

The 1950s and 1960s

CARCANET

For Beetle,

and our children.

Always.

First published in Great Britain in 2001 by
Carcanet Press Limited
4th Floor, Conavon Court
12–16 Blackfriars Street
Manchester M3 5BQ

A CIP catalogue record for this book
is available from the British Library
ISBN 1 85754 535 4

The publisher acknowledges financial assistance
from the Arts Council of England

Set in Monotype Bembo by XL Publishing Services, Tiverton
Printed and bound in England by SRP Ltd, Exeter

Contents

Introduction

I may have dreamed of opening the bowling for England, but I never intended to be anything other than a writer. During my adolescence, in the 1940s, such an ambition was more unusual, and lonelier, than it is now. Creative Writing courses were unknown; authors rarely made a living. Had I sought his advice, 'Oily' Malaher, the Careers Master at Charterhouse, would have advised that authorship was ill-rewarded, and ill-regarded. Literary O.C.s were renowned for unflattering descriptions of the *domus Carthusiana*. No wonder that I was keen to be of their number.

Robert Graves's *Goodbye to All That*, for instance, was notoriously lacking in the school spirit, yet the classical education he received in Godalming was at the root of his poetry. With a little help from Suetonius, it also enabled him to make his fortune with two pseudo-autobiographies of the emperor Claudius. Graves' idiosyncratically annotated, best-selling register of Greek myths was no less evidence of the benefits of the education to which he could never wholly say goodbye.

Like Graves, I spent my young years doing Latin and Greek proses and verses for a succession of capable, rarely inspiring beaks. A classical education was the assumed course for young scholars. If it was no preparation for anything so banausic as getting a job or even changing a fuse, composing proses and verses in the style of Cicero or Ovid, Demosthenes or Euripides, did at least foster the habit (or intention) of accurate imposture which proved invaluable in becoming a writer. The Old Man of the Sea is the unsaintly but engagingly mutable patron of anyone who aims to impersonate a variety of characters.

The Classical Sixth had only one period of English a week (taken by the Games Master who had to be occupied somehow), but even without it we should have been introduced, at a tangent, to a wide range of English prose and verse. Translating Macaulay, Froude, Ruskin, Matthew Arnold, Herrick, Gray, Junius, Gibbon, Tennyson and many other worthies into their equivalents among the most eloquent of the ancients offered an early, involuntary, experience of de/reconstructing a text. If the study of relativity or nuclear physics might have been more relevant, as they say today, what we did seemed an unquestionably good idea at the time. Especially since, if we came to do it well enough, it would secure us entry to Oxford or, if all else failed, Cambridge.

The Charterhouse library was both well-stocked and warm. Even the corners of the big room remained hot in the rigid winters of the rationed late Forties, thanks to the unusual, two-hearthed central fireplace. Smoke was ducted downwards, through a sort of S-bend, and then piped under the floor before escaping up a chimney at the side of the building. Periodicals were ranged on the flat top of the fireplace. My preferred reading was always Harold Nicolson's *Marginal Comment* in *The Spectator* (its founder, Joseph Addison, was a Carthusian, as if I cared). The ease of Nicolson's delivery, and his lordly diffidence, reminded me of Somerset Maugham. I had no notion that both men might have adopted their man-of-the-worldly stance the better to cloak the homosexuality which both of them practised, but to which neither confessed until after it was no longer a crime. Was I inclined to mimic their acerbic civility in the hope that it might mask the Jewishness which had set me apart from most of my schoolfellows?

Until I was seven years old, I lived in America, where I was born. When he was transferred to the London office of Royal Dutch Shell, my father – who had been born in England – consoled me for our leaving New York by saying, 'At least you can now grow up to be an English gentleman, not an American Jew'. He was not ashamed of being Jewish nor was he disposed (like some other members of his sprawling, eccentric family) to conceal the fact. He saw no more contradiction in being a Jew and an English gentleman than St Paul had when, as a Jew from Tarsus, he announced '*Civis Romanus sum*'. Pre-war America, on the other hand, openly marginalised Jews as well as Negroes. England, my father liked to think, was more civilised. Its then unquestioned conviction of cultural superiority subtended a tolerance only faintly flavoured with condescension.

The assumption of an educated style was a respectable form of assimilation. As Dr Johnson proved, mastery of the Classics offered a regular way for outsiders to establish their claim to preferment. A first in Greats, we were promised, opened many doors. The cult of the ancient world was never the preserve of nobs, though the hierarchy had its share of prigs. The freemasonry of classical scholarship, from which small practical dividend is to be expected, is still generous with time and advice, even to eternal amateurs. A club without premises, its membership is by self-invitation.

Books were my escape from a loneliness with no other available cure. It was a relief to discover that all genius was misunderstood. I was prompt to conclude that the only enviable crown was composed of thorns. Art made a virtue of rejection. You did not need to be in a team to read a book. I got through the whole of *War and Peace* one summer term while walking, head down, between classes. It was not the first adult novel I ever read. During one lonely holiday, I had happened on a sepia-illustrated copy of Somerset Maugham's *Of Human Bondage* in my parents' flat in Putney. The plump image of Miss Wilkinson revealing her stays while in the process of seducing Philip Carey was meant, I suspect, to emphasise her brazen want of charm, but it still excited me. When you were a solitary male of fifteen in 1947, you were glad of what visual stimulus you could find outside the air-brushed nudes to be scanned, furtively, in the monthly *Lilliput*.

Philip Carey's misfortunes were both very readable and – because so unremittingly grim – finally rather comforting. I had the company of a public schoolboy even more ill-favoured than I. Philip's club-foot was an inescapable blight, more difficult to conceal even than Jewishness. Maugham was so pitilessly sympathetic to his hero that I guessed that he had used his own experiences to furnish his story. With a growing sense of liberation, I realised that my own adolescent *angst* could be dignified, and even treasured, by being transformed into fiction. Self-pity might be modulated into irony; pariahdom could foster an accurately disillusioned account of the futility of the human condition. I could hardly wait for further indignities to plume my eligibility for authorship.

In the hungry years that followed, I read many other – and not a few better – modern novelists, but Maugham had abidingly instructive qualities, not least that of nicely turned clarity. I am not alone in owing Willie a debt, though – as Gore Vidal has shown – it is often repaid in mature resentment at ever having had time for anyone so trashy. Such disavowals recall what Maugham once said about Norman Douglas: that the subject which he read at Oxford was 'biting the hand that feeds him'. Maugham's work is like the ladder in Wittgenstein's *Tractatus* which, once used, is cast away. He was not, in truth, a great writer, but he combined urgency with durability, intelligence with professionalism. You are free, as he would say, to take him or leave him, but he did what he set out to do: he did not compile a few precious volumes but a solid, enjoyable *oeuvre*.

In the autumn of 1949, I went into the Charterhouse bookshop, which did not usually carry popular authors, and saw a copy of *A Writer's Notebook* for sale. Maugham's usual Arabic emblem was on the cover. I bought it at once. It was a providentially instructive purchase. I was like a man who knew only that the hands of a watch went round and who discovered one of those models with a transparent back, through which to observe the intricate mechanism and understand the means of its precise rotations. The old magician had consented to reveal at least a part of how he contrived his tricks.

Maugham's text consisted of prudently abbreviated extracts from jottings from as far back at the turn of the century. There was something of his usual cunning in the apparent artlessness with which the Old Party (as Maugham prophylactically called himself) failed to excise a measure of the callowness of his apprentice years. If, for that reason, he appeared more naïve than the chin-up novelist whose portrait had recently been painted by Graham Sutherland, he also managed to seem surprisingly, and engagingly, vulnerable. The knots of imperfection were part of the pattern in his carpet.

Maugham declared that he had never intended to publish what had been assembled only to serve as *aides-mémoire*. His notes were often scribbled when he was on his travels and recorded off-the-cuff impressions which could later be worked up into stories, plays or novels. Tersely interpolated comments indicated where, for example, a few quick paragraphs had later been elaborated into *Rain*, the famous short story about Miss Sadie Thompson and her 'corruption' of an English missionary during a drenched stop-over on a tropical island. Graham Greene once said, with reproachful admiration, that Maugham had done more than anyone else to foster the impression of the man of God as a repressed and joyless humbug. After my enforced experiences in Charterhouse chapel, I could hardly wait to join him.

I immediately bought myself a notebook and, in my first entries, sought to reproduce Maugham's tone of world-weary detachment. Since I was working for the university scholarship which I was to take later that same Quarter (the Charterhouse year was divided, quaintly, into three Quarters rather than terms), I had no time for sustained entries, but I found sporadic opportunities for acid emulation. André Malraux said that people became artists less through looking at life than by looking at art. Mimesis is the source of most apprentice work. Originality comes later. Meanwhile, there was delectable duplicity in detailing the crassness of my fellow-Carthusians without their suspecting that a nascent Old Party had come their way.

The addiction to notebooks has never left me. It was not my intention, any more than Maugham's, ever to publish them. I set myself to depict things as they were, not as they were said to be. If I meant to be unguarded and direct, I should have realised that the adoption of a style, no matter how perspicuous it may seem, affects everything described in it. Even Christopher Isherwood's camera had a very specific lens, and blinked more often than advertised.

Since I have been unable to find my Carthusian notebook (I daresay it is just as well), the present cull begins at the end of my first year at Cambridge in 1951, when I was not yet twenty years old. Nineteen was very young in those days. In the Long Vac, I went to France, and the Mediterranean, for the first time. It was a romantic and enlightening journey with the girl I loved. She figures little in my notebooks, but she is at the heart of my life. For all my programme of disabused vigilance, I saw France not as it was, but as a lover does.

Our Parisian guidebook was Eliot Paul's *A Narrow Street*, a genial memoir of *entre-deux-guerres* Bohemia. The post-war Left Bank had become the home of black-trousered existentialism (a philosophy which, I liked to think, sanctioned unlimited sex), but St Germain-des-Prés was also redolent of the artistic life which I longed to inhabit.

I bought my first *cahier* from the *Librairie* Joseph Gibert, in the Boul' Mich. I have relied on the same source ever since. Spiral-bound, the pages are squared, like enlarged versions of the graph paper we used at school, with forty-two horizontal lines to the page. I always fill them from margin to margin. That very competent professional C.S. Forrester, with whose Captain Hornblower I sailed as a boy, recommended this way of writing to abort any temptation to hurry to the bottom of the page with spaciously laconic dialogue. Notebooks are distinct from journals or diaries. From the beginning, I resolved to avoid what the French call '*états d'ame*', the self-conscious parade of one's feelings. I proposed both to observe *and* to comment, but as far as possible to avoid my own shadow falling into the picture.

Terence Reese, the great bridge player, advised beginners to adopt the *posture* of mature confidence. By sorting and holding one's cards as the masters do, the novice can acquire an attitude conducive to mastery. An initiate who sits confidently is not thereby empowered to make the subtle bids or execute the refined squeezes which mark the expert, but he is already positioned to do so. A young writer can do worse than to adopt something of the same determined intentness. If he can later transcend what he began by aping, so much the better.

I have excised some of the most naïve as well as the more over-written paragraphs. Hindsight has been applied to little of what remains, apart from the correction of some of the howling infelic-ities. If I appear to deliver a portrait of the young novelist as a priggish outsider, there may be some truth in it. It is not, however, the whole truth: during my twenties, when I still sought to make my tone seem maturely caustic, even to myself, I married and became a father. As the years went by, I learnt to love my wife, and my children, and hence life itself, in a way for which Mr Maugham, and my own apprehensions, had hardly prepared me. Since these pages contain neither diaries nor confessions, my family life is depicted only in very brief and, I fear, sometimes petulant vignettes. How blessed we were in those sunny years when I thought that bad reviews were the worst thing that could happen to me.

Part of the pleasure of being a writer is to create a persona which others take to be indistinguishable from the man himself. Equally, of course, it is part of the reader's fun to divine more from his words than the author intended. It may be that, if the dots are joined up, a clearer profile of the artist will emerge than he ever intended. However, what is said here will give a misleading impression unless it is understood that, as I became a professional writer (i.e. managed to live by writing), I grew more likely to resort to my notebooks when stalled in the doldrums than when occupied with demanding, and substantial, work.

I began making notes with apprentice eagerness; I persisted because I was interested to discover what my unguarded self had to say. These pages are not fair copies of fully formed ideas or consid-ered *pensées*. The act of handwriting supplies a style, and exacts revelations, distinct from what comes of using a typewriter or a word processor, but what is written in private is not written in a private language. Neither spontaneity nor sincerity is a method in art. These *cahiers* comprise a form of mediation between me and my selves. The truth emerges; it is not presented. Perception is an act; what men take to be reality is a construct, not a given. One's own 'inner' reality is no exception.

In publishing these and, I hope, subsequent notebooks, I admit to being driven by a certain vanity (without it, how could anyone find the lonely resolve to become, and stay, a writer?), but I have also realised that their pages resemble the report of some private detective – no wonder Graham Greene made use of them so frequently in his fiction! – who has been tracking me all my life, pretending to be me. Their accumulated verbiage amounts to an involuntary dossier on what I have secretly been doing and thinking. They do not always put me in a very admirable light, but there they are and I must stand by them.

The cannibal strain runs through literature: each generation consumes what it admires and becomes whatever it has digested. Ambitious writers pick and choose whatever diet appeals to them. If these pages serve to remind some young person as callow as I was (if such people still exist) that writing is not about markets or advances or prizes or fame or fortune but about a certain kind of personal testimony, the wish to leave honest marks on the page, that will be excuse, and dividend, enough for making private pages public.

F.R.

1951

Ramatuelle. In the early evening we walked along the high road. The village was a turban scarfed around the summit of its hill. Piles of cork, unsleeved from the raw tree-trunks, stacked by the roadside; insects chatter and scrape. Beyond the village, the silver necklace of the sea, polished by the sweep of the Camarat lighthouse.

In the deep night we bathed on the long white beach at Pampelonne. Afterwards we made goose-pimpled love on shingle that stuck and freckled the skin. We walked back through the vineyards, past the farms, heralded at each one by vigilant dogs. There was a villa on the main road blinded with shutters. I called it 'eyeless in Gaza'.

The villagers go into St Tropez in the bus for fresh milk and other food. The village shop sells only eggs (sometimes) and tinned goods. Women collect water at the spouting fountain in thin-throated tin jugs.

The *Auberge de l'Ancre*. The villagers spoke of it reluctantly. An English couple, who had come to Ramatuelle for the day, told us that they went there for supper. Asked what there was to eat, the *patron* chuckled and eventually said, 'Curried chicken, as much as you can eat, *mille cinq cent francs.*' Could they get a drink first? He directed them upstairs to the bar. The room was filled with couches on which couples reclined, smoking what seemed to be reefers. A waiter asked them what they wanted. When they asked what there was, he said, 'The usual.'

The couple fled. In the village café they asked us how we were going to get back to St Trop. We said we weren't; we were staying there. They said, '*Staying here*? What do you find to *do*?' We were in love; there was plenty to do. A Swede whom we used to see on the rocks above the beach at *L'Escalet* called out to us, 'Adam and Eve...Adam and Eve.'

Cambridge. D. opened her handbag and I happened to see that it contained a piece of lavatory paper. I asked her why. 'Oh, to remind me there's more to life than the things of the mind.' Who but a Newnham girl would need, or select, such a reminder?

1952

A child was collecting shells in the shingle-strewn bed of the river. What little water remained jittered between boulders like fat, smooth muffins. The road looped round the river, crossing it where it narrowed. Whitewashed political slogans were scrawled on the concrete of the bridge.

Pisa. A chocolate-and-white palace like a child's bilious biscuit. Flat-faced houses fronted the river. They had the emptiness of lost glories. The front halls smelt of tobacco and old women. Many bridges crossed the river, few with traffic on them. An occasional tram flipped left or right from a bridge and resumed its even course to the station or the *duomo.* A little Russian church, meretricious with pinnacles and statues, crouched down by the river, under the big houses with their blank façades, like milady's pooch, pert and distinct, in some smug bourgeois painting.

Fontainebleau. The tram was olive green, with straw-mat seats. The conductor was an old man with a wispy moustache and a tired square cap. He collected the fares and put them in a leather satchel. We swayed and jolted through the back streets of the town, past recondite mansions, little cafés and general stores. In the early morning, the café owners hose down their tables and chairs and rely on the sun to dry them before the customers arrive. Snails could have overtaken us. It was a place that seemed to be waiting to die. The old conductor and the tram seemed necessary to each other; when one died, so would the other. We had to run to catch the train.

Lyon. We tried to leave our luggage at the station but were warned that it was '*déconseillé*'. The man was unwilling to say why. Later we discovered that a strike was imminent. If we had left our bags, we should have been sentenced to stay in Lyon until the *grève* ended.

The nearest cheap hotel was beside a heavy steel railway bridge. You went through the restaurant to the office. A large dog growled. We were advised that it was trained to bite anyone who stroked it.

The *patron* was scarcely able to write and had protracted difficulty in filling in our *fiches*.

To get to our room, we had to go through a glass door to the adjacent stairs. They were of greeny stone and, in the evening, very dark. There was a lavatory on each half-landing: an enamel covered hole in the floor. When you pulled the chain, the whole floor flooded with dark water. The bedroom contained a double bed, a wardrobe, a single chair, a basin (behind a screen) with one tap. A bare bulb hung from the ceiling. 650 francs.

Heavy, bent old ladies, in black, shapeless dresses, walked the narrow streets on knobbly, distorted feet.

Lucca. The station is outside the fifteenth-century walls. You walk along tram tracks, through a strait gate into the city. A wide drain divides the rich quarter from the poor. The people were suspicious because I wore a beard and looked fierce. They stopped in the street and watched us go by. Once I shaved the beard, they lost interest. The young girls wore crosses round their necks and kept their bodies covered. Old ladies wore black dresses and cloth shoes. During the day, men wore jeans and T-shirts, but in the evening they changed into suits and ties for the ritual *passeggiata*. Radios play popular music all day. The heat is oppressive and dry as earthenware. The woman who owns the *Pensione Ardea* wanders about with her eyes almost closed and clutches a shawl around her shoulders.

Bagni di Lucca. The bridge used to be named after the Virgin Mary, but now they call it '*ponte di diavolo*'. It is arched like an angry, petrified cat. The upward slope is a sunny ladder to paradise; it soars as if never to descend. At the top of the arch, however, it falls in a warp to the left and ends deep in shadow, by the grassy railway line. The bridge is cobbled and steeper than any other bridge. It is solid and unbudging, but you feel oddly insecure until you reach the far side.

At *Viareggio*. The pedlars tramp along the hot beach, in broad straw hats, leaning away from the wide, heavy baskets on which they tote their goods. From where you lie on your rented mattress, they seem up to their knees in sand. '*Bomboloni, gelati, aranciata!*'

The Impressario. George Black is Alfred's brother, and Albert his; their names are indissociable. G. is well-dressed, in a slightly 'off' way. He wears monogrammed shirts and his fleshy face sports a small moustache. The brothers' office contains two wide his-and-his desks; standard lamps with fat cylindrical navy-blue shades. Above the mantlepiece, a large chalk portrait of Sid Field; in the corner, a white mini-piano; on the shelves, reference books with photos of actors and actresses, taken years ago.

G. is courteous, offers cigarettes and seems on good terms with members of the profession whose calls he takes. All he wants is to please the public. He had just been to Paris and caught up with an Apache act. 'As soon as I saw it,' he told us, 'I thought of it.' The dancers asked four hundred pounds a week. Robbery, right? He memorised their routine and is getting a cheaper troupe to perform it. He thought a sketch in which some children end up burning an RSPCC inspector at the stake had a 'splendid twist'.

The Foots' house. The lavatory has an original Henry Moore on the wall and a bookcase to the left of the throne; serious books in it. The lounge is grey-walled, L-shaped; many books, cheap and fancy editions thrown together without class consciousness. A Henry Moore and Renoir, of a small pinkish woman; not very good. Marble fireplace; glass soot-screen; black cat. Crimson curtains in box pelmets; three chairs and a sofa, all upholstered in beige plaid. Squat lamps and flowers in squat pots. The ostentation of wilful modesty. Michael refers to the House of Commons as 'the boys' club'. Before he goes there, he checks in the mirror to be sure that his red, woollen tie is not straight.

1953

Grenoble. The bus crosses a steel suspension bridge and goes up a long street to the central square. The terminus is flanked by tinny cafés. Mountains rise sheer and sharp; a castle on a spur commands the valley. It is a quiet town. In the evenings the populace come down to the cafés by the river. The other guests in the *pension* were all French. The Grenoblois are hard-working artisans; there is no industrial unsightliness. The people are methodical, tidy and not given to ostentation. During the war, so I was told, they killed just one German a night.

Peter Tranchell. Renowned for his naughty, deadpan wit; one of his monologues begins 'It is spring and we are beginning to feel ourselves again.' We went to his house above Castle Hill to be instructed in how to write Footlights lyrics. He took the whole thing very seriously and was surly with anyone who sought to be amusing. It was, he said, wrong to write 'In the nice quadrangle/ The vice squad wrangle' because it was clear that the rhyme was contrived. Better to say 'The vice squad wrangle/In the nice quadrangle': the more improbable phrase should always come first. Sound advice, but for a famously sardonic person he did tackle his task with rare solemnity.

Another Footlights musician was famous for walking along Trinity Street and, if someone inadvertently bumped into him, calling out 'That'll be ten shillings'. One night he picked up a paratrooper. The next morning he walked across First Court to breakfast wearing a red beret.

1954

J.G.W. Davies. He once bowled Don Bradman for a duck. He talks
about 'the boy, the wife' etc... He has no doubts and despises
whoever does. The four 'secretaries' at the Appointments Board do
not much like each other; they are united only in the criteria upon
which they judge about-to-graduate applicants for jobs. They dislike
Jews, ugly people and swots; they admire Blues, club organisers and
Presidents. They noted of one of my acquaintances that he was 'Jewy
and wore Jewy-cut clothes'. Luckily, I don't want a job and chose
never to go near them.

A few years later, Bernard Levin wrote in *The Spectator* that there
was no longer any sign of anti-Semitism in England (as we then
called it). Perhaps he confused his own success, as the pseudony-
mous political columnist Taper, with evidence that Jews were no
longer subject to discrimination or disparagement (he should have
heard what his targets said about him behind his back). Since I
had a sheaf of the Appointments Board's disparaging remarks
about Jews, both undergraduate and potential employers of grad-
uates, I dared to write and tell him he was wrong. One of the
Secretaries had even confessed, as if it were no sort of confession
at all, that he felt 'instinctive' hostility to 'the Chosen Race'.
Levin was promptly on the war path and published the more
contemptible comments in his 'diary'. Lord Rothschild, he told
me, '*s'interesse*'; he was sure that heads would roll. Fairly soon,
however, B.L. (and his lordship) lost interest in the cause, not
least because the revelations were received impenitently by the
Secretaries. Certain assurances were, it was promised, given that
such things would not be said, or at least recorded, again. But no
one resigned. When I mentioned the matter to Bernard several
years later, he had more or less forgotten about it. He told me
that he destroyed all his correspondence at the end of the year
and kept no record of what had been written to him. I asked him
if he was not afraid that he would forget or destroy what might

have proved interesting to posterity. He said that he had small interest in it.

Tony Becher and I went to dinner with Charlie Broad. The professor was sitting, reading, in an armchair on the far side of the enamel stove in the fireplace. His domed forehead shone in evening light that glimmered through the sash windows overlooking Trinity Great Court. Clusters of undergraduates were making their way to Hall. 'Now then, come along, boys,' he said, and showed us where to hang coats.

A serving table stood under the window, a tureen on the lower shelf. The dining table was already laid for supper: two glasses at each place; at the corners, a lamp-like candle-holder fringed with beads; the centrepiece a silver bowl filled with budding anenomes. Broad poured us sherries and sat us in armchairs. We talked of the weather and of travel. He took annual holidays in Sweden, but he was about to go to the US for a lecture tour. He had had to fill in many forms about his politics. One of his destinations was Delaware. Maryland had regarded him with particular suspicion and required him to swear not to subvert the constitution of the state by force. 'I never swore to anything with a clearer conscience,' he said.

The other guest arrived, Simon someone, a fleshy undergraduate whose family evidently included old friends of C.D.B. A gyp came in with a two-handled college tray with high edges. It contained hot dishes and a basin of soup. The gyp put the tray on the floor and unloaded the plates and a silver chafing-dish onto the serving table. Broad thanked him in an amused way, as though it had struck him that it might well have been he who served the food and the gyp, a Pole I think, who gave the orders.

Broad went into the scullery and lit the gas and heated the soup to which he added some grated cheese. 'I think we can begin,' he said, as he decanted the soup into the tureen. 'Raphael, you might cut some bread, would you?' He lit the candles and stood behind his chair. We went to our places and stood by them. Broad had the reputation of being an atheist, but we all seemed to fear that he might say Grace. On the chimneypiece was a framed canvas with a Biblical quotation on it in faded Indian ink. He regarded us (and our thoughts perhaps) with a blue twinkle of amusement and then he said, 'Shall we sit down then?'

He is a small, well-polished man with those china blue eyes and a long thin mouth. He wore a blue suit; small, puffy hands emerged

from white cuffs yoked with heavy gold links. In town, Tony and
I often see him in sports jacket and grey flannels, a fawn scarf around
his throat and a green snap-brimmed trilby. Once he told us that he
was off to buy yoghurt, from which he cultured fresh supplies. It
was, he assured us, the only scientific experiment which still interested him since its results were unpredictable. Under identical
conditions, dissimilar consequences followed: if A, then B, but also
if A, then not-B.

After the thick, meaty soup, chicken with rice and cauliflower;
a Rhenish wine with it. The candles shone gaily, deepening the
shadows in the room. A mahogany bookcase at the far end was filled
with fat works by philosophers from a longwinded age. When Broad
criticised MacTaggart, it took two volumes of some five hundred
pages each one. Now he himself is to be the subject of a volume of
critical essays, to which he is to add the customary responsive
chapter. This tome will be a weighty addition to what he calls 'the
library of moribund philosophers' (the editors prefer the adjective
'living').

Broad said that he had become especially fond of ice cream since
he started wearing false teeth. It used to give him 'tuthache', but
now he could enjoy it without painful consequence. It was followed
by cheese and Madeira. A Victorian silver biscuit dish opened in an
elaborate manner: by lifing two handles at the centre, the lid slid
round and underneath the vessel.

When we returned to our armchairs, cigars were offered. Broad
extinguished the candles and lit the lamp on the table by the fireplace. Tony raised the tactful topic of Comic Verse, on which B. is
said to be expert; he quoted extensively from Lear, Hood and
Belloc. He took us to see a first edition of *Ruthless Rhymes* which
he kept in his bedroom. It was lined with books, mostly philosph-
ical.

Later he told a story about W.S. Gilbert. He was informed by a
young man who had listened to a rigmarole of conceited remi-
nisences that 'self-praise would never get him anywhere'.

'On looking at you, young man,' was Gilbert's reply, 'self-abuse
doesn't appear to have got you very far.' B. reddened as he told the
story, but laughed loudly.

We set about leaving at 10.30, though he seemed happy to have
us stay all night. After the others had made their excuses, he said,
'You don't have to go yet, do you, Raphael?' I did.

Charlie Dunbar Broad's style of philosophy had been outmoded by Russell and Wittgenstein, but the latter had no little respect for his philosophical taxonomy. Although C.D.B. disagreed thoroughly with the former's pacifism, which led Trinity to withdraw his fellowship, he dissented from the action taken against him. He had been one of three most assiduous of the young Russell's students, and the most 'reliable'. Broad's principles were, in some respects, more honourable than his opinions: a puckish appetite for shocking people led him to declare himself, in print, to be an admirer of the racial theories of the late Adolf Hitler, but he never practised the anti-Semitism which he seemed to preach and, to judge by his attitude to me, he either failed to recognise or had no aversion from individual Jews. What he seems most obviously to have shared with the Führer was an admiration for blonde young Aryan men, which was, no doubt, why Sweden was his regular summer destination. He was a witty man whose indexes are unusually amusing. That of *Five Types of Ethical Theory* has an entry which reads, 'England, Church of, The author's respect for.' When he lectured, he repeated everything he said; he repeated everything he said. I have copious notes of his lectures on Berkeley, but although I recall vividly his saying 'I shall list seventeen objections to this theory; I shall now list seventeen objections to this theory', I could not now say what any of them was.

The great actor was in his fifties, but still very good-looking. He took his new knighthood with becoming seriousness and saw himself as one of the pillars of the artistic world. He signed letters to *The Times* about the salvation of ancient houses and, especially, theatres. He championed poetic drama, though he and his wife preferred to appear in more popular work. He liked to be thought of as an intellectual, but he remained childish: his relations with others consisted largely in giving and, preferably, receiving compliments. Though solicitous and courteous, his sentences often started with the first personal pronoun.

His eyes were dark and lustrous. The front rows of matinées were said to be filled with women who booked their seats weeks in advance in the hope that his mobile eye might fall upon them. When other actors had lines to say, his habit was to turn his head slowly in order to give the audience a long opportunity to see him full face.

'Is it…all right?' he asked.

'Oh yes,' she said, smiling, 'it's perfectly all right.'

She had been ready to make love before he arrived. But she had not known that he was coming.

Later: 'Do tell me you love me sometimes.'

'Oh I do, I do. Sometimes.'

D. was away for most of the earlier part of the term. His illness became less real to us than when he was there, hollow-eyed and with his clothes sagging from his thin shoulders. When he came back he took care of himself. We thought it meant he was getting better.

I went to see him in the London Clinic. It did not have the usual smell of a hospital. There was a notice in the hall reminding those who were about to pay their twenty-eight guineas a week that all proceeds went to the improvement of the facilities. It is the smartest place in London to die. D. was on the eighth floor; a cheerful nurse took us up in a deep lift.

D.'s room had double doors, despite being small. All we could see was his head above a bank of flowers. He was in good spirits and often squeezed out that giggling laugh of his. We stayed for a couple of hours. We kept it light, and he seemed very bright. Yet it was hard to avoid the feeling that one was visiting the condemned cell: the prisoner might not look unwell, but he was going to die all the same.

In Cambridge, the comments have been unfeeling. Brickell said, 'Oh'; Bricusse went as far as 'Oh dear!'

A man should make up his mind, the philosopher told them. So they shot him.

David was cheerful today, when I phoned him. He is out of pain and eating good meals. Unlike other of his 'friends', I have seen a good deal of him. Why? I cannot help wondering to what purpose I may one day put my altruism. He is quite alien to me, a grey, emaciated figure in a hospital bed; now ill, now better; now hopeful, now desperate. What good am I to him?

D.'s mother told me that he has 'a great chance' of never being ill again. The relief makes the terror of one's apprehensions seem almost wilful: a cruel dramatisation which allowed one to partici-pate, safely, in a tragedy. When she told me the news I leaned over and squeezed her hand. Yet I do not think she likes me and I am not sure that I like her.

Pat Burke. She took Leslie and me to the French pub. Her complexion is shot with stage make-up, but her keen eyes are set in well-moulded sockets and her jaw is firm, fretted with down. She is a member of the C.P. In her husky voice, she told us, contemptuously, of the tricks of the Binkie Beaumont establishment. The 'queers' form a clique who can decide, as in the case of Sonia Dresdel, to run someone out of show business.

An independent producer took an option on *The River Line*, by Charles Morgan, and asked Pamela Brown and Paul Schofield to star. They took the play to Binkie and he advised them not to touch it. The independent had to relinquish his option. The next day, Binkie acquired it and put Brown and Schofield in the play.

Another impressario leased one of Binkie's theatres for *The Big Knife*. The agreement was that if the takings fell below a certain figure the show would close. By the time Binkie wanted the theatre for one of his own productions, the requisite drop had not taken place. The other impressario began to hear that people couldn't get tickets for *The Big Knife*. When they rang, they were told that nothing was available. The impressario himself called and was told the same thing. Binkie had instructed the box office not to sell any seats. The takings would fall below the cut-off figure and he could repossess the theatre.

The day the Tripos results went up was sodden and dank. I dropped off the bus at the corner of Caius and went through the iron gates of the Senate House. There were few people about; no one I knew. I glanced quickly at the glassed board and saw my result, and Tony's First, and I walked quickly away down Senate House Passage. I carried a brown paper bag of books, which I had to return to various libraries, through Tree Court and out onto the Backs.

The Backs shone with beady rain; the river was pimpled with it. Beyond the Wedding Cake the heavy sky sagged with rain.

Out of the Blue, the Footlights May Week show, went for a week to Oxford before opening at the Phoenix for two weeks (which was extended to three). While we were staying in Oxford I again met W., with whom I had been at Charterhouse. He was engaged to a girl called Louise who, when we met, looked keenly at me. She told me that she had expected me to be 'very rude'. I had apparently been the subject of many Oxford conversations. She seemed disappointed that I behaved less scandalously than she had been led to hope. When W. said that he had something he had to do, she asked me to go for a walk with her.

We went through the great gate of Christ Church, under Tom Tower, and through to the river. Heavy heat lay on the meadows, gauzing them with yellow and blue and white light. In the shade of the trees by the old farm people were lying, in twos and threes, reading or sunbathing. L. took me down to the Cherwell, which flowed between the shady banks from which Zuleika's suicidal fans had pitched themselves into the water. Suddenly she said to me, 'Do you think I'll be a good thing for W.?'

I was astounded, and a little touched. I said, 'I scarcely know either of you. It'd be utterly impertinent of me to answer.'

She shook her head, as if she knew that I had an opinion but was refusing to give it. She told me how jealous W. was; they had broken off their engagement and then resurrected it. She seemed to be trying to tell me that she was a more volatile woman than I imagined. She had been to Cornwall on a holiday and had met some man, already married, and became 'involved'. She was 'rescued' by a flying visit from W. and S., a school friend of his.

S. told me later that someone of 'strong character' would always be able to 'overcome' Louise. It seemed that I too was regarded as a 'strong character' by the 'posse' of Old Carthusians who surrounded W. I felt that I could kiss L. if I wanted to, and that she would not be sorry. Somehow what she was telling me was an invitation to do so. I didn't.

She and W. married and had six children. Louise became a Justice of the Peace and W. a businessman and then a lecturer in the North East. A few years after I met L., they invited themselves to stay with us in our rented cottage in East Bergholt. We were poor; they were presumptuous. Not long afterwards, I wrote a novel called *The Graduate Wife*, elements of which derived from my sour impression of them. They were the only friends (not excluding the dedicatees) to write and congratulate me on it. I imagined that they must have been blind to the *à clef* aspect of the book. Thirty years later, they invited themselves to visit us again, for the day. We had a very amiable time. As they left, they said, 'Now you can write another book about us.'

I once hoped to go to Christ Church, but my candidature for a scholarship 'closed' to Carthusians was embargoed by George Turner, the Charterhouse headmaster in whose gift it was, after I had written to a visiting preacher and called him a Nazi for preaching an anti-Semitic sermon in the chapel. The Provost of Guildford told Turner that he would never have said what he said if he had known there were any Jews in the congregation. Turner said that I should write and apologise for insulting a guest of the school. When I refused, I was not allowed to sit for the Christ Church scholarship, which was awarded to Robin Jordan. After I was awarded an Open Scholarship at St John's, I wrote to Turner saying that I was leaving Charterhouse and had no need of his favours. He did not write to congratulate me, but my last report advised me to abandon my grievances and suspicions and, instead, to launch myself into the great adventure of ideas which constituted the scholar's life. Fat chance.

I incorporated the preacher's sermon into the beginning of *The Glittering Prizes*. If a writer is lucky, and patient, nothing need ever be wasted.

After the show at the Phoenix we went to dinner with Victor Gollancz. He had, I suppose, heard about my Evelyn Waugh and Graham Greene number, in which E.W. says, during a litany of publishers, 'Victor Gollancz?' and G.G. replies, 'No thanks.' Big laugh. V.G. called B. and demanded two front row seats for himself and Ruth. I understood it to be quite an honour that he also asked us to dine. I did not know it was the couple's wedding anniversary.

V.G. has a fine patriarchal air: high-domed forehead, tufted with angry white hair. A cigar smoker, his brownish face seems to have been kippered; the eyes, dark and softly commanding, are half closed under bushy brows. His ears have hair growing from the lobes up towards the orifice. The hirsute impression is broken only by the clear foreshore of his head. He walks with the measured pomposity of an elder statesman, expecting people to know who he is, and to defer. He hands you the menu and forbids you to have certain things: potted shrimps are disgusting, and so are oysters.

Ruth's great virtue must be patience. V.G. is egotistical, self-willed and passionate. He has another satyr-self, whom he calls Moses. He is known to have loud dialogues with Moses (a person-ification, B. told me, of his nose), whose desires he is powerless to resist. He is a generous man; people come on begging missions to

Henrietta Street and seldom leave empty-handed. Yet he stamps his feet in rage and frustration at his secretaries (not B., whom he called 'Sheba', as in the Queen of). Guy Ramsey told me the clerihew: When Victor Gollancz/Gets up to his prancz/Sheila Hodges/ Dodges. But not always, it seems.

He talks about his achievements and acquaintances with *almost* endearing artlessness. He tells Jewish stories with sociable facility. You are tempted not to notice his wife's knowing, and forgiving (I suppose) passivity. She has lived in the shadow of something which, if not greatness, is at least as demanding: its counterfeit.

In the taxi, he asked what kind of job I was planning to get when the show was over. I said that I was going to be a novelist. He advised me very strongly against it.

Jonathan Miller. He received rave reviews for his solo performances in *Out of the Blue*. He seemed to think that his success warranted long public accounts of his medical studies. He could not entirely hide from us the nobility of his decision to refuse the many stage offers made to him. *Vogue* commissioned a page of humour from him and Marghanita Laski spoke well of him. He can be charming and compassionate and, a moment later, unnervingly steely.

Jock Jacobsen. He was in Leslie's dressing room after the show. He had come to see Jonathan Miller, but decided to sign Leslie. Leslie said I was his writing partner, so he wanted to sign me too. He promised us that he came from where the money was. He had been a small-time variety agent, but he and his partner, Norman Payne, had been bought up by MCA, not least because they represented Max Bygraves. He wore a tailored macintosh and a broad-brimmed hat which he kept on indoors. His face is grey-brown. When he removes the hat, his ridged head is carefully covered by what is left of his shiny brown hair. His eyes have the effortful weariness of a con man who can't get anyone to believe him and scarcely believes himself.

We visited his office at 139, Picccadilly. A big little man with a battery of telephones and secretaries, he calls up people of importance just to prove that he knows them. The ensuing conversation does not always confirm that they know him. He undertook to make Leslie and me his 'personal responsibility'. We were not overwhelmed, not least because it emerged that we were the first writers he had ever agreed to 'handle'. When addressing both of us he called us 'fellahs'; individually, he called Leslie 'Leslie' and me 'um-er'.

Had it not been for L.C.B., I should never have had the nerve, or the entrée, to have anything to do with showbiz.

The crooner. He was a young man, nice-looking who served in his father's fruit and vegetable shop. He was unfit for the army and joined a dance band when he was eighteen. He played drums, badly, so they gave him the vocal spot. He was a sensational success. Girls went crazy about him. He took to wearing flash suits and cut his hair in the American style: oiled and brushed back in languid curls. He wore gaudy ties and drove a large car. A record he made, entitled 'My Empty Arms' sold a million copies. Girls took him to be the epitome of virility. His version of 'I Want You' sold even more copies than 'My Empty Arms'. The concert halls rang with the shrieks of his fans. He said in an interview that he owed his success to his sincerity: he couldn't sing a song he didn't mean. One night he went with a fan and had a sexual fiasco. His next record was entitled 'I've Got the Sweetest Little Sister in the World'.

At Crockford's. Julia Locksmith is an elderly habituée of the two shilling room. Her nose has an arrogant, querulous hook, like that of a bird of prey no longer dangerous but still predatory. She is hung with diamonds. Her bracelet is said to be worth twenty thousand pounds. She keeps a handkerchief tied round it so that, should anyone touch it, her attention will be tickled. She carries two gold cigarette lighters which she treats as her children; she talks baby-talk to them.

One of the class players had a duplicate partnership, for several years, with a woman to whom, eventually, he suggested that they both get divorces and marry. She then divorced her husband, but the man decided that he was not going to break up his marriage after all. The lovers continued their affair but the breach of trust destroyed their bridge partnership.

Whores in London. 'Come and talk to me, darling,' you hear them say, again and again. Men walked past and occasionally one went, furtively, into the chemist's which was still open. If the whores are sedulous in soliciting every passing man, they make no effort to be seductive. They never display their breasts. They wear buttoned coats and platform shoes; only sluts wear sweaters.

As evening approaches, they meet in the street and chat for a while before dispersing to their stations. They stand, walk a few steps up and back and stand again. They yawn, without shame, in the face of prospective clients. If they have any expression, it is one of primness. Occasionally a man stops and talks to one of them. However strong his desire may be, it seems to require a good deal of persuasion for him to give a pound or thirty shilling to satisfy it.

Beatrice Lillie. Leslie, Robin and I called on her at 55, Park Lane. The foyer covers have 55 embroidered on them like a royal device. 175 is on the eighth floor. No one was there when we arrived. Eventually a short, frail figure in a dustcoat, huge white-rimmed sunglasses and a tea-cosy for a hat came across the little bridge leading to that wing of the building. Bea said later she rented the apartment only because she loved the little bridge. She was followed by a corpulent young man, with many chins, wearing yards of grey flannel.

There was much business opening the door. The flat is small, but expensive-looking: mirrored tables, glass-framed pictures in 1930s style. On a table a regiment of glass doorstops; a huge bowl of pink roses; a bookcase with a few yards of books in it.

We were there to decide what numbers Leslie should do if he agreed to take part in *An Evening With Beatrice Lillie*, which was to open at the Globe Theatre. We suggested a few ideas which Mr John Phillip (the corpulent young man) deemed 'brilliant'. For the most part, he rehearsed what Reginald Gardner ('Reggie') did in New York. Bea told many stories with total lack of narrative skill; she was embarrassingly unfunny. She smoked Chesterfields incessantly. When Leslie said that he didn't smoke, she said that he couldn't be in the show with her. John Phillip kept telling her that she was a genius; his repetitions had the oracular unctuousness of the speaking clock. Bea was scatty, but friendly and unaffected. Apparently, she never plans what to do on stage; she goes on, and it happens.

She trotted in and out, chattering and blinking and making little clicking noises in the back of her throat, as if in a Japanese play. We had to remind them that what Reggie did was not necessarily what Leslie should, or could. Of course we were right, they said, but there was that orchestra thing Reggie did that Leslie had to be sure and do. As we were leaving, he told Bea that she had given Noel every good idea he had ever had. This she denied. 'Bea darling, you're a genius,' was the last thing we heard J.P. say. That she did not deny.

Leslie Bricusse did appear in *An Evening with Bea Lillie*. He received the most savage notices I ever read. It must have been hell for him to go out every night and perform to theatre-goers impatient for Bea, but he carried the whole thing off with conspicuous courage. His just reward was to meet all the famous people in Bea's orbit. He never looked back.

I had collaborated in writing some of the material which Leslie performed to his unamused audience. I was grateful for the few pounds of weekly royalties to which I was entitled, according to the contract, for the duration of the run. When the show went on the road, the cheques ceased to arrive. When I queried this, I was shown the contract my friend Leslie had drawn up; payment was stipulated only during the *London* run. It was my introduction to small print.

Vernon Paris was a friend of my father's in India. Forty years ago, he had known two sisters and was alarmed at the prospect of seeing them again. My father said, 'It can't be as bad as all that.' 'You don't understand,' V.P. said. 'I was in love with one of them.' 'I don't suppose that'll bother her.' 'Maybe not, but I can't for the life of me remember which one it was.'

In the underground. A young man got on with a Negro. The white was pink and bony, with horn-rimmed glasses. Each of his grey, watery eyes seemed to swim in its own tiny bowl. He wore a grey double-breasted jacket which belonged to a suit and a grey cardigan which recoiled from its buttons like a gentleman from the hands of some inferior. Jacket and cardigan were spotted with black grease, but they were clean compared with the khaki trousers. The turn-ups were turned down in a twist of unravelling threads, the black shoes cracked, with flapping soles. The Negro was a handsome fellow with a purple-brown suit. He talked in a sing-song voice. He said 'In my country' quite often. The white man sat away from him and turned towards him as if he were trying at once to keep away from and to protect him.

I was fortunate enough to be given a Studentship for Creative Writing on leaving Cambridge. It was an annual university award, administered by my college which did not officiously advertise its existence. The previous beneficiary was Thom Gunn. Hugh Sykes-Davies vetted the candidates. I did not know him, but he had a reputation for eccentricity. He had a feud with the St John's

Housekeeper, who had accused him of keeping his curtains drawn so that they faded in sunny weather. He suspected her of spying on him so he would take off all his clothes before suddenly throwing the curtains open. Since he was an unyoung man of mottled complexion and a certain obesity, she might well have been unsettled by the sight of his nakedness.

He was fully dressed, and laconic, when I went to see him. I said I wanted to be a writer. He said, 'Why not?' And that was pretty well it. H.S.-D. had written a novel or two himself. One was called *Rats* and featured a hero who decided that rats were more intelligent and less destructive than human beings and went down a sewer to join them. H.S.-D. was a member of the Apostles. In the 1980s, when Anthony Blunt was exposed as a Russian agent, he was asked what he would do if Blunt came and knocked on his door. The author of *Rats* replied that he would say, 'Hullo, Anthony, come in and have a drink.'

The Harper Wood Studentship gave me three hundred and fifty pounds with which to go on my travels. I went alone, which was painful but, I thought, true not only to the spirit of the clergyman who was giving me the opportunity to avoid paid employment for the next year or so but also to the advice of Somerset Maugham who had himself gone to Spain, alone, at about my age. I planned to go first to the Riviera, then to Spain and Morocco, and thence to Italy and, perhaps, to Greece.

Sir Bernard and Lady Docker were on the plane to Paris with me. They stood in the bar before the flight and drank whisky. He is a tallish man in a grey suit, chin disappearing into his collar, with an air of genial imbecility. Lady D. was wearing a beaver-lamb coat and a little flat fur hat. Her eyes shone with the certainty of someone who knows exactly what she is doing and where she is going. An interviewing journalist was given all the answers she wanted without having to put any of the questions. Lady D. has poise, if not breeding; she might be one of Colette's courtesans. The black dress hangs perfectly. An elderly secretary (her mother?) holds a great hank of silver fox, fine as candy floss, in case the rich shoulders get chilly.

When they went out, first, to the plane the crew greeted them effusively. Sir B. cracked a new smile and raised a hand in acknowledgement. The Dockers (and I) were seated with backs to the engine, so to speak. Food came to them first, and they had a complimentary (?) bottle of champagne. They had seventeen pieces of luggage and were met at Orly by a huge Daimler with an attendant van for the bags. The secretary went in the van, without the silver fox. On the flight, Sir B. mentioned, in his vapid way, that BEA has helicopters now. One of the sycophants said, 'You could have one, Bernard,' rather as if he were selling picture postcards. Sir B. thought them not quite safe enough yet. He and his party did not go through customs with the rest of us.

As I searched for somewhere to stay, the heavy case swung clumsily against my legs until they were bruised and swollen. I took to carrying it on my back like a load of coal. In the metro I felt so lonely and unhappy that my privilege seemed a curse. However far away B. may be, she is on the trip with me.

After a couple of days in Paris, I took the metro to the Porte d'Italie and started to hitchhike. I got several short lifts which took me beyond the *pavé* which, in those days, lasted as far as Melun. A Citroën van, of the grey corrugated variety, picked me up on the N7 and I seemed to be on the way to the South. However, we had not gone far along the tree-lined *route nationale* before my driver tried to overtake a truck as it began, without a signal, to turn left. We were driven off the road, between two trees, and into a field as corrugated as the Citroën. We bumped and lurched across the furrows and stopped. The driver turned to me and said, '*Il faut trouver une autre voiture.*' I tramped back to the roadside and resumed cadging.

My last lift of the day took me to Lyon. I decided to avoid the expensive centre of the city and walked, with my too heavy bag, all the way across the bridges, past the railway station and on out towards the southern suburbs. I went into a small hotel/restaurant with a bright bar. I was tired and lonely. The first thing that I heard, from among the workmen in their blues drinking in the bar, was '*Ce n'était pas une vraie défaite. La France était vendue en Quarante. C'était les Juifs. Ils ont vendu la France. Que voulez-vous? Pour ces gens-là, ce n'est que l'argent qui compte.*'

A day later, I arrived in Juan-les-Pins. In early October it was largely deserted and shuttered. I found a cheap hotel by the railway line (the trains hurtled by, with shuddering loudness, right outside my window) and began to write a novel on an unlined quarto pad. It was based on the note I found I had made about a

crooner. I started to write *Obbligato* more because I told myself
that I had to write something than because I was infatuated with
the showbiz of which it was a naïve, but not entirely false, picture.
My caricature of Jock Jacobsen, called Franco Franks, may have
been grotesque but it prefigured the manipulators and power-
brokers who would come to dominate the business in the second
half of the century.

I had published a few stories in undergraduate magazines and
composed supposedly sophisticated numbers for the Footlights,
but I had not yet written anything which even I could imagine
would appeal to the adult market. I had done only a few pages
of *Obbligato* when I realised that, if I could finish it, it would be
published. It was as if someone had graced me with a competence which more embarrassed than exhilarated me. I had no
illusion that I was writing anything worthwhile, in the literary
sense, still less that I was blessed with remarkable talent. It was
simply that, within a few days, in that room with the trains batting
by the window, I discovered that I could write a book, even
though it contained nothing about my benighted adolescence,
the wickedness of the *bourgeoisie*, my sexual longings or the fate
of the Jews, the things which had primed my determination to
be a writer. *Obbligato* was quite funny, but I laughed at my own
jokes, as I composed them, quite as if they had been delivered to
me by someone else.

While I was staying in the *Hôtel des Voyageurs*, I sent a letter to
Somerset Maugham, whose *Of Human Bondage* had spoken inti-
mately to my lonely fifteen-year-old self and whose notebooks
inspired me to begin my own. Maugham's sardonic style seemed
appropriate to my own (as I thought) disillusioned condition. I told
him that I should very much like to visit him. He replied at once
to my 'undated' letter, in his own hand, inviting me to tea, should
I still be on the Riviera. He warned me, however, that his house
was rather remote. He did not see how I should get there unless
perhaps I had a motorbicycle. It was arranged that I should take
the bus to St Jean Cap Ferrat where someone would meet me.

I sat on a bench in the sunny little *place* where the bus deposited me.
The only other person in the square sat next to me. He was a neat
man who seemed to be waiting for someone. We sat for several
minutes without looking at each other before he said, 'Mr Raphael?'
His name was Alan Searle. He was Mr Maugham's secretary. We

walked to a grey Citroën with a uniformed chauffeur which had been idling in the shadows.

Maugham's famous Moorish talisman was branded in the low white wall of the villa Mauresque. The front hall had austere black and white tiles and an unshowy twist of staircase, with an *art nouveau* balustrade. I was shown into the drawing room, past a great grey Picasso of a dying harlequin and other works I had no time to identify.

Like the narrator in Maugham's *The Voice of the Turtle*, I waited for my first glimpse of a legendary man of letters. In the story, a distinguished man appears, 'every inch a poet', but he turns out to be a retired brush merchant. Maugham's narrator has called at the wrong house. I had not: when a small, surprisingly brisk man in dark grey flannels, with a Paisley scarf at his throat, came striding into the room, Alan Searle said, 'Here is Mr Maugham.'

He shook hands with brisk cordiality. My bold deference was met with uncondescending hospitality. When he sat next to me on the chintzed sofa, I had no sense of being coldly appraised. 'Now,' he said, 'we must see about getting you some tea. Or perhaps he'd prefer a cocktail?'

It was four-thirty. 'Tea, please,' I said.

A white-jacketed manservant brought tea and *petits fours*, badged with preserved cherries. After the stale bread in my *pension* breakfast, they tasted like manna. For some uneasy reason, I asked for my tea with lemon; he took it the same way. He asked me what I was writing. I told him that maybe it seemed a strange thing to be doing on the Riviera, but I had started a novel about someone who lived in Putney. 'Not at all,' he said, 'Old Kipling, whom everyone despises so much these days, was quite right when he said, "What know they of England who only England know?" It's only when you get away from a place that you can describe it. You recall the salient features and all the incidental details f-f-fall away.'

I mentioned that I had written the 'book' of a musical comedy which, it seemed, was about to be put on in London. He said that it had taken him ten years to get anything of his on the stage. When he was last in London, he had seen *The Boy Friend*, Sandy Wilson's skittish pastiche of a 1920s musical. He understood that it was a great success but, he said, 'I didn't enjoy the joke as much as I should. I couldn't share it, you see, because I stopped going to musicals in the nineties of the last century.'

After tea, as he was telling me that I should get a job, so that I might have some experience of 'the rough and tumble' of ordinary life, he started to light a cigarette. The match jumped from between his skinny fingers and fell into the crevice between the cushions of the sofa. He was suddenly an old man, flapping at the fugitive ember in elderly panic. I felt pity and affection for him as he recovered his dignity.

He asked me how old I was. When I said, 'Twenty-three', he said, 'You've got plenty of time, plenty of time. You won't go into the BBC, will you? There was a man called Carn or something of that order who won the Maugham Travel Award some years back. He went into the BBC and nothing has been heard of him since.'

He recalled another writer – was his name Dahl? – a dozen of whose stories he had read recently. The first couple were promising, but only four of the rest were up to standard. 'And that's not enough, you know.'

Not long before, he had called on Max Beerbohm in Rapallo. 'I was shocked at the change in him. He looked a very old man. He must be eighty-nine, of course, but he looked about a hundred and fifty. We were all young together, you know, in those far off days. Do people still read Max?'

I told him that I had read the essays and the parodies; *Zuleika Dobson* was being made into a musical comedy by a Cambridge friend of mine. Maugham nodded without pursuing the matter. Perhaps he was more concerned about whether we read *him*. He feared that the Edwardians (which he pronounced to rhyme with 'guardians') were dying out. Who knew how the fossils were to be filed by the new curators of the literary world?

He was soon to go to London to see his doctor. The ones in the South of France were altogether too casual. 'They advise me to let nature take its course. At my age that's the last thing one wants.' His trip was necessary because he had fallen over while extinguishing a fire in his garden. His ribs were still strapped up, which did not inhibit him from laughing heartily when I confessed that I carried an Old Carthusian tie with me, in case I needed to establish my respectability if I had to call on the help of some British embassy.

I said how much I envied the range of his reading. 'I've had a long life in which to acquire it,' he said. 'But there are still gaps. Books in Swedish and Portuguese must be rejected at once.' His work was interrupted by, on the average, five manuscripts and some four hundred letters a week. They came mainly from young men and old ladies. 'They frequently enclose photographs of themselves, but rarely any stamps.'

It seemed an odd grumble when you were sitting in a room hung with Monets and Pisarros, Manets and Renoirs. We talked about bridge. His appraisal of the top players seemed accurate enough: he particularly liked Kenneth Konstam and rightly declared another famous player 'very rude and unpleasant'.

I told him that I intended to hitchhike from Juan-les-Pins into Spain. When Searle asked how I proposed to get about inside Spain, Maugham said, 'He'll take the omnibus. You'll find the people in Spain wonderfully polite and charming. Alan, we must give him some maps, and that list of *paradors*.'

They had been in Spain recently and 'stayed at the most expensive places we could find. You see, I have some quite large royalties tied up there and I wanted to spend them while I could. At the end of our trip, I asked for the account. They refused to bring it.'

'They said they were so privileged to have Don Guillermo with them,' Alan Searle explained, 'that they couldn't possibly accept any money.'

Maugham asked Searle to be sure to give me a letter to a man who would, he said, 'open all the doors in Madrid'.

After I had been at the villa Mauresque over an hour, and thought it proper to take my leave, Maugham said, 'Would you like to look at the pictures on the way out?'

He led me past an ormolu console, its slab of marble supported on the spread wings of a Napoleonic eagle. I wondered if it was the one which he once invited his brother to admire. The Lord Chancellor looked at it for a moment and then said, 'A bit florid, isn't it?'

He stopped in front of a large canvas of a crouching man, in the sprint-start position. Could I guess who painted it? I swear that the name Toulouse-Lautrec came into my mind. There was something about the modelling of the head which betrayed his hand. For fear of seeming foolish, or a smart alec, I shrugged. 'Toulouse-Lautrec,' my host said. 'Sir Kenneth Clark is the only man ever to have identified it.' I felt faintly like Max Kelada, in Maugham's *Mr Know-All*, who consented – just, and with a palpable effort of will – to swallow his pride and look a fool in order not to compromise the young girl whose pearls he knew to be the valuable gift of an admirer rather than the cheap string which she desperately wanted her husband to believe that it was.

I took the train to, but not into, Spain. The gauge changed, and so did I, at Portbou. The Spanish train had varnished wooden carriages like those in the newsreels I had seen of recruits waving with naïve cheerfulness as they went off to the Civil War, less than twenty years before. Spain was sullen with the '*tranquilidad*' imposed by fascist force. Barcelona swarmed with Franco looka-likes: mean moustaches, pouting chests with trim ties and gold tie-slides. Catalonia was an occupied country, its language proscribed. I imagined, frowningly, how it had been when Orwell paid tribute to it, but what could I do? I took little square Renault taxis to see the Gaudis and I wrote passionate letters to the girl I had left behind. A Cambridge friend had promised that in Barcelona you could get a woman for one and ninepence, but I was too faithful, or too squeamish, to test the market.

After a few days, I took the train to Madrid. Maugham's letter of introduction seemed a piece of great good fortune, but by the time I needed it I had lost both the letter and the crucial man's address. The only doors opened for me in Madrid had to be unlocked by a '*serreno*', the nightwatchman who, in the 1950s, still patrolled the streets. Without one of his keys, no one could hope to get into the big apartment buildings after dark. You gave him a peseta or two for his trouble.

A day later, outside the Prado I met Herbert and Judy Oppenheimer and their three year-old daughter Linda. Herb, a recently graduated architect, had been awarded a Guggenheim. They were driving through Spain looking at buildings. They were about to leave for Toledo and then go on to Andalusia. Would I care to join them? Would I not!

Ubeda. Dining alone in the parador gave us an illusion of propri-etorship. After breakfast, Herb and I were loading the Simca when we met the son of the last private owner of the castle. Its severe Renaissance front and barred windows faced onto a broad, paved courtyard where he had parked his baby Seat; its bonnet was pendu-lous, like a Hapsburg's upper lip.

The property had been sold to the state in 1927. With his round, heavy head, like a polished bean, and a front tooth missing, the dispossessed aristocrat seemed to symbolise the decay of his family. His good English had the rueful cadences of those who have known better days. He asked why the Oppenheimers didn't hire a *muchacha* to look after Linda, who is three. A local nursemaid would work fifteen hours a day, gladly, for between a hundred and fifty and three hundred pesetas (two or three pounds) a month.

At a level crossing on the Ubeda–Linares narrow gauge railway. We had to stop while a train shunted back and forth five or six times, taking a run at a gradient perhaps. A throng assembled around the Simca. They smiled at Linda and offered us cigarettes. The children were often misshapen: skin eruptions, oozing ears, gummy or already damaged eyes. Others were lovely: dark eyes, curling lashes. They stared enviously, but without malice, at the fat American child.

Between Jaén and Cordoba. Women returning from the fields, walking on firm, brown legs with long purposeful strides, like the militant females in left-wing Italian films. Big straw hats and nun-like cowls over their faces.

Cordoba. For breakfast flat cakes of crumbling meal dusted with sugar (*tortas*). It started to rain on the drive to the Mosque. The long side walls, divided into a series of arched stalls, are not impressive. Then you come to the front of the building, on the far side from the river, and there is a great Moorish gateway of tawny stone. Through it, a court of orange trees (*naranjos*) and a black-and-white pebbled path leading to the entrance of the *Mezquita.* Inside, to the left of the gate, a goldfish pond, replenished by a pump. Women take water and carry it away down narrow, cobbled streets to their bleached houses.

Inside, the ceiling and shell of the cathedral are suddenly exalted. The doubled Moorish arches seem not to need their pillars. They leap and support the roof with no effect of effort; like formal foliage, they rise apparently independent of the marble trunks below them. Arches stride away, uncountably, in all directions. The desecrated, roped off Mihrab evoked more awe than any crucifix or statue. (In Toledo we saw an exhibition of Virgins; the only one of merit came from the Congo.)

The cathedral pillars – pink, white, mottled with black, quartz-like and marble – had all been cannibalised, probably from a temple of Janus. In the centre, the highly ornate chapel of the Christian cathedral is a wilfully tactless intrusion. The reticence of the ruptured mosque comments, with stylish sarcasm, on the presumptuous rhetoric of Christianity.

You are always aware of the arrogance of the Church. I never met a polite priest. At Ubeda we were told that 'the Reds' destroyed many religious ornaments; they were woefully unthorough. Of all that I have seen, only one ghastly piece of work achieved its effect: in Toledo cathedral some Baroque artist has plastered the pillars supporting the lantern and frescoed them with figures that thicken into three dimensions. Statues step up through the domed opening and climb into the pink heavens until they seem to stand on the naked air. Concealed light from the lantern gives an impression of lurid infinity. It is perfectly appalling. Who could dream up anything in worse taste? But what showmanship!

The synagogue in the ghetto. I imagined that the ghetto would be grim with sewage, the consummation of Christian vindictiveness: a sordid prison. The streets are picturesquely cobbled. Wrought-iron gateways lead to flowered patios. Gleaming copper hangs from the beams or from painted metalwork; ferns and palms in plump pots; slim metal garden furniture among trellised bougainvillea: purple, scarlet, blue. Terracotta walls back wide marble stairways to the first floor: plants in little boxes, suits of armour in open windows. An old woman, in black shawl and shapeless canvas shoes, stirs a pot of linens. The washing of less opulent tenants hangs, heavy with rain, on lines across the boxed sky.

The streets are sharp and white; the dun cobbles and the black ironwork of the elaborate gas lamps, the pastels of the tiles confirm their neatness and charm.

The synagogue. It is clean and void of memories. Some wall decoration remains, but it is a square, blanched, lifeless room. No black elders; no bewigged women looking down from the balcony where they were once sequestered; no light, no ark in the niche. A garrulous old guardian, with a single tooth, announces 'Monumento nacional. Antigua sinagoga Ebraica'. He tells you where the Torah was kept and how it was wrapped. I nodded, implying that this stuff was more familiar to me than it is. Nothing is left of a great culture but this dusty room and an old man spewing platitudes mixed with spittle. They have killed or expelled us and put decorum in our place. The Jews, we are still told, must learn to behave better. Must they? How many people have we driven from their homes; burned, murdered, crucified? Before the walls of Jerusalem, Titus crucified seven thousand men who had defended their city. Eso no es lo peor; far from it.

The house of Maimonides is a museum of bullfighting. It is built round the usual central courtyard, with an open gallery on the first floor and fine long rooms on different levels (shades of Frank Lloyd Wright).

Manolete was killed by a dying thrust from a bull to which he had already given the *coup de grâce*. As he acknowledged the applause, he took a *cornada* in the groin. He died shortly afterwards.

Ecija. A Baroque town between Cordoba and Sevilla. Main square thronged with men in blue overalls, smoking and talking. Few women. The place was bright and cheerfully overblown: in the *plaza central*, paunchy porches and rambling terraces hang over the restaurants and bars beneath them and squeeze the church into insignificance. We bought a picnic and ate it among thistles at the side of the road. Three youths hung about, hoping for cigarettes and something to eat. We gave them all we could spare, but they didn't leave. I said, 'Better tell them if they're waiting for the car, they're wasting their time.'

What they got was a game of football with Linda's rubber ball. Two of them (in flat pudding-like berets) were quite talented; one of them kicked his shoe off scoring a goal. The third was a clown: when he lashed out with his left foot, he connected with his right; when he tried (pretended?) to head the ball, it struck his knee. The ground was stony and uneven; I fell and split my jeans and barked my shin. The Spaniards were amused. A big diesel truck, towing road-making machinery, puffed slowly up the road. The cabman leaned out and called '*Olé*'.

Sevilla. The Giralda tower. It's said a horseman can ride to the top. The ascent is up a series of brick ramps rising, at right angles to each other, in a shallow gradient.

The shadow of the tower is improbably large across the city. You can see the steeply-tiered seats of the bullring; slim pillars support brick arches and the tiled roof. The bells of a church are protected by green wooden hoops which project, basket-like, beyond the line of the façade. Masses of white houses: roof gardens and strings of washing. To your right, the river with sizeable steamers and moored barges. Trams whine through the tight streets or along the wider boulevards beyond. By the river, dirty children play on heaps of rubble and run onto the unfenced railway. Men in greasy caps and blue overalls lounge against the bridges. Dingy warehouses confront wide cobbled squares; clapboard bars and coffee-stalls with folding wooden seats.

In the cathedral, I tried to get into the sacristy, where all the best paintings are, before the service was over. An outraged priest invested the word '*Hombre*' with evictive force.

We bought bread in Alcala de los Panadores and searched for toma-
toes and fruit. The market was closing; what was not sold was black
with flies. We bought a hand of bananas and picnicked outside the
town. Herb believed the Rosenbergs were innocent. Certainly they
had not deserved the death sentence. Greenglass, the chief witness
against them, had everything to gain by giving evidence the FBI
wanted. As it was, all he said was that he had heard of a man called
Julius who was some kind of a 'leader'; the name Rosenberg was
not mentioned. Klaus Fuchs' middle name was also Julius. Greenglass said that 'Julius' had memorised and passed on information
about the mathematical formulae needed to make an atomic bomb.
Yet Rosenberg had failed every mathematical grade in the state
schools. Einstein and another physicist, Harold Urey, of the U. of
Chicago, pointed out that it was inconceivable that such a man could
remember abstruse information. Trial by newspaper, judicial
partiality, public hysteria and inept defence, combined with presi-
dential pragmatism, led to the executions. The Supreme Court said
that if the defence had been properly conducted, the case could –
at one stage – have been thrown out and, had it not been, they
would have had to allow the appeal. Three Supreme Court justices
dissented from the judgement; all liberals. The Rosenbergs, Herb
said, could never have been convicted, on the evidence, by an
impartial jury. America was on the way to Fascism: you had only
to compare Judge Medina's attitude to the trial of Communists with
his conduct of the Federal anti-Trust case over which he presided
at the same time.

What about Willie McGee? It seemed likely that he was having
an affair, and had had for a long time, with the white woman who
said he had raped her. When people began to talk, the scandal forced
her to accuse him of rape in order that she not be branded a nigger-
lover.

Linda cried and cried. We stopped for coffee and ate cakes which
we had bought in Sevilla. As we left, the waiter smoothed out the
crumpled paper from the *pasteleria* and punched the box back into
shape. Poverty.

'Snide' is US slang for 'sarcastic', as 'fruit' is for queer, 'light' equally;
'rocks in your head' means you are stupid. Herb applied 'snide' to
Russell, a young American whom we met at the Parador San
Francisco in Granada. They had no room and he appeared to advise
that 'the neatest of you' go to the Alhambra Palace and ask them to
suggest a hotel within our means. My English accent abated his arro-

gance. Typical, Herb said later, of an Ivy League snob. Granada was wonderful, Russell assured us, as if we might not have heard. He was planning to be here until at least – I expected him to say the following year – 'Monday'. He writes travel pieces for *Holiday* magazine.

From the Pension America, you have to walk only a few yards down the hill to the Alhambra. In the Court of the Lions: a circle of lions, with water-pipes in their mouths, surrounds the central fountain. In Moorish times, only one lion at a time had an issue of water from his jaws; as the hour changed, so did the source. Under the sultans, the court was filled with exotic plants; now it is appropriately red-gravelled (Alhambra means 'red').

Ceilings like fantasticated candlewax. The Moorish recipe for the plaster contains white of egg, which renders it proof against the weather. When Christians tried to repeat it, in order to efface the original moulding with its texts from the Koran, the added plaster fell off.

The guide said that the sultan used to throw an apple into the pool and the harem all dived in. Whoever got the apple also got the sultan, for a day. One of the sultans went away and, on his return, was told that his wife had been seeing too much of a certain powerful family's chief. For weeks, nothing happened. Then he invited the whole family to dinner. For dessert, he had them all strangled. On the oak beams above the dining table, creamy leopards prowl.

Russell said that I absolutely *had* to go back, see it all by night. The fountains were dead. It was shadowy and cold. I tried to read Shakespeare by what I could cadge of the moonlight. I managed only a couple of shivering sonnets. Nuts to Russell.

One of the Americans at the *pension* was an Air Force doctor in plain clothes (olive-coloured nylon shirt, no tie, fawn seersucker suit) with a heavily pregnant wife and a year-old baby boy. The doctor had volunteered to avoid being drafted. The son of the *padron*, a lame, dark youth with high cheekbones and long sideburns over them, took us in a mixed party – French, American, Spanish – to see, and hear, the gypsies on the Sacro Monte.

The caves have whitewashed entrances and are lit with yellow gas lamps that flare up in the night. The 'Zambra' took place in a large room shaped like a deepish U, lined with wicker-seated chairs;

glaring electric light; worn red tile floor. Bedroom beyond; kitchen to the right; whitewashed walls stippled like the arrested surface of a breeze-chafed pond. The main room was hung with copper dishes and baskets; posed theatrical photos in black wooden frames: gypsies of all ages, including one of the famous Antonio.

We sat down, feeling awkward, looking at the few gypsies already present; two guitarists strummed listlessly. Our lame guide whispered that the dancing would probably be bad. More gypsies came in and sat down; the odd castanet was clicked. You could see an old iron bedstead, chromium-plated, with a red cover, in the bedroom; a tired tiered dress hung on a wardrobe. Bare bulbs shone.

A fat-armed gypsy with an elusive brassière came in and sat down, yellow flowers absurd in her towered hair. Others, older, wrinkled, with rounded noses and thin reddened lips, wore similar yellow flowers; the girls had paper or plastic flowers, broadpetalled, blue, pink, and scarlet. Finally, six elderly gypsies, in washed-out costumes, began to dance. The others clapped; so did some of the tourists. The guide pressed his palms together in ritual hope. The routine might have been the sad opening chorus of 'Why go to Granada?' You felt like a visitor to a brothel: alien, wishing you weren't with people you knew, insufficiently excited to forget your embarrassment. I felt I was doing something brazenly cruel and craved darkness. Painted smiles girded the leather faces as the dancers went through their convolutions to the thin guitars and clumsy clapping. It was like some hopeless audition.

The cave was hot, and airless. A young gypsy girl sat beside me, mouth heavily rouged, and clapped with petulant servility as a solo dancer replaced the sextet. She whirled and nearly fell and clicked her castanets, brows contracted. A few calls of 'Olé' and the hollow, cup-palmed clapping gathered pace. More gypsies arrived and more chairs were brought, and more. A new young girl, fourteen or fifteen, very slim, no bosom, darker than most, luminous black, accusing eyes, pride in her shaken, lustreless hair, thin fingers with crescents of whitened nail, stared unblinkingly over our heads, serving a different god. She snapped her fingers and the clapping resumed. Her technique may have been bad, but she was a born dancer, paltry repertoire hot with wilful resentment. Her heels spurned the tiles as she jumped forward, skirt raised, rapping the rhythm with her heels; claps and cries. Suddenly she would stop; hands writhing in the silence, eyes frowningly on them, eyes dark and love-ready, flicking across the audience now, available for a moment and, then oh no: then private, guarding the flame within.

She bent back over the floor, red mouth, white teeth, face knit yet reposed; beauty. Then she moved her hands again, arms so slowly moving, as she watched and watched them. Up again, shaking her shoulders, eyes narrowed and suspicious; more clapping, sharper, demanding. The cries of the onlookers were in earnest now: clapping in a crescendo, the dancer's hair tumbling over her nose, dark eyes, knit brows, red lips, heel rapping and rapping; head flung back, virgin eyes dark with knowing innocence; then the hair flung forward again: climax, stillness, applause. The god spent, all that was left was a shy girl who nodded to the company and went to sit down.

The weary-bosomed trolls, their sadly gay dresses dragged together by straining hooks and eyes, managed somehow to sustain the humid gaiety. A girl of twelve, with broad flat feet and the wide-apart hazel eyes of a Velásquez princess came in and danced, mouth pursed, brows drawn in concentration, breastless chest arched, hair long and lank and brushed back. A young boy danced with her; almost a dwarf. The angular, haughty postures of his puny body and the slanting contempt of his little eyes left you uncomfortable at how perfectly he mimicked the man he would never be. He beckoned to Linda and the little American girl seemed possessed; she writhed like a Bacchante. Kindled by the clapping, her eyes caught fire, legs twitched, hands straining to clap in a kind of sexual paroxysm.

An old man with a long nose and sad, small eyes in a pale face quavered some flamenco; he was said to be the most inspired of the singers, but his voice was past its best; when the singers are young, their voices are suitable but they lack the wisdom. You can never hear a perfect flamenco singer.

When the girl danced again, briefly, it was more calculated. You wanted to give her your heart, but she wanted only pesetas.

In the Sierra Nevada. Driving out of Granada, you reach ten thousand feet without difficulty. Rough slate plates were strewn like bulky shale, sharp cushions of colourless grass between them. We picnicked (dry sandwiches, raw wine from the *pension*) on a glistening, serrated rock up the road from a slate-roofed, black-shuttered mountain inn. A dog came and yapped at us, petulantly, as if starved of anger. Herb and I threw stones at an upturned slate further down the slope. We showered it with earth but never hit it. Thoroughly chilled, we went to the inn for coffee.

In the lounge, a round deal table on a single central leg; wooden sofa, leather seat. Two men had drawn armchairs into the tall, wide fireplace with a stove set in it. We sat on stools near them and were brought coffee, toast and marmalade. A child's book lay on a chair: the alphabet at the beginning and an idealised word-portrait of *El Caudillo* at the end, preceded by a similar eulogy of José Antonio who was shot by the Reds. Franco's coup had been '*por Dios y España*'.

A tall slim man with dashing white hair came in and warmed himself. A New Zealander who lived in Switzerland, he had come up with a handsome, dark-faced youth from his hotel. He told us that the cold made him feel 'like a feathery willow'. Not for the first time, one imagined. He thought it very 'quaint' of his companion to want to come into the mountains with him.

Tangier. In the casbah, a Moroccan in a faded brown shirt and dirty trousers took me to his favourite coffee place: up a cobbled alley faced with blank walls. The café was cruciform: dark-stained doors open onto three rooms forming the arms of the cross. In the right-hand room, a man was lying unconsciously asleep on a bench against the wall; another sat by him, in a fez and a brown *djellaba* (collar and tie underneath); he held a violin upright on his knee, sawing it without any effort at tunefulness. Black table and a few chairs, bulb in a glass shade, unglassed window onto the alley. In a corner, a boy smoking a long bamboo pipe with a tiny red clay bowl.

The room across from us was spread with thin coconut matting; a low stone bench ran around the walls. Electric light shone on the faces of several Arabs sitting or reclining as they smoked pipes similar to the boy's. On the sawdusty ground in front of the bar, several glasses on their sides. The landlord, elderly in a dirty suit and yellow apron across pyjama-like trousers, brought me a tall glass of black coffee; equally dark tea for my companion who told me that he did not work; he smoked marijuana all day to dispel the blues.

In its dried state it is pale green-blue. You pull away the diamond-shaped leaves and remove the tiny yellow seeds. The stalks and the seeds are too strong to smoke. The leaves are chopped finely, like parsley, and left to dry. The bluish smoke tastes mild and when you have finished your bowlful you blow down the cob and the dottle pops out onto the floor. The boy fills it and you go on smoking. The violinist looked alarmed when I was offered a second pipe; he warned me to be careful, but the other Arab and the boy laughed at him. They smoked all day. The unconscious Arab rolled off the narrow bench and thumped on the floor, without waking.

The boy walked me back to the Hotel Bristol. We made an

appointment to visit the brothels that night, but the marijuana made me sleep so soundly, so dreamlessly, and for so long, that I missed the tour.

On the train to Fes. Two Jews shared my compartment, as well as a heavily built European, in horn-rimmed glasses, reading André Maurois in Spanish. One of the Jews was tall and British, in a brown pebble-dot suit, baggy but quite expensive, and a floppy brown homburg hat. When removed, it revealed a black skull cap. He had a brown beard, pale skin and harsh hair brushed back from a shiny forehead; dark brown, lustrous eyes; nose rounded and fleshy, lips full and soft, the lower one falling open, with a dip in the centre. He sat most of the time open-mouthed; when he spoke it was in a very British accent, though sometimes with middle-European consonants. His hands were like soles: broad and white; colourless nails trimmed and devoid of dirt. His companion was Moroccan/French; olive-faced, smallish eyes, mouth almost blue, nose curved to a dark upper lip; profile almost semi-circular. He wore a skull-cap and scanned a Hebrew book from time to time. The other man quizzed him, like a member of an investigating committee, about the conduct of Zionist affairs in North Africa. He seemed unsatisfied by the replies. His only commendatory remark (not infrequent) was, 'He's a very *clever* boy.' When I asked him if by any chance he knew the Test match score, he seemed quite shocked.

The skull-cap and the European dress, the suit bagging about his wide hips, rumpled, grubby collar, heavy, dusty shoes, were distasteful. I found myself wanting to say, 'All right, you're Jewish; now stop trying to look it'. He seemed to see himself as a kind of Lawrence of Morocco.

They bought a screw of peanuts from a vendor at one of the stations and hunched together, cracking and crunching. They whispered together over each other's shoulders, like French generals at an investiture. I wanted either to dislike them or to be taken into their conversation, now Hebrew (I supposed), now English. I was a child who had failed to be chosen in a pick-up game. 'Clever,' I kept hearing, 'he's a *clever* boy.'

When the brown man opened his big brown suitcase, to get some apples, I saw that everything in it had been compressed into tight cylinders, as if he were toting a range of sausage-rolls.

I quote such notes as these not from any illusion that they present my young self in a pleasant or even youthful light, but because it would be dishonest to hide what a prim prig I could be, and often was. The tone and attitude are worth recording (or confessing) only because few people in their twenties today can have anything in common with the kind of person, and writer, I was trying to be. If emulation is often the better part of originality in young writers, beginners now follow raunchier and braver examples than were available (or appealed) to me. Before the watershed of British confidence at Suez, in 1956, we had neither shame nor doubt when adopting an air of well-spoken condescension. My attitude to the Englishman (if that is what he was) in the compartment was one of wonder at so flagrant a declaration of Jewishness. I should not have denied my own, but neither faith nor conviction disposed me to advertise it. In something of the same spirit, Somerset Maugham – whose homosexuality I had never suspected, and of which I had no sense even when I visited him – concealed his appetites during his entire career as a playwright and novelist. Only when he became indifferent to his audience, and careless of what people thought, did he abate his reticence. Style was wholly at odds with the man in most writers of the time. As Mr Eliot had announced, individuality was not of itself a sign of talent.

When I re-read the careful, tabulating and often pedestrian account of my solitary journey I feel a certain irritation with my young self, and a certain pity for his buttoned apprehensions and want of unguardedness. I do not entirely blame him; I had become what a scholarship boy was expected to be: grammatical, inhibited, and as correct as possible both socially and intellectually. There was no market in heterodoxy; the ruling ethos both prevailed and, in every sense, paid. I was governed by a super-ego compounded of my father's expectations of me (even though I argued fiercely with him) and of what examiners and editors, not to mention Gentiles, found acceptable. If I considered myself a socialist (and had done so ever since the General Election of 1945) it was because I had the naïve idea – which of my ideas was *not* naïve? – that the Left, a church without a metaphysic, would outlaw anti-Semitism and put an end to one-sex schools. My belief in socialism was less revolutionary than a desire to belong to a movement which would, but only incidentally (never from favouritism), deal with injustices too intimidating for me to confront on my own.

The po-faced vigilance of my notebooks was wilfully adopted. I dreamed of being recruited to a literary regiment where rough accents and partisan attitudes were a bar to membership. My attitude to the Jews in the compartment may be read, by some people, as proof of some visceral self-hatred, but no such deep, or perverse, emotion determined my remarks; I was simply thinking, and writing, according to the conventional proprieties of the day. Feelings did not come into it. Only with age have I dared to be increasingly outspoken. I am younger now; I was much older than that then.

In any event, I suspect that writers and artists are often less fuelled by passion and hot emotion than romantic aesthetics would like to argue. Ambition in the arts more often resembles entering an examination than it does plunging into the dark night of the soul. How just is it that the confessions of Anthony Trollope, Arnold Bennett and Willie Maugham that they made it a rule to compose a certain number of words each day did more damage to their reputations than did the Fascism, Stalinism or fellow-travelling of the trimmers, opportunists and noodles who invoked the rights of genius to excuse, and even to ennoble, opinions and actions which would have disgraced a clerk?

We had to change trains at Petitjean. The thickset Moroccan bought me a drink at a wood-framed bar. A yellowing notice said that it was forbidden to serve Moslems with alcohol. Discrimination? No; the legal enforcement of a religious injunction.

As darkness thickened, we passed Berber encampments with fires burning. A lone Arab had pitched his tent under the embankment. As we passed, he came out and shone a torch at us. Why?

The pulsing flame of Petitjean oil refinery came up out of the night, the cat-cracker and other installations lit by bright bulbs strung along steel girders, like a fleet on review. The compound is fenced with wire mesh; the lights flare grey-white as if through the uncooked white of an egg. A lifeless city built by a madman out of some unearthly Meccano set.

When he laughed, his whole face seemed to come away from his teeth, leaving them to grin independently.

I drove from the station in Fes in a two-horse cab, very smelly, driven by a blanket-robed Arab who uttered wheeing cries to encourage the horses. Red lanterns shone on either side of the cab. The single bench seat at the back was covered with a hooped awning of rainproof plastic, red and cracked. The entrance to Hôtel de la Paix was under a portico in a boulevard with a double row of palms down the centre.

My guide was an Arab who had been a sergeant pilot in the RAF. He wore a plum-coloured fez with a tassel and a fawn linen robe. He showed me testimonials from English and American tourists, both signed in full and bearing the legend 'To Whom It May Concern'. The word 'bargain' was used in inverted commas, as if it were untypical of the author to employ such a term, or to pay less than top price.

The old town is surrounded by walls, some dating to the eighth century, others the twelfth. The battlements are as tall as three men, the tops serrated like an improbable saw. Between there and the French town, what was the Sultan's summer palace (he visited it no more than two weeks in the year) and is now a barracks for French native forces.

A bren-carrier lay in the ditch, a politely curious crowd of Berbers and town Arabs around it. A French officer was trying to be offhand about its removal, as if it had been deliberately tipped there to test his ingenuity. A plateau stretched out like a tight skin from the battlements; a Berber camp, a few dark tents, a brown and white dog, women carrying children tucked, like newspapers on a wet day, under their bosoms and hanging there; seated men in a large double circle in white robes like a huge tyre for a gangster's Packard. In the centre was a story-teller. I asked my guide what the stories were; he said traditional tales from the 1,001 nights, embellished – if the raconteur was good – with individual flourishes.

The French supervise the *souks* where workshops and stores are combined in tiny alcoves. Pools of dirty water; reek of urine; beggars in the dust and rich men astride mules with turreted saddles. The *souks* are arranged so that there is a clothiers' quarter and then a potters', then a leatherworkers' and so on. The streets are narrow; sometimes you have to go in single file or even sidle between white walls. The tight doors of the houses are cedar which gives off a faintly scorched odour. The lintels are not more than five feet high. Many have little brass hands for knockers, fingers down, for luck.

Among the brassworkers, one was making trays. He took a disc of brass, like a cymbal, and laid it across a vice and took up a small chisel, like a wedge, as blunt as the wrong side of a knife, and a light hammer. Looking about him as he did so, as one might while holding a skein of wool for another to wind, he tapped the wedge and tooled the surface of the tray with a pattern of leaves which involved an intricate flow of curving lines which could be ruined by one false stroke. He subdued his material with a kind of humble contempt. How did he manage to bite out a circular design with a straight-edged, quarter-inch of straight steel?

The salesmen all told me how lucky I was: it was out of season and they needed money badly. The deposition of Mohammed v by the French, and the riots and repression which have followed it, ruined the tourist trade. My guide did not quite convince me that he was arguing my case when we bargained. He had the habit of leaning up and quickly kissing a seller's forehead to clinch a deal I was still disinclined to make. I bought a silver bracelet but refused thin teapots, coffee pots, coasters, gongs, animals, chandeliers and incense-burners gaudy with green and white and blue and red enamel.

Behind the old Arab market, with blackened cedar arcades, now a police station where a single fat gendarme leaned, in blue shirt-sleeves, over the first floor balcony. Below, on the left, the ironworkers make grilles for windows. Their forges are black as funerals. Squashed against the back wall squats a boy clutching and pumping the double bellows with both hands so that, like alternate lungs, they breathe first one, then the other, on the hidden fire. The tip of its tongue darts, like the pulse of an insatiable passion, quick and thrusting at the bolts of iron pressed up to it by the smith's tongs. When the arm of iron is red, he draws it out and beats on it before its heat can run away. He hammers it into curlicues, flexing it with no more than the hint of effort you apply to bend a sheaf of spaghetti in a pot of boiling water. Behind him, the dark child, feet packed away in a curve of dark toes and pink soles, pumps and pumps as though he were priming his own heart.

After the bridal dresses, with their cinctures of gold twine braided on linen and the grooms' costumes (white belts), we came to the dyers' quarter. Pools of colour lay like fractured rainbows in the roadway. Big vats of natural dye bubble under corrugated iron roofs, cadging their colour from boiling flowers and leaves. Hanks of wool bleed green and yellow, red and orange. Women drown fresh bolts of white in the vats and prod them to stay down, like old memories dumped into oblivion.

Potters live under the walls, dabbing black designs with ink-bruised fingers on raw jugs and waspnest urns. Then there are the

spice sellers, fat sacks slumped in front of them, umber, burnt sienna
and yellow and grey, leaf and powder, stalk and seed, dry as the old
men by the big city gate.

Between the old and the new town – literally middle men – live
the Jews, in their black cowls. Their houses resemble those in
Toledo: open wooden balconies on the first floor; tall windows
below (Arab houses are closed and secret). The Jews are detached,
superior, and vulnerable.

In the mosque, the tomb of one of the great sultans (perhaps
Moulay Idris himself). Beside it, a parade of grandfather clocks, all
showing different times (for prayers). They are presents from nobles
and other sultans for the great leader's obsequies. The floor is
covered with bamboo mats.

When it comes, the sunset blushes quickly, a tissue filter pinking
the distracted clouds. At five-thirty the light is lit on the principal
minaret, puny and commanding. Crowds hurry to prayer in one of
the one hundred and thirty-four mosques in the city, some grand
and elegant, others like the small, dark box near where ironworkers
fill the brazen air with their hammering. Donkey carts with lanterns
bobbing fore and aft clop along; an Arab sits sideways on a donkey
kicking its neck with its heel in rhythm with its agreeable movement. The Muezzins' cries rise as the sun crumbles into ash. The
sky glows hollowly in its wake. Night has fallen.

Meknès. In the New Town there are boulevards and broad side-
walks, cafés such as you find in provincial France. The *colons* behave
as if it *were* France: they sit in cafés, they shake hands with each
other. The buildings are white and sheer and impersonal. A beggar's
chalky eyes are turned upwards, staring blindly above the level of a
man's head. A stream runs, fast, towards the wall of the Medina.
The road curves up into the old town and breaks up into pot-holes
and cracked concrete channels, fenced with white bars resting on
X supports. A hotel, grey, with a broken electric sign, trailing wires:
HOTEL MODERNE, *tous conforts*; door propped open with a stick.
Inside, flies and blackness; radio playing Arab music. An Arab café
adjacent: soiled wooden benches and old card tables. A *tabac*, black
door like a scabbed sore; flies, flies; dung in the road; clothes matted
with sweat. Smell of cloying sourness from dark stores and restaurants. A truck blows thick fumes as it climbs towards the Medina.

The gate is narrow, a high triple Moorish arch. You cannot see
through it. Traffic is faced with a blank wall: an enemy would have
to make an abrupt turn as he entered the town, so does everyone:

hooting and impatience. Inside, a broad rectangular courtyard, domed like a shallow breast, where the native buses leave for Moulay Idries, the sacred town which Europeans must leave by nightfall. Shops built into the walls on two sides, each in a hoop of stone: pottery, cedarwood planks, bolts of brown dates. The shops seem to be shrivelled by the sun, hardly big enough to enter.

The *souks* are dark and smelly; palm branches across the alleys, dried and blackened from the summer. The road is dirt and mud. Mostly vegetables for sale; iron-workers, in wooden shacks like kennels. Bakers thrust long shovels into the ovens, discs of dough on their flat tongues. The ovens glow in the darkness. Women bring their own uncooked loaves to be baked, five francs a time. Bolts of raw dough, covered by a damp cloth, are carried on slabs of wood on their heads. The poor use oatmeal, sprinkled with carraway seeds.

The baker's heavy grey dough turns to gold and brown when cooked. The loaves lie like plump, dimpled coins on the dark shelves. No rich, veiled Arabs on fat mules here. The houses fall away towards the lower wall. Children grub about on the exposed flank of the hillside and piss, fat bellies protruded, in the roadway. The houses are white, rough-plastered, small; washing hangs across the little *patios*. A radio plays in the *tabac*; the rest is silence. Human excreta and furry flies at the single-arched exit from the town. The road drops away towards Rabat on the coast. Donkeys' hoof-prints in the crusted dung where the town ends. A band of rough brown earth surrounds the walls; the grey undulation of fields begins.

La Comédie Humaine. The *librairie* is owned by a Russian émigrée who writes novels and memoirs under the name Jacques Croiset alias Princess Kubowsky (?), which may have been her real name, or not. Her Parisian publishers are Plon. Many paperback novels; a table with various art books and memoirs: Malraux etc. Her own books on a basket-seated armchair; more on the upper shelves and, in leatherbound editions, in a cabinet behind the desk. Skira art books, glossy and virginal. A gallery above the back of the shop with more shelves.

The assistant was a Frenchwoman in a blue windcheater, tweed skirt, stout stockings, thick-soled, flat shoes. Angular face, dark spectacles across a sharp, bony nose; thin, sardonic mouth; no make-up.

The princess was delighted to meet an Englishman. She had me sit down and told me that she had escaped to England in 1941. She had had a wonderful time as a journalist in London. She met Cyril Connolly. A short thick woman, in her black suit she looked like puff pastry in a black pie dish. Fair hair, cut short over her podgy face, thick flat nose, fleshy cheeks, large shapeless mouth, blue eyes, chins depending from a big jaw. She reminisced and laughed (too much) at the same time, as if she were shaking sugar on her memories. Legs and arms like bolsters; skimpy bolsters, but bolsters. She feared she had not been a success in London. Her husband – now in Brussels trying for a job with some international agency – said that she talked too much and was too inquisitive for the British. Maybe; I found her the least inquisitive novelist I could imagine. I was her mirror, not her source. During the two days I hung out with her, she never asked me why I was in Morocco, nor what I had done or planned to do. She did, however, warn me, urgently, against making a joke about a Foreign Legionnaire's képi. He would be dangerously offended by any such jest. It was not the most useful advice I could think of.

She had bought the shop four years earlier, for four million francs (her life's savings, after losing all her money in occupied France) and now she was broke. No one wanted to invest here. The trouble in Morocco had cut tourism to almost nothing. That was why her husband, a Pole, was in Brussels.

She was affable, but I was not at ease. She thought there was no such thing as justice; there might be divine justice, but human never. She seemed to think that because the Germans were beasts they could not be blamed for the concentration camps. She told me about a Russian woman, a writer, not Jewish, who was in one of the camps. A girl of fifteen was included in a list of those who were to die. When she began to cry, the woman said, 'Don't take it so hard. Death is not such a terrible thing.' The girl was unconsoled. 'If it will help you,' the woman said, 'I'll come with you.' The girl nodded; the woman took her hand and they went into the gas chamber together.

I have no idea where Jacques Croiset heard this story, or how. In the sense that I hope that it is not a fabrication, I should like to believe that it is true. It seems now to have acquired a legendary 'truth' which might dispose a sceptic to wonder about it. However, I was told it at a time – only a decade since the *Shoah* – when such events were little discussed. Five years still had to pass before Raul Hilberg's *The Extermination of the European Jews* tabulated the truth and obliged the world to pay attention to what had happened. I should be glad to hear more precise details: who the Russian woman was, and what exactly happened, where, when; and how we know of it.

Jacques Croiset told me that she won the *Prix de Paris*, whatever that might be, for her 1949 novel *Europe et Valérius*. In the evening she took me for dinner at the house of a Moroccan prince, Moulay Ta'ib. A friend of his escorted us from the Medina gate, a slim Arab with an inch-long beard along and under his jaw, like the strap on a guardsman's busby. Conjunctivitis puffed his eyelids and pinked his eyes. The low cedarwood door to the house was in an unlit side street. The hall was angled sharply to the left, like the city gate. Pairs of shoes on the floor as we turned again into the large central room. It was bare of furniture; a basin of washing by the wide fireplace; an open doorway to the kitchen and the women's quarters. High beamed ceiling continuous with that in the small, oblong room into which we were led, a linen curtain in the square archway. Bare whitewashed walls. In the smaller room, a radio on an inlaid table, a cheap clock and a mirror on the wall above them; legless couches, the lowest not more than eighteen inches high, on which we were put. The couches are hard-soft, covered with floral, blue-green linen, very inviting, with plump pink cushions. Shoulder-high blue tiles around the walls. A brass table on short wooden legs adjacent to the couches so that you could sit round and eat; a small, taller table with an ash-tray.

Our guide wore European dress and shoes, as did Moulay Ta'ib, who joined us only when we were seated on our cushions on the dining room floor. Being a relative and supporter of the Sultan deposed by the French, Moulay Ta'ib and his friend, who had sworn not to cut his beard until Mohammed v was reinstated, were in financial difficulties. The princess had helped him to get some official position in the executive. Moulay Ta'ib was short and dapper: dark leathery face, the colour of roast turkey, fine-featured with dark, amused eyes; neat brown hands. His hair was almost cropped above a sharp, shining forehead.

He curled his small feet, in grey socks, under him as he sat between us on the highest couch. Arab women never dine with men; you are unlikely even to see, let alone be introduced to, an Arab's wife. Moulay Ta'ib's nephew, a thin boy of twelve or thirteen, with a wide face and humorous black eyes, waited on us in a grey suit and dark tie.

First, he brought a silver basin and a kettle from which warm water was poured over our hands and towelled away. Our guide cut flat loaves into six. Pieces of lamb came on long spits, on which they had just been grilled over a wood fire. You tore out the centre of your bread, gloved the meat and drew it off the spit. Only the right hand should be used; the left must never hold food. As soon as a spit was empty, another came. I ate freely, thinking that this was all we would get, but when we arrived at the end of the new spits for old, in came a huge bowl with lumps of meat and spiced cabbage leaves swimming in gravy. You heaped a mixture on your bread and popped it into your mouth. It was bad manners to have your fingers touch your lips. I had to drop a piece into my lap and hurried to put it in my mouth, with my left hand. Nobody struck a gong, but I was as ashamed as if they had.

Moulay Ta'ib and his friend ate with clean dexterity. We talked easily, uninterrupted by the clash of plates and cutlery. After the big bowl was removed, another came, heaped with grapes. Then the basin and the warm water, now with a piece of soap, to get rid of the grease. We reclined on the pink cushions and smoked cigarettes. Tea was next; only the master of the house and his closest friends could make it. It was an honour and an art to blend the various kinds of mint. They came in gilt coffers, with a gilt teapot of chased metal and sugar crystals like hunks of salt. The mint is put in the pot, with lumps of sugar, and water poured from a large, thin-necked kettle. The mixture was left to stand, then tasted. More of one or another kind of leaf is added to perfect the brew. Then it is passed to the visitors to fill their glasses. Many glasses were drunk; fresh mint being added before more boiling water is poured over it.

Moulay Ta'ib had read Spinoza, Descartes and Plato. Philosophy interested him greatly. He was well-read but naïve. He thought the French should stay as the administrative servants of the Sultan (Mohammed v, of course) who would have supreme and total jurisdiction. At times he said that he hoped that the French would kill them all, because salvation lay in dying for his country. We talked till 1.15.

Notebooks rarely tell the whole story. I make no mention of leaving the house. Moulay Ta'ib's friend must have taken Jacques Croiset home in another direction. I had to find the way to my hotel, in the European quarter, alone. There was a curfew and no one in the streets. I was stopped by a suspicious and (at first) unfriendly French foreign legion patrol. I refrained from any jokes about their képis. They inspected my passport with no immediate signs of deference. I felt at once alarmed and aloof. What did Morocco and its problems have to do with me? I flirted with danger without truly believing myself at risk. I could imagine being thrown into jail, but I never thought it would happen. Nor did it. The patrol escorted me back to my hotel. I marched along with them, invisible swagger stick under my arm, quite as if they had recognised me as having been an ex-Under Officer in the Charterhouse JTC.

I had to wait almost an hour for the Tangier train. When it came in, I was in a hurry to get a seat ahead of the crowd of Arabs. We were an hour out of the station before I realised that I left my blue sack, with all the presents I had bought, shaving things, sweater, etc. on the marble seat on the Meknès platform. A woman said, '*Je l'ai vu là, un sac bleu, n'est-ce pas?, sur le banc et je me suis dit...*' I smiled and shrugged. I could've killed her.

The ticket collector called the station, asking for a taxi to bring my sack to Petitjean, where we had a forty-five minute halt. At Petitjean, he called again. '*Le sac toujours à la gare? Je comprends.*' To me, '*Votre sac est toujours à la gare de Meknès, monsieur. Le taxi va partir tout de suite. Taxi trente-neuf.*' However soon that was. I decided to wait for the taxi and hope to catch the train up at the border of Spanish Morocco. The taxi was not authorised to cross it.

It was 4.30. The taxi would take an hour to arrive. The station yard was rough, bare and muddy; the Hôtel Terminus and its dusty garden to the right. Facing me, the refinery, less sinister than baffling in the daylight: tubes and cannisters, dials and gauges, towers scaled by ladders and topped with curling pipes, platforms with heron-necked lamps. Sentries with rifles in boxes along the road; guards on the gate. The service road was flat and deserted. A sentry forbade me to walk along it.

No sign of the taxi. Mad with frustration, I beat my fists on a concrete bench by the roadside. How could I have been so foolish? Trucks came and wheeled into the refinery. Why had I gone and booked passage on the USS *Constitution*, sailing from Gib. in two days' time? Had I not, I could have returned calmly to Meknès and taken the next train. I thanked God that B. was not there to see me fuming, but I wished she were.

I remembered how serenely I had observed the Berbers outside the refinery as I sat smugly in the train on my way to Meknès. Their camps are surrounded with a plaited grass fence about five feet high. The shanties are pitched on a slope for the sake of drainage and built from corrugated iron, bent tins, broken packing cases, sticks and mud. Some are thatched, others roofed with tin sheets or sacking, their intersections held down on wooden frames by bricks, branches and wash-tubs. Children roll in the dust; dogs and fowls wander in and out of the doorways.

Now I was mortified by my ineptitude. I sat in front of the infernal refinery. An incessant flame flew its hot, ragged banner in the darkening sky, black at the edges like charred paper when a flame surges back greedily for what it has already seared.

5.45. There was no chance of catching up with the train. Yet I could not resign myself. I felt a fool, and I was. Even alone I could not take a joke of my own devising. I had so hoped to be able to go on as if nothing had happened. I cursed and cursed and then I walked to the crossroads where taxi 39 had to come, if it came. I peered down the highway from the island in the middle. Cars rounded the island and drove on up towards the frontier. The sky reddened. The sign on the Shell station was turned on. 6.00 p.m.; darkness. Arabs and Europeans left the refinery on bicycles, laughing together. An old Morris came, slower than walking pace. For a moment I thought that it was just my luck that this should be my taxi. My luck was not that good. The Morris contained about five hundred and forty Arabs and plodded like a metal donkey.

The highway pulled away from me like a tight belt spooled around the island on which I stood. Cars blinded me with their lights; I couldn't see what they were until they came up to me. Suppose taxi 39 went to the station by another way and failed to find me. I watched cars coming from that direction as well, smiled at their drivers as they swooped by. One skidded suddenly, curving gravel into weals. He had not seen a group of cyclists. No one was hurt. He accelerated away. I hung about and hung about and then I was running and running, back to the station yard under the long flame. No one could tell me anything. I flung myself on on a concrete pier by the refinery gate and cursed and cursed. I wanted to cry. An Arab woman with a baby (and more troubles than mine) watched me curiously as she passed, burdened, on her way.

At 6.30, taxi 39 arrived. He had the sack in the *coffre*, he said. I made him open the boot and show me. I took the damned sack out of the car and held it. They said in the station that there was a bus from Arbaona, at the frontier, at 8.00. I demanded that my taxi-driver take me to it. It would cost 8,000 francs. I sat by him in the big Ford and we drove through the night, the sack on my knee. The driver asked me what was in it that was worth his coming all this way. It occurred to me that he might think it was worth dumping me in the desert and making off with the treasure.

'*Que des cadeaux,*' I said, '*pour mes parents et ma fiancée. Rien de grande valeur. Des choses personnelles.*'

We drove into a small village and down a side road and stopped outside a dark hut.

'*Attendez, j'ai de quoi faire.*' He got out of the car and whistled in the darkness. A light shone in a doorway. He went in. What could I do? If they were going to rob me, then they were. It was, after all, the Reverend Harper Wood's money with which I had bought the bracelets and slippers and other baubles. Put it down to experience. As long as they didn't mean to kill me.

The driver and two men came out and went to the back of the taxi. The boot was opened and the men took some boxes out. The driver came back to my window, '*Excusez-moi, monsieur, ils sont mes cousins. J'avais de quoi leur livrer. Ne vous inquiétez pas.*'

Inquiet? Moi? We drove on after I had refused tea. The headlights picked out plodding native carts with red lanterns on the way into Arbaona. I sat and glowered. I knew there wouldn't be a bus; and there wasn't.

We went to the *Douanes*; it looked like an underground station, full of strip lights and policemen. A dignified old Arab was persuaded to give me a lift into Tangier in his huge, chauffeur-driven car. '*Vous avez de la chance, monsieur,*' said my driver.

'*Vous croyez?*'

When I asked for a lavatory, the policemen said they did not have one. I felt the old man take my sleeve. He led me outside and pointed to the gutter. When I had finished, he led me to his limousine and, when the chauffeur opened the door, indicated I should precede him. I hesitated. '*Subito!*' he said.

The radio played as the great car's headlights split the purple night and the old man hummed and burbled in his throat, shrivelled away in the far corner of the back seat. He was clearly rich and important. There were salutes as we passed. The car must have been sixty horse-power; it was built like a battleship. The old man wore a turban with a little yellow soft hat, like a rabbi's, secured in its folds. He was commanding, but kind. On his orders, the chauffeur stopped to pick up a couple of women and their bundles. They called him '*effendi*'. When we arrived at the Tangier frontier, he had his chauffeur take care of all the passport formalities.

On the ferry to Gib. Half a dozen cars, few passengers; a lounge with metal tables and chairs with red leather seats. I talked all the way with Mr True, a furniture salesman – 'Only the best!' – from Hampton's of Knightsbridge. He was broad, round-shouldered, medium height; small light eyes; trim, sensual lips that yielded a dark yellow, gold-capped smile. He wore an unbelted macintosh and a floppy brown hat, brim turned down all round as if he expected at any moment to go angling. Plenty of initials on his briefcase. He had been on a six-week tour of North Africa: Addis, Aden, Oran, Tunis and Cairo. 'I'd like to have gone to the Varsity,' he said, 'not to study, you understand, but to play games and all that. I'm a rugger man actually. My school switched in '26, just as I arrived. Know why? No? Well, you have to have ball sense to play soccer. Ball sense, either you have it or you don't. But rugger! You can take a boy without an ounce of ball sense, bung him in the scrum, all he has to do is stick with the ball. You know: kick it and run in a forward scramble. Chances are a keen boy'll be quite useful at rugger where he'd have been hopeless at soccer. That's why they switched.' He clearly thought he had been robbed.

'I'm a Surrey man myself,' he said. 'But that's not why I'd like to see Lock in Australia. Wardle, he's a defensive bowler, but Lock! There's a matchwinner for you. I know Bill Edrich. Met him in business. Reckon he lost ten thousand pounds by turning amateur. Only did it because he thought he'd get captain of England. Yes, I reckon he'd've had as good a benefit as Compton if he hadn't jumped the gun. Reckon he doesn't make above ten thousand a year in his job. I would've coughed up: can't help liking old Edrich.'

'He drinks, doesn't he?' I said.

'Not only drinks, old boy. That's why they didn't dare take him on the tours. Every time they did, his wife divorced him afterwards. Some people have all the luck. Only joking. I like to combine business with pleasure myself. These Arabs, you know, they're incredible. Reckon they're impotent if they can't function sexually about five times a day. In Addis I saw this local doctor giving these natives a shot in the behind. Smack!' He crashed his fist into his palm. '"Drop your pants," this doctor'd say, and then, smack! In went the needle and off they went.'

'What did he give them?'

'Oh it's quite harmless. Vitamin B, something like that.'

'What's wrong with them then?'

'Wrong? Nothing! They can only come twice a day so they think they're impotent. One of our chaps was out in Saudi Arabia for three months, without the wife, you know, planning the furniture for one of the big nob's palaces. They think nothing of spending four hundred thousand pounds on a single palace. They kept putting things off but he stayed and stayed. The Arabs were amazed at him.'

'His persistence?'

'No, no, no. They couldn't understand how anyone could go more than three days without his wife. I think they kept him hanging about to see how long he *could* go. You know, if I had my life over again, I think I'd like to go up to the Varsity and then become a journalist. You know, I often think of things I'd like to write up. Never do. I suppose you need to be born with the gift.'

'Not at all,' I said. 'Only sub-editors have to be born with the gift.'

'Really? Anyway, that's what I'd like to do if I had my life again. Sports journalist. What a life! I'm keen on sport, you know, and I think I could make a sporting journalist, get on with people and so on.'

At Gib. he gave me his card and said that if my ship was delayed I should come and look for him at The Rock. He could lend me some cash if I was short of pounds.

A few years later, I put the furniture salesman in a story in which he left his luggage at a station in the middle of Morocco and felt the same fury and the same apprehensions about the taxi-driver as I had. I cranked up the tension (and had him mix some local pleasure with his business) but I didn't change a lot. The story was published in *Town*, a smart magazine which is unlikely to have been Mr True's kind of reading. If he had seen it, he might fairly have claimed to have been maligned. He would probably have faced the situation with greater resource, and certainly with better humour, than I did.

Gibraltar. A policeman in British p.c.'s uniform on the quay. Gib. is like a great tooth in the wide jaw of the bay. The slopes are so steep that there are no buildings on them; bushes in the cracks of the slate. Pipes run down (from reservoirs?) to the town ribboned along the water. You go through a tunnel in the old fortifications and there is a big barracks; married quarters opposite. Guardhouse with a gleaming regimental emblem hanging on a tripod in front. No admittance except on official business. NAAFI across the gritty, rust-coloured parade ground.

The streets are narrow and crowded: Spaniards, army wives, sailors, soldiers and off-duty officers in flat caps and three-quarter length overcoats or macs, cavalry twill trousers. They appear advisedly inane: no military secret could possibly be divined from the monumental expressionlessness of their faces. The shops are crammed with English goods (Player's at 1/5d for twenty). I bought *The Observer* and *The Sunday Times* in a dark brown teashop full of army wives and squawling children. *An Evening with Beatrice Lillie* had opened that week. Ken Tynan's review called Leslie Bricusse 'a flaccid comedian from Cambridge... ruthlessly cut he might escape obloquy.' Unnecessarily harsh, I thought. It was splendid to have a cup of English tea again.

In the evening, on the way to board the *Constitution*, I saw the officer of the guard, a lieutenant in blues, with a peaked cap piped in red, inspecting the guard, assisted by a tubby 2nd lieutenant in the same rig. A beefy sergeant was in charge of the protracted proceedings. The lieutenant's shiny face wore a grimace of exulting arrogance. His sidekick had difficulty keeping step. He always halted a good half second after his superior, like a badly attached shadow. Spaniards in berets and overalls walked past on their way home across the frontier, shaking their heads.

The ferry had a small saloon with bilious green benches. Not many passengers were going to the ship, but a number of Gibraltarian residents were going to see them off. One of them, in check suit and flat cap, wished me *bon voyage* as if he were my C.O.

The gangplank had a roller on the deck of the ferry. With the motion of the boat it moved back and forth across the planks like a drunk on roller skates. In the darkness, lights shone through the portholes and windows of the bulging ship as if cut in a fat pumpkin at Hallowe'en.

I had to share a cabin with an Italian. There was a shower and three kinds of water: hot, cold, ice. The lavatory flushed with the plunging zeal of a porcelain Niagara. Closets with plastic hangers; dressers with tight drawers; many light switches: touch the wall and it's show time.

In the saloon, there are grey chairs with yellow tables and yellow chairs with grey tables. Choices. The Vulcan Bar has lurid volcanoes on the walls. Italian immigrants re-emigrating sit about as if on a ferry. Many have the decrepit air of impotent elephants going home to die.

I played my cabin-mate at pingpong and beat him easily. Later I was beaten 21–19 by a young American who crept up and hit you on the shoulder in a friendly way unless you were very careful. I eat a lot, but without appetite; I have paid for my board. This morning I had griddle cakes and a lot of maple syrup. My cabin-mate has sad eyes, thin sideburns and greying hair. He shakes his head at meals and pushes the dishes away as if they were just what he had expected. The steward's attitude is, 'If you don't like things you can go some-place else.'

'But I can't.'

'In fifteen years there's been no complaint and then you had to come along. I don't need this. I have a lovely girl waiting for me Stateside etc.'

5.12.54. Dad's birthday. Soon he will retire; his life's work is over. He has seen his son through university and he has completed a great number of years with a Big Company. His service promises him security, but in many ways he considers himself a failure: he has not achieved a high position nor has he acquired wealth. He has been dogged by misfortune, especially bad health. He has been in pain and he has been humiliated sexually by its nature and source. It must be galling to listen to J.'s allusions to his prowess, to R.'s particular desires and his adept satisfaction of them. J. is compensating the shame of his first wife's infidelities, but stories of his coital jamborees cannot be what C. wants to hear.

My mother once told me that Dad had an illegitimate child. It was on board ship coming back from the US in 1948. She said that he had been ensnared by what she called 'an older woman'. It was when he came down from Oxford and had taken up dancing. I remember what I was told through a distorting swirl of emotion. I think my grandfather paid the woman a large sum of money to go away. Had my father agreed to this, or desired it? I fancy I was told that he had wanted to marry the woman. This came out not because my mother wanted to condemn C. but to draw attention to her own secret griefs. Displeased by my too obvious regret at leaving Mary Jane in New York, she required me to direct my sympathy at her. I did not feel any disgust at my father's ancient behaviour (he was a young man, after all), but a certain antipathy to my mother. I can hardly bear to kiss her goodnight. I take no comfort in her arms; not for me the sinking of the filial head on the maternal bosom (she never breast-fed me). When I see her brusque with dad, I hate her for it. When I watch her repel his affection, mock his kisses, shrug off his embrace, I am filled with unvoiced pity for him and revulsion from her. When he tells me how much she has gone through, I am unmoved; I think of how much she has had and how little she has given. She tells me how much she needs security because she never had it as a child. Her father went bankrupt and she could not go to college. She has filled C. with uncertainties, wishing always to be 'able to do something to make her happy'. His hopes and fears are visited on me. He watches me as a gardener his favourite plot, anxious to interfere where he would do better to wait, wanting to clear weeds and clumsily obstructing what he is keen to see flourish. He seems cold at times; his green eyes glitter as if with poisonous hatred. As a terrible loneliness seems to possess him, he wants to resurrect the old Jewish family concerns; he will say that he is the head of the house and talk of his old father and how he would have wanted him to say prayers or have had us all go to services. Yet intellectually C. is agnostic, an uncertain rationalist, coldly contemptuous of men's ways, sneering at morals and doubting motives. He is torn by conflicting logics. In anger, he seems hateful, frightening; a sudden vision of lunacy paralyses the onlooker. Yet he is gay and fun, full of happiness, kind and sociable, laughing, dancing, oh so lovable that one is full of joy for seeing and knowing him. *Then* my mother loves him and you know that she too cannot resist his charm. What strange beast is caged in with him? What flays him, leaves him distraught, sullen, doubtful? Is it her petty miseries or some fault in himself, a fatal reticence, unwillingness to be open to solace? Sometimes he appears to be trying to construct out of me the being he wanted to be. How easy he finds it to resolve in me the uncertainties which beleaguer him! His marriage is like an imperfect electrical connection: at times the bulb burns brightly, beaming at all around; at others it flickers and fails and darkens everything. When they are happy, laughter fills the flat and makes happiness seem available to all. Then there is emptiness, rooms without spirit, misery and rootlessness. We seem then to have no home, no being, voyagers on a dark sea full of perils whose weathering brings only fresh disasters. Here is all the sad consequence of Jewishness, the terror implicit in creating because only in the creation of individuals can any faint hope or salvation be found. We are weaker together than we are when we are alone. The struggle is endless; there is no resting, no sustenance; life, environment spring alone from each separate one's efforts. We have no common purposes. To the Jew the land is no mother and the bosom of the earth gives no pap.

Americans will believe anything you tell them, even – if it is sufficiently disguised – the truth.

The last night out, there was a farewell dinner: paper hat, garlands,
rattles and bells to play with. Americans think they are giving you
a treat if they let you behave like children. It seems that they all long
to be kids again, or never cease to be. Such occasions license their
latent infantilism. There were streamers and yards of coloured paper
cellotaped to the ceiling. Sausagy balloons were similarly adhesive
to the walls; round ones were bunched under the lights.

After dinner, an accordionist played Neapolitan songs and, inter-
mittently, sang them to the frenzied delight of rattlers and squeakers
and the clanging of bells. The Purser, tall, Germanic, with a balding
egg-shaped head and a nose like an ant-eater, all smoothness and
whiteness, played the double bass. The ship's photographer, short
and thick with wavy brown hair and a handsome, apish face, was
master of ceremonies. He crooned and got the words wrong and
did a tap routine. His hair flopped about; he waved his arms and fell
about the floor like an unhinged gollywog, oh and he smiled, he
smiled and smiled. Afterwards he came back to the microphone,
panting. It squeaked – naughty! – as he adjusted it in order to gasp:
'After doing that, anyone else would be out of breath.' He stopped
and waited for the laugh. It came second post. 'OK,' he said, 'now
we've had a request, but in spite of that, the Purser is going to do a
solo.' The microphone was tilted towards the double bass and the
Purser dum-dum, dum-dum-dum-dummed while the drummer
drummed and didn't look at anybody.

Someone sang a song about Sorrento and then the photographer
bobbed up again, sweat darkening the armpits of his light jacket,
and told us to stand up. He started us off singing 'Old Macdonald
had a cow'. He seasoned it with burps and Bronx cheers and every-
body sat down and he laughed. Children ran around and popped a
few balloons and the Purser asked (not for the first time) why they
weren't all in bed.

When the band packed up, the children pulled the balloons from
the walls and collected the hats people had left behind. The Purser
suddenly reappeared, with a fat German bulging behind shell-
rimmed spectacles. They had lighted cigars hidden behind their
backs. They would go up to a child with an armful of captured
balloons and, while one talked to him, the other popped the
balloons. In a few minutes, the room was filled with children crying
their hearts out. The Purser and the German stood and laughed. I

wanted to go and hit the bullies, but instead I just walked over and stood and looked at them. They seemed to realise they had gone too far. The Purser started removing more balloons from the walls and trying to force them on the children. They were made even more miserable and redoubled their cries. Having expiated his sin, the Purser became very tough and mature and told them they must shut up or go to bed. They stood, open-mouthed, tears running down their faces, holding balloons they didn't want. The Purser went around the room tearing down the decorations and peeling cellotape from the walls. He whistled as he did so and removed children tenderly from his path.

I was reading Nietzsche on deck when a woman in a red suit came by and started talking to me in Italian. I smiled maliciously at her. She talked for a while and then went away. I did not understand any of what she said with such urgent volubility. She was shiny-faced, with hairy legs, pointed nose, wide contorted lips. As we closed on the dock at Genoa, she must have caught sight of the person waiting for her. She started to shriek and run about in short spurts, as if trying at once to find and escape something. She cried in gasping convulsions and plunged her head in her arms as if the sight of her friend was too exciting to bear. Everyone looked embarrassed. She resurrected her head and resumed the panting animal sobs which wracked her body. Her fur fell to one side and she dropped her umbrella, stooped gasping to recover it.

The man on the quay was short and stocky, in a belted macintosh and a soft hat. He raised his arms above his head and waved, more friendly than passionate, but even this electrified the woman, who panted and groaned as if delirious. She turned and pointed to him and cried out again. When the gangplank was lowered, she ran down it, scampering, half-falling, towards the dumpy man who had inspired such passion. An American woman told me that the woman had tried earlier to talk to a young Lebanese. When he said he spoke no Italian, she dealt him a vicious kick on the shin which resulted in a 'terrible wound'. I had a horrifying intuition that the stocky man in the soft hat was not the lover she imagined but some unhappy relative delegated to escort her to an institution.

The *pizzeria*. *Pizza* is a flat piece of dough oven-cooked and loaded with cheese and tomato and, if you wish, little sprats. The owner, in a white coat and walrus moustache, stood at a counter to the right of the door. Bolts of white dough were passed to him on trays and he worked them incessantly, beating them thin with his fists, flouring them the while, and then spreading grated cheese from a tin jug. Behind his right shoulder was the white-tiled oven; the mouth glared orange in the grey light. A boy put the *pizzas* on a long wooden paddle which he pushed in over the embers of the wood fire inside the oven. The uncooked flaps of dough were flipped nimbly onto the black floor within. They swelled like omelettes; the cheese melted and the tomato blistered appetisingly. Wooden tables, paper cloths; the menu stuck on the wall and obscured by a coat on the peg above it. The walls were yellow and peeling, tiles the insipid white of cottage cheese. The children ran about, collecting plates and glasses. The kitchenmaid rinsed them in cold water and rubbed the dirt away with stubby fingers. The owner's wife, heavy bosom in a brown blouse resting on the counter, stood behind a cash register of much the same shape, and colour, as what you could see of her.

A Pieter Breughel in the Naples Museum. A round painting of a venerable figure in a blue-black cloak, face almost hidden by its fall, walking with the aid of a stick. Behind him, hunched down in villainy, a boy, perhaps fourteen or fifteen, fat and deformed, face coarsened as if by a goitre or some glandular deficiency, or excess. His expression is brutish and sly. With a wide-bladed butcher's knife, he is cutting the old man's red purse strings which hang from the lower folds of his gown. The purse hangs like a heart towards the ground and you have the feeling that the cutting of the string is also the cutting of the old man's lifeline. He is about to be deposed from his serenity into a bloody death. The monstrous child is encased in a strange pair of hoops which intersect at right angles. The circular motif of the canvas is repeated in the bizarre cage in which the boy is moving. The cage has a cross on top. Behind, there is a windmill and sheep grazing; a shepherd unconcerned in the background. The ancient worthy's calm assurance is sweetly at odds with the sly worldliness of the hunched boy-villain about to do him in.

H. told me that he was 'just waiting' for someone to call him a homosexual. If anyone did, what would he do? 'Get married at once.' It is surprising no one yet has. He is soft-looking, though his beard has lately toughened. His friendships resemble those of a woman: he is more pleasant than men usually bother to be; he gives compliments. He makes mutual plans ('You and I are going places')

and yet his affection never seems to come from the heart; it is businesslike. A woman will sacrifice friendship for love; H. will sacrifice
it for himself: he is in love with his own ambition. Granted this
sacred, inalienable passion, he is as charming and as generous as need
(his need) be. He genuinely resents any reproach which questions
the primacy of his personal interests. He will spend hours trying to
convince you (and, more importantly, himself) that you are being
illogical in not seeing the virtue in some action on which he is
already determined. What makes a moral solipsist so fervent in the
justification of his intentions? The possibility that he just might need
you again.

On the way to the Museo San Martino. Narrow cobbled streets
with tall, tall houses falling like cliffs to the ground; no pavements.
Washing hung across the streets in the rain like flags at regatta time.
The postman put the mail in wicker baskets which top floor tenants
lower on strings and then hoist again, careful to avoid the washing.
Vegetable-sellers with high, tilted carts trundle through the alleys,
harness gleaming silver on the horses' backs.

    From above, the streets fall away like fissures too narrow to walk
in. Tenements face each other so closely that D. and I saw a woman
pass a highchair, perilously, through an upstairs window to the
woman opposite. The shops in many of the houses are also
bedrooms; fish and vegetables are sold in doorways through which
you can see the big double bed, the image of the Virgin above a tall
dresser with a lace runner and an oil lamp. The rain has the effect
of a disease, ageing the city, emphasising the dirt and decay.
Innumerable arches run with moisture and the dark mouths of the
shops are like the entrances to sewers. Fat priests with fastidious
umbrellas pick a distasteful, tiptoed way through the poverty.

    By the water's edge, barefoot youths fished, for squid I was told,
squatting on the black rocks. Black water surged through the many
channels, boiled up towards them, almost wetting their behinds, and
was then sucked away. They dangled hooks between the rocks, but
caught nothing. They finished their sandwiches and went home.

You take the narrow-gauge railway to Pompeii from the Circum-
Vesuvianum station; rows of wooden-slatted seats in the third class.
Men come through with *giornali* and *caramelli*. On one side of the
train, the old suburbs: a white-grey house with peeling plaster, damp
on damp; fading advertisements and political posters. On the other,
the land slashed plain and flat and concreted for new apartment

houses, in pink and yellow uniformity. Washing has already started
to grow on the occupied balconies. Stick-like saplings are tethered
to poles in circles cut in the concrete. Some cars are parked in the
loop at the end of a new street. A woman in a red coat, high heels,
walked away into the uninhabited area on the arm of a man in a
check coat. Going where? Why?

How happily will Naples' tenement-dwellers be transplanted to
the serried impersonality of urban planning? Will they gladly forsake
their ancient vines which scale the rain-bruised walls of the old
quarter and are coaxed towards balconies and dormer windows?
Will they gratefully exchange gnarled city trees for skimpy suburban
saplings in concrete gaiters?

The country comes at last. Carts rut the sunken roads; hamlets
fall open to cobbled *piazzas* surrounded by the marble and streakily
whitewashed formality of official buildings. The green, arrested
fountains of cypresses plume the skyline. Vesuvius is an inverted
cone, its top the hot end of a giant cigar when the ash has fallen,
leaving the hollow tip with a burnt brown cuff around the grey
embers. There is a grey fall away from the summit, then creviced
cliffs, scabbed with lava from the last eruption which still seems to
ooze from the cracks. The surface is darkened like milk that has
boiled over and scorched the stove. Greenery begins below the
barren summit, low yet bushy, like hair below a tonsure line. Soon
white houses thicken like dandruff among the trees. Big dilapidated
villas close on the little railway. After thirty five minutes, Pompeii.

Men cluster round the entrance to the *scavi*, trying to sell postcards;
some obscene. You go up a steep street and under a damp arch. The
road is of round muffins of grey volcanic stone, like elephants' feet,
veined with mud. The city looks bombed, scythed off at a height
of about eight feet, though temples and a few houses rise above it.
The grey and brown volcanic stones are dry, as if roasted. Water,
like the people, seems to have gone into exile. The fountains are
empty. You wonder how water ever reached them. There are step-
ping stones across the streets, but you cannot believe that mud was
ever a problem; perhaps they were there because carts had gouged
the road so deeply. If aristocrats used chariots, the bourgeoisie must
have been powerful enough to demand the crossing stones; mer-
chants wanted pedestrians to be able to move easily about the city.

The place brings home the faintheartedness of classical teaching
at Cambridge. What good are appraisals of literature and 'character'
without reference to the architecture, art and social habits of the

ancient world? This squeamishness in the classics dates from Victorian times; anthropology, for instance, revels in disreputable details. It is idle to chide Catullus or Juvenal for obscenity or Ovid and Martial for lasciviousness without appreciating how accurately they reflected the habits and attitudes of their contemporaries. *Equites* are often portrayed as patricians without a pedigree, but the House of the Vettii, for example, proves that the senatorial order must not only have feared the insolent (and growing) wealth of the mercantile class but also detested their blatant vulgarity. The House of the Vettii has at the front door a wooden box which, through the prudery of the authorities, covers a painting of Priapus weighing his elongated prick on the scales. It has the blunt scurrility of a barrack room joke: just the kind of thing R. might have drawn, had his conversation had fingers. The guide also showed us (the male tourists) a series of paintings, locked away in a side room which he called 'the fuck room'. They depicted a menu of positions for sex; a new use for the dull grammarian's term 'conjugations'. The guide said that the pictures were 'very interesting, were they not?' 'The most interesting things I ever saw,' I said, giving him a cigarette. I only wish they had been.

There were more of the same in the brothel near the Stabian *thermae*. The men are all red-brown and muscular, the women inclined to fat and very white. The pictures were almost medical; they seemed more instructive than titillating, as if the women did not want to have their time wasted by incompetence. Many of the poses show women in the dominant position; I suppose they reflected the services on offer. There were five *cubicula* in a room no bigger than the average drawing room; each with a bed and a stone bolster. The partitions between the work-spaces were about seven feet high, space above; cash desk by the door with a slotted urn for coins, a seat for the madame. Upstairs, there were private rooms for the rich or the more demanding. The guide made sure we understood the merits of the various positions and was given cigarettes for their names.

Many bars and taverns; even shops supplied refreshments. Big pots of wine (and oil) were let into the counters and were dispensed, I suppose, with a ladle or by dipping the buyer's vessel into them. You expected the owners to return and accuse you, in coarse Latin, of taking advantage of their temporary absence.

8.12.54. The end of the 'Marian year'. At 5 p.m., from the terrace of the hotel: a vast procession, led by a blaring band, moving up the

Via San Felice and turning left, in front of a small crowd, to continue down the Via Medina. After the band, a parade of ordinary people, in ranks of six or seven, wearing brown and dark blue suits and modest dresses, led by a man with a flag; there were several contingents, similarly marshalled. A thin fence of citizens watched them go by; so many people seemed to be on the move that there was no one left to admire them. The parade split into two lengthways and spawned parallel columns, each four abreast, marching up the sides of the wide street,leaving the middle clear for the standard bearers and the marshals, mostly priests. There were platoons of schoolgirls in black smocks and white Eton collars, shepherded by balloony nuns in black habits, rushing about, restoring the dressing like holy sergeant-majors. After the schoolchildren, older girls, under a blue-green banner with a forked tongue; four outriders held streamers attached to the points of the flag to keep it at fullest stretch. They were so zealous that the child carrying the flag was almost hauled to the ground.

Darkness was coming. There came a section of nuns, some starched, some in black wimples, carrying unlit candles. After them, girls in virginal dresses that shone in the gloaming; fresh, earnest faces, budding mouths and white hands seemed all there was of living flesh (they resembled the figures we saw in Toledo). As the evening thickened, people brought lamps and easy chairs onto their balconies. Down the road towards the Corso Victor Emmanuele, the army changed its nature: file on file, like glistening coils of jewels, the marchers came with lit tapers sheltered from the breeze with paper muzzles. The light brought the dark; people lost definition, all you could see was the show of black robes, the velvet setting for the gold stars of candle-light, the twitching but unfailing army of the Lord. 'Ave Maria,' they all sang, the deep voices of the priests, the innocence of nuns and virgins. Broken-stepped but unstoppable, slowly and deliberately they were borne past us up the hill until the whole road was filled with the dazzle of tapers. Half-closing the eyes, one saw twin snakes of gold light, chains of stars, pressing up the slope under the urgency of the chant, pausing then resuming as if under the hand of a celestial conductor. A loudspeaker van surged up the open centre of the road, telling bystanders to come to the Piazza del Plebiscito to be addressed by the archbishop.

When the leading lights had disappeared, a row of priests in white vestments, others in black cloaks, scampered along; some had doused their tapers, one or two hurried down sidestreets as if they had had enough. The remaining ranks broke up; the procession lost dignity. Earlier contingents had the serenity of martyrs proceeding to their deaths; the stragglers lacked coherent conviction. Then a whole new army appeared, with tapers lit. Like an orchestra which falters and then recovers its unison, the parade resumed its majesty. But the magic was lost: the hurrying humanity of the marchers had become too obvious.

At last came the dignitaries, fat old men stumbling slower and slower as the length of the march sapped their small energies. Finally, up strutted a squadron of swordsmen in blue cloaks, policemen alongside, and the image of the Virgin in an illuminated truck of the kind that usually carries bricks but was now cloaked in greenery, floodlights flaring through it. More swordsmen and then a great crowd chanting 'Ave Maria'. Behind this culminating concourse, the lights of automobiles and buses. Laggards were hooted aside by drivers as they jostled behind the Image. The secular usurped the clerical without a pretence of respect; soon the street was the usual unmannerly rush of nocturnal traffic.

In the train from Naples to Rome. Hill towns on the razor's edge of sharp hills; road zigzagging at acute angles up the mottled escarpment. Pinks based with green and umber, whites refined by the weathering water, the blend of buildings with landscape marked man's conquest of the earth. Where was that woman walking with her basket under her arm along a mud-caked lane? To what small cottage did she move so slowly, so certainly, head high as if with the discipline of a vessel upon it? Black cattle shifted ponderously over the thick green, turning their heads to the train like stately buffoons. Acre on acre, mile on mile I've seen it these last weeks, the common world of the peasant; the humility and indomitable purpose of man on earth: gates, fences, hedges, herds and flocks and their solitary guardians, soon their killers, consuming the redivival bounty and breaking the stony paucity of old soil, yoking and yoked. I saw them in the cracked mud of the Moroccan desert, among the bitter dunes where the sea lashes the attentive shore, patient in their sorrows, honest in their dishonesties, true to their destinies. I saw creaking carts on the bald stoniness of Spain, real people beneath dungarees and robes. It's easier to be ignorant of the city than to leave it. Horace even in his most artful verses meant what he said; Virgil in his Georgics and Eclogues voiced genuine sentiments with urbane hypocrisy. Politics and commerce ask, and offer, nothing compared to the insatiable demands of country life.

I am slightly, but perhaps unworthily, embarrassed by the callowness of my paean to the peasantry of the Mediterranean world
which I was discovering for the first time. I was embarrassed even
then, but determined to tell myself, in terms which I do not care
to parade, that I had a duty to tell the truth, to 'voice vulnerable
thoughts' and be 'fearless of the opinions of others, preserving at
all times (my) integrity'. Nothing more clearly dates my young
self than the elderly terms in which I expressed myself, even to
myself. I did not profit from the revolution, or at least rebellion,
which would give the young the liberty to litter the prints with
the kinds of expression which, in many cases, they had had
shouted at them by drill sergeants during their National Service.
It seemed then that individuals had been given their unhibited
voices, but the new style was, in some ways, as full of cant as the
old; it was bolder, but not noticeably braver. Conventions of one
kind replaced those of another, and called themselves unconventional.

It would be pretty to be able to say that I have always observed
the callow purposes I recommended to myself, but without them
I should still see no point in being a writer. I never hoped for
success, or for reception into literary high society; I wanted to be
published, and performed (and not to have to get a steady job or
have a boss). My callow resolve was to say what I thought was
true, especially if this involved what other people did not want
to hear or have said. I prescribed for myself a programme of wilful
solitude, believing – a little too credulously – that Cyril Connolly
was in earnest when he called a hotel bedroom the writer's spiritual home. In truth, I had had more than enough of solitude,
though I took small pleasure in the adhesive company of a man
called Dick Knight whom I had met on the USS *Constitution* and
with whom I shared a bedrooom in Naples. He slept in a vest and
I so disliked the smell of the man that I resolved never again to
sleep in the same room as another male if I could possibly help it,
though I have been happy to make an exception of my own sons.

I neither liked nor disliked Dick. What was strange was that,
as so often in life, I found it impossible to break a relationship
which I found irksome; it has been the same with collaborators
and casual acquaintances. I suspect that I had been so unnerved
by certain experiences at school that I have never had any confidence in my ability to recruit new friends. I also greatly fear that
those whom I do not disarm with genialities, however spurious,
may join the gang of those who will combine to humiliate or

destroy me. I know perfectly well that such alliances are unlikely, but I can never be quite as outspoken as I should wish. Sometimes this dread of unpopularity can hardly be distinguished from cowardice and I despise myself both for it and for agreeing to certain commissions which I accept less from greed than from the fear of never being asked again. What I have always most disliked in myself is an inability to break decisively and openly with people and to speak out as unhesitatingly as I should.

It was part of the cant of my Cambridge contemporaries, inspired by Mr Eliot and by Frank Leavis, that 'criticism' was a noble pursuit. Although I did not read English, and was never admitted to the counsels of those of my generation who were to dominate the literary world, I was, and remain, sufficiently impressed by their opinionated confidence, to have done a good deal of literary journalism. I have not infrequently been accused of 'boldness' in saying undiplomatic things about figures who might more prudently have been flattered. Certainly, I have rolled few logs and have often dropped bricks, but even here I am more conscious of my timidities than of outspokenness. I have certainly not entirely honoured the callow resolution I made as the Naples train slowed and stopped at Termini station, that I should remain indifferent to fashion and listen only to my conscience, but my vision of being a writer has not greatly changed: I never intended to have a career; awards and titles are no part of an artist's proper ambition. Those who have been said to deserve them by juries of the kind of people available for such activities should ask themselves why they attach importance to such verdicts.

The Pantheon in the rain, a chained off circle of wet in the middle. The coffered mass of the unsupported ceiling threatens to thrust the walls outwards; solemnity without repose. Raphael's tomb is in a low-arched recess and is permanently illuminated, unlike the adjacent tombs of the kings of Italy.

Babington's tea room in the Piazza di Spagna. Despite the high prices, we were seduced by the promise of waffles. The air is imported from Cheltenham Spa: green cups, white inside, paper napkins tucked in them; copies of the *Tatler*, *Illustrated London News*, *The New Yorker*, Xmas puddings on the mantelpiece; elderly aproned waitresses.

I overheard two Englishwomen talking about bridge. There was a club near the English cinema on the Via xx Settembre. In London, they played at the Ladies' Carlton Club and were impressed by my mention of Crockford's. They were in Rome for the winter, staying at the Grand Hotel (Marlon Brando stayed there, they told me). Meals cost 3,000 lire each. They did not think it possible when we told them that we lived for five days on what they paid for luncheon. They did not consider themselves rich, but roughed it at the best hotels, confident of bedbugs, larceny and indecent assault anywhere else. One of them (small, black-suited, dark-haired) asked me where I went to school. When I told her, she said she thought I was a Carthusian because Carthusians had a particular way of enunciating. My speech has, it seemed, been determined by an institution I cordially dislike.

When I told them how much I had admired Fes, the other, tallish blonde woman said that thirty years earlier her brother had been dying in a sanatorium in Switzerland. Of course he didn't *know* he was dying, poor lamb, but an hour before he died, on New Year's Day 1924, he had said, 'When I'm better I'm going to take you to Fes.' She still hadn't been. Perhaps they would fly there next week.

In the Villa Borghese. A Vasari nativity. Shepherds and the radiant child, apparently conscious of the momentous nature of what is happening under a flood of celestial light. But behind the stretched neck of an ass, beyond the bar of the manger, is the balcony of the hostelry. On it are leaning a couple, arm in arm, so human and so modern that they might be Elyot and Amanda in the first act of *Private Lives*. They are entirely concerned with their own affairs, maybe wondering what the commotion in the stable means but caring not at all what it signifies.

On the corner of the Borghese gardens above the Piazza del Popolo children play football in the late afternoon. They are of all sizes, some athletically attired, others in macintoshes, long belts trailing towards the ground. Poorer children tie together a bundle of rags or old brown paper. They all play very fancily, juggling the ball from foot to foot, flipping it back over their heads when it seems to have passed them. Another favourite spot is the dry moat of the Castel San'Angelo, where there are opportunities for fancy footwork, including the ricochet pass to oneself. If they made up a side, it would have ten forwards and a goalkeeper. They spend all their time in close passing; no one wants to be a defender.

The pedestalled policeman at the piazza Venezia *conducts* the traffic. He has lean, flexible hands in white muslin gloves and each finger has independent jurisdiction. Under a dark blue topee his eyes flash approval or disappointment, pain when a motorist fails to respond with an alacrity and elegance equal to his. He faces down the Via del Corso and never looks in any other direction; he *feels* the traffic amassed behind him, and when you think that he has forgotten it, his arms are raised and, with a gesture at once restrained and compelling, he releases it. What timing! As the traffic passes him, he flutters his fingers, reassuring the motorists of the rightness of his motion and the significance to him personally of even the smallest ingredient of their concert. He commands a stupendous ensemble: ranging from the solemn percussion and double basses of the great oblong buses to the insolent piccolos of the Vespas, to which the varied horns of Cadillac and Fiat add a trenchant obbligato. He reminds you of an Indian dancer; you would not be surprised to hear that he was reviewed in the newspapers.

The threatened BEA strike means Beetle may not be able to be in Paris on the 26th. I shall be crazy with disappointment if she isn't. How long it took me to learn to trust somebody else! I was so used to loneliness and so accustomed to hostility.

I sat on the steps above the Piazza di Spagna to read the letters I collected from American Express. The flower sellers were unloading fresh spiny Christmas trees from trucks parked against the boat-shaped fountain in the centre of the piazza. A boy darted through the traffic to the fountain and drank the hard cold water from one of the spouts, shook his head, and ran off again.

Children were playing on the landing halfway up the Spanish steps. They were throwing ivy berries at one of their number, the best natured it seemed, who occasionally responded to their salvoes with one of his own. One child, fat, in tweed shorts, blue jerkin, thick-rimmed glasses, played with particular intensity. He employed any available subterfuge, from distracting attention by pretending the game was over to faking friendship in order to approach close enough to be sure of hitting his smiling target. The fat boy threw with vindictive viciousness, his face contorted with beastly effort. A smaller boy, whose energy made me suspect (wrongly) that he was a disguised dwarf, threw his berries with savage intensity, aping the malice of the fat one. I felt that I could have been at school with either of them. The fat one reminded me of Robin Ewart Gladstone.

On the 23rd of December 1954, I took the night train to Paris. I took a room at the Hôtel des Deux Continents on the Rue Jacob, where Beetle and I had already stayed several times. On Christmas Day, I had lunch with our oldest friend, Jacqueline Weiss (whose family came from Strasbourg) and counted the hours till the 26th, when BEA would indeed bring Beetle to Paris. She would, her endlessly reread letter told me, be wearing a new green coat with a little fur collar. Jackie and I ate turkey with chestnut stuffing at the Pré St Germain, up the boulevard from the café Flore. She had taken rooms in Crimée, in a flat belonging to relatives of the owners of the Deux Continents.

On Boxing Day, I went to the Invalides to wait for Beetle's bus from the airport. It never occurred to me to go out to the airport. She came towards me with her head slightly to one side, as she always did, and we were together again, and happy.

I had enough of the Revd. Harper Wood's money left for us to be able to stay in Paris while I wrote my novel. In January, however, we flew back to London, very briefly, and got married. When we returned to Paris, Jackie Weiss said that we could not possibly stay permanently in a hotel and offered us the rooms in Crimée which she had found for herself. She was the best of friends.

We spent that cold winter in the flat of a blind man and his disobliging wife. Beetle got up to make porridge, as she has so often since. I went down the passage for nuggets of coal and then lit the stove which was our only heating. I had rented a big upright Royal Sovereign typewriter from a place near the Opéra and on it I typed the pages of the novel I had started in Juan-les-Pins. Beetle shopped and cooked lunch on the gas in a pantry whose wallpaper became increasingly freckled with grease. I took for granted that my art took precedence over our life. She did not disabuse me, nor has she since. I worked, and have ever since, with regular determination. I had taken Mr Maugham's industrious habits for a recipe.

In the evenings we went by Métro to the cinema or to the opera. Cheap seats were easy to get at the unfashionable *Opéra Comique*. Sometimes, after visiting a classic cinema off the Rue St André des Arts, we shared a pot of hot chocolate at the Café Flore; a grog (like Inspector Maigret) when it was particularly cold. In the early days of 1955, Pierre Mendès-France was ousted from the premiership. I took it rather personally, less because he was a Jew than because I was a steady reader of *L'Exprèss* (then a hairy-papered minority sheet), in which P.M.-F. and Jean-Paul Sartre often wrote. François Mauriac contributed '*Bloc-notes*' on the back page. He displaced Harold Nicolson, whose *Marginal Comment*, in *The Spectator*, was my favourite weekly reading at Charterhouse, as the model for what I took to be the dispassionate reading of current affairs by a mature literary mind.

If we did not go out, we read (Moravia's *Woman of Rome* made a suavely erotic impression) and then went to bed, often early. This was due, in part at least, to our neighbour downstairs. He was a *poids lourd* driver who left his articulated lorry tilted on the pavement outside our tenement, sometimes with the cab in that broken-necked position which, in those days, seemed unique to France. Our small sitting room, where the stove was, had a parquet floor which creaked even when crossed in stockinged feet. He slept, or tried to sleep, immediately below it. If we so much as entered the room after 8.30 p.m., he would shout from below, '*Il faut dormir*'. I was strong for workers' rights, but I did not believe that they included sending the world early to bed. For some time, we did our best to honour our neighbour's un-nuanced demands. One night, however, after my daily coinage of jokes had failed to make Beetle laugh, I walked over to take them back and was greeted, if that is the word, with the usual yells from downstairs. Something snapped: I knelt on the floor and barked into the parquet, at length. I stopped, and then I did it again. There was no response. We never heard from our *routier* again. A few years later, long-distance lorries began to carry on their radiators the image of a racy girl with the slogan under it, '*Les Routiers sont Sympas*'. I was never entirely convinced.

We stayed in Crimée until March of 1955, when I came to the end both of my novel and of the Revd. Harper Wood's three hundred and fifty invaluable quid. Our blind landlord had never seen the grease marks on the pantry wall, which had become epidemic, but his wife took furious exception when, belatedly, she saw them. I was of the view that they constituted fair wear and tear in view of the six pounds a week we were paying, but Madame Lambel did not share it. She summoned the downstairs neighbour to lend muscle to her objections and I denounced him, with juvenile recklessness (and British chauvinism) as '*monsieur l'agent du Gestapo*'. My reading of *L'Express* had given me the dangerous illusion that I knew how to speak to the French in their own language. My sarcasm did not shame or embarrass its target. In spite of having the flu, and high temperatures, Beetle and I were evicted into the snow. We went to the Hôtel de la Sorbonne and then to London where, thanks to her parents' generosity and her own savings, we were able to pay 'key money' for a tiny basement flat at 9, Chelsea Embankment, the same address as George Weidenfeld into whose flat I was one day admitted by the Welsh janitor. Can I be right in remembering that it had a *fountain* in it? We had to keep the light on all day in our basement. At night, if you turned it on suddenly in the living room, roaches studded the carpet. The great thing, for me at least, was that we were living in Chelsea, which was, I liked to think, a borough of artists.

1955

'Binkie' Beaumont's offices in the Globe Theatre. The only way up is by a tiny lift in which two can be squeezed. It goes slowly and you are pressed against your companion. The offices are divided by wooden partitions, except for Beaumont's. His foyer is hung with framed bills of past Tennant productions. There is a strong smell of perfume. Billy Chappell, our producer, came up and met us before our audience. He is short, like a jockey, with glassy, yet lively, blue eyes and a boyish old face. He was dressed like a juvenile lead in an Edwardian musical: check tweed suit, waistcoat with little lapels, buttons covered, like those on the jacket, in the same tweed. Like all these people, he drawled nasally and preciously but also in a clipped tone which seemed to emphasise the drollery of *absolutely every word*. When you laugh at what he says, he seems embarrassed, as if you have given him a better reception than he deserves, which you probably have.

Binkie was older than I expected, fleshily sleek, with whitening, copious hair, cool, damp hands. He smiles with seasoned charm, forcing bonhomie into his grey-brown eyes. The mask never slips; that is how you know it is a mask. I could gather nothing of the chances of his putting *Lady at the Wheel* on the stage. No one could have looked more impartial; he would sentence you to death or give you the keys of the kingdom without any change of expression. His smile was a frown; his frown a smile. He spoke always of 'ladies' as a carefully brought up left-winger will refer always to Negroes. One is very careful about things that do not come naturally.

Binkie's desk is in front of a window through which you can see the backs of the letters advertising *An Evening With Beatrice Lillie*; charcoal drawings on the walls of elegant ladies in cloaks with stars on their bosoms à la Ivor Novello. A spindly black anglepoise lamp on the wide, fat desk; facing it a green wing chair, high-backed and so deep that Billy, who sat in it, perched on the edge like the boy in *Vice Versa*. His conversation with Binkie had a coded innocence like the pre-arranged small talk of spies. When Binkie spoke to me, I felt embarrassed not to be one of their club. It was like being a fourth who did not play bridge, not reprehensible but manifestly unsociable.

Ken Tynan gave a party at Larry Adler's house in Norfolk Street, St John's Wood. It was a big house with a lantern over the front door. A maid let us into the hallway where there was an electric xylophone; flattened geraniums figured in the wallpaper; there was red paintwork on the stairs and the glass doors to the kitchen. We arrived after midnight (it was Leslie's last night at the Globe) and the parquet-floored double drawing room was already smart with theatricals. Ken, tall and languorous, saluted us with limp hand-shakes. It was as if you were being dared to reach over and touch something nasty in a penny arcade. He is very pale, with a pendu-lous face, loose lips, observant half-closed eyes. He wore a grey suit with a white shirt and a torero's string tie throttled in a leather toggle like a dissolute scoutmaster.

John Barber, the *Daily Express* drama critic greeted me with pleasing extravagance. Dark eyes and sensitive face give him an air of courageous intelligence; you expect a bold and perceptive wit. His work shows no sign of it: in print he is banal, superficial and commonplace. His wife is a charming Indian. It needs courage, I suppose, to have an Indian wife. It seems that they have decided not to have children. J.B. is vulnerable, alert and innocuous.

Elaine, Ken's wife, wore a vivid red dress, and looked aggres-sively sad. When a singer called Annie Ross, the guest of honour, did her jazzy stuff, Elaine urged her to add some other song from her repertoire (to prove how well she knew her?). It made Elaine seemed less a sophisticated hostess than a kid who wanted to prove that it was her party too.

As the evening progressed, the masks slipped; tiredness did for glamour. Spivvy, a fat negroid lady, sang chic cabaret numbers and people tried to laugh. Hermione Gingold, tattered and magnificent in a flowery blue garment which offered glimpses of soiled under-wear, received the tribute of countless young men as she sat on a prolonged brown sofa. 'Is there room at your feet?' they asked. 'There is *always* room at my feet.' Diana Dors, whose dress might as well have had 'Coming home with me, dearie?' written all over it, and Pamela Brown were there. P.B.'s eyes were bright and unseeing, like a drug addict's, eyes that are there to be looked at not seen through. As we left, Hermione was behind the xylophone in the hall, pecking out 'Stranger in Paradise' and singing it in a heavily garlicked French accent.

I went to see Hermione about the radio series which Roy Speer wants me to write for. The flat is in Capener's Close, off Knightsbridge. You go under a brick arch and find three or four pink and white houses. A dark-haired, podgy secretary with a very delicate manner opened the door of number 4. When I asked for Miss Gingold, she waited, it seemed, for the password. Finally I was asked up. The banisters were tall golden rods which reached right to the ceiling. My coat went in a putty-green cupboard and I was shown into the drawing room where Lady Eulick Brown greeted me expansively. Hermione said 'Hullo' in a suitably welcoming way. She was like emery paper trying to pass itself off as cotton wool. Lord Eulick Brown was a tall, disjointed fellow in a grubby brown suit; lean face, prominent nose, long white hands, the fingers held apart from each other as if they were drying. There was a hint of cynical humour about him, but his wife was earnest and thick. She wore bi-focals, the smaller lens set like a bull's eye within the larger; at the centre, the black pin-head of her iris, as if an expert marksman had just plugged her. She blinked at you and you were not sure if she was shy or not yet convinced that you were really there. She had crisp, dirty brown hair and a yellow-white face, thin-lipped, high cheekbones. She was as voluble as he was silent. She thought it was scandalous how much publicity Hermione Baddeley got from *la* Gingold.

Hermione wore a blue dress with a pink rose at the throat and long pink gloves. She kept saying the dress was too tight and she was quite bursting out of it. If she said anything at all amusing, Lady E.B. leaned back and grinned as if sub-titled, 'You see? She's done it again!'

We talked in an alcove, an appendix to the drawing room, fenced from it by a screen of black tubing. I sat in a red swivel chair, the others on spindly, cushion-seated little chairs. On the wall was an appalling framed relief: lengths of wire crossed over two raised squares, one red, one white. A white bakelite house phone with impressive buttons stood at her ladyship's elbow.

The main room had a series of French windows giving onto a concrete terrace. In the far corner, on a black marble pedestal, was a two-headed statue which appeared to have been fashioned from petrified pigeon shit. Low furniture was pitched here and there on a lot of white carpet, like rafts on a sea of dusty cream. The walls were black. Over the sofa facing the French windows was a peculiar section of arrested vomit which stood out from the wall like the gold leaf on an officer's cap; spangled below this macabre excres-

cence, pieces of coloured metal. The whole thing looks like a very
thin fakir stretched in a joint-cracking pose on a bed of nails on
which a few rose petals have been casually distributed. There was
nothing in the whole place which indicated that it was intended to
be inhabited by sane beings.

We had tea in Rosenthal china cups, decorated with stripes and
little lozenges, like cough sweets on the ends of fishing lines.
Hermione's blonde young man 'Miles-y!' arrived during tea, having
just fetched her poodle from the vet's; one good poodle deserving
another, I suppose. H.'s darling had had a swelling in a place he
simply couldn't *mention*. The dog stayed downstairs; H. had never
bothered to house-train it and it lifted its leg *everywhere*. H. didn't
mind, but Lady E.B. *did*. It had to be left in the yard where it flirted
with the Browns' terrier with which it was terribly but futilely in
love.

My Cambridge friend and fellow philosopher Tony Becher and
I wrote a weekly monologue for *Grande Gingold*, Hermione's
radio series. We shared a fee of twenty-five pounds; a fortune
which paid the rent on Chelsea Embankment and our grocery
bill.

At the weekend, Tony would come down from Cambridge,
where he was working for the C.U.P., and concocted an advice
column for the next week's show, I typed and delivered it on
Monday morning and waited for Hermione's response. 'Darling,
is that you?' 'Hullo, Hermione.' 'I've read the script, darling, and
it's *all wrong*.' 'Oh dear, what don't you like?' 'The *script*, darling.
Will you come round first thing in the morning?' 'When's that,
Hermione?' 'Eleven o'clock.'

I would report to Capener's Close and Hermione would be
my tutor. I thought at the time that she was demanding and dictatorial. In fact, I now realise, she was patient and educative and
invariably right. The scripts improved. They were performed to
a live audience at the Playhouse Theatre. Miles-y, a nice young
man called Miles Rudge, did another segment, in which Ken
Connor and a genial, obese actor called Alexander Gauge, were
featured. I think David Jacobs was the regular announcer.

I enjoyed losing my virginity in professional showbiz writing.
Luckily, Hermione could squeeze a laugh out of the bloodiest
audiences, with the flimsiest material. I had the satisfaction of
corpsing her once, on mike. The script required her to give a

recipe for whale meat, which had recently been a part of the national diet. Hermione was required to say 'You may wonder how to get hold of some whale meat. Try your fishmonger. He will probably respond, "Whale meat again? Don't know where, don't know when."' It is not, I concede, a line which will recommend me to mercy at the final judgment, but Hermione was suddenly, and very untypically, convulsed by it. The show could not go on for several minutes (seconds?) which remain utterly unforgettable to me. She tried to start again, but again had to turn away. The audience, luckily, caught the contagion, so all was well.

Someone remarked that Ken Tynan was at the top of the ladder. I had to say that it was true, but that he had set the ladder against the bottom of the tree.

They came to dinner and I took them for intellectual heavyweights. He wore a city suit and removed his glasses to reinforce a point. They took the world very seriously. I tried to have the same attitude but I did wonder at times whether flippancy did not have its puncturing place. A small boy frowns solemnly over an examination question at which an adult merely smiles. The smile need not be superior; it shows only that a certain stage has been passed by the one, and not by the other. I wanted to respond solemnly to solemnity, but found myself saying only, 'Oh dear!' Really, how *could* he think so much of Hegel? I have never read any Hegel, yet I know that he is worthless. He *had* read him, and still thought highly of him. He was very worthy, but not very worthwhile.

I have abbreviated this note, but not eliminated it, as it deserves. I should like to believe that, in the last few sentences, I was being straightfacedly ironic at my own expense, but I fear that I meant every insufferable word. Nothing could more damningly, or succinctly, declare the complacency which Cambridge engendered. I was not, I should like to believe, alone in presuming to 'know' that certain philosophers were not worth reading. Leavisites were similarly schooled to dismiss many authors (Shelley and Milton for contemptible instance), and nearly all living ones. I have now read some Hegel. I cannot, however, pretend to have done so on the Damascus Road; I remain unconverted.

The unsubtle economy of nature.

He cudgels you with quotations; he cripples you with allusions; he inundates you with palace gossip. His conversation may be intended to be informative, but you are more punished than enlightened. At first, you retaliate with a paradox, but he has two for the price of one of yours. He crams on the pace. You parry with an epigram; he caps it. In despair, you surrender with a truism and find that he has no answer to it. A quick platitude flattens him. He is a sucker for the commonplace. His face breaks into fat sections like a peeled orange when pressure is applied from above. A fierce blast of laughter comes out which reminds you of the snorting blare of the horn on a very red sports car.

Ruth Ellis was hanged this morning. I daresay she was a vulgar little tart with a predilection for wearing crosses round her neck, but to sentence her to die at such and such a time, in *that* way, is to make her into a dying goddess. At the thought of her death (imagine the ham-fisted hangman paying off his cab), one sees the death of the world itself. The sunny morning of a London July is dead for her, and should be for us. We elected to destroy the world when we decided, after thought, as a rational act, to destroy a human being. London shuddered in the heat, and so it should. Executions are unnatural crimes.

We rehearsed *Grande Gingold* during the day and did the show, live, in the evening. We had to follow the same routine on the very day when Ruth Ellis was hanged. We were filled with shame and horror, but the show had to go on, and did.

Arrowsmith was form master of the Remove when I went to Charterhouse. He walked with a limp, swinging his foot as you might a weight at the end of a rope. His aquiline nose started like a keel from between his ruddy brows. He had a habit of saying 'Ah, my dear sir!' in a loud, affected voice. He told us the joke about a wicketkeeper who was like the ancient mariner: 'He stoppeth one in three.' Mad about cricket, he took the first eleven for fielding practice. The passer-by could watch 'the Arrow' toss a ball in the air, limp a step and smack it once more along the turf to the Bloods waiting, with stinging hands, in an arc under Verite steps. When he hit steeplers for them, they took minutes, it seemed, to come down from the stratosphere. It was said that when he was ill, he sat up in bed wearing an I Zingari blazer, O.C. pyjamas, a first eleven cap and a club sweater.

Last night I was introduced to Brian Trench, my father's boss, at Crockford's. He was an O.C. and knew R.L.A. 'He was said to be a very good Classic, but I can't remember him playing much cricket.'

Trench shakes you firmly by the hand and wrinkles his nose like a politician answering an awkward question with frank evasiveness. He came to ask my advice about Oxford scholarships for his son. I could not help very much, but it was all the same to him because he knew everything and everyone already.

In the years that followed, preceding my father's retirement in 1960, Trench made made C.M.R.'s life an increasing misery. Nothing so confirmed my resolution never to work for a big company as the slow humiliation which was piled on my sick father. He had made a great mistake, as far as Shell was concerned, by refusing a promotion, in 1945, which would have entailed our return to New York. He persuaded himself, over the years, that his decision was determined by the fact that I had just gained a Charterhouse scholarship and was destined, it seemed, for some success in the English educational system. I suspect that he was motivated no less by the dread of having to tell his mother that he was quitting London. She was a permanent invalid, having taken to her bed in the 1930s with what some of her doctors (whose services she did not retain) diagnosed as acute indigestion. I learned to play bridge when I was eight or nine by watching her and her husband (who died soon after the war) and my parents playing on Sunday afternoons. I sat for hours at one corner of the table, adjacent to a dish of Lyons violet chocolates for which Amy had an insatiable appetite). She never liked my mother, less because she was American (which was no recommendation) than because she had taken her only son from her. He regretted her hostility to Irene, but could not bring himself to challenge it openly. He waited for his mother to come round, which she never did.

After he had declined to be promoted, and transferred, my father became a slight embarrassment to Shell. He was over-qual-ified for whatever was available in London and so was shunted

into 'press relations'. Many of his contemporaries became directors of Shell, and he was regarded with affection and respect by
most of them, but his own prospects were aborted. He showed
no open resentment at his new, somewhat menial job and, in
time, came greatly to like, and be liked by, the journalists whom
he entertained, stylishly, often at the Berkeley in Piccadilly.
When Trench was put in charge of the new department charged
with Public Relations, it seemed that he and C.M.R. were well
suited. Perhaps they had too much in common. Trench was not
used to subordinates with minds of their own and he found many
ways to irritate and undermine my father who began to accum-
late a self-justifying dossier of Trench's pompous and sometimes
ridiculous memos and decrees. This was meant to be a comfort
but merely to open it, as he often did in the evening on the dining
room table, became a trigger for obsessive and repetitive bitterness. The persecuted not only suffer from what they cannot
change; they become tiresome too. My father had the satisfaction, such as it was, of outliving Trench, but contrived no other
revenge.

In the underground. A young man got on with a Negro. The Negro
was a handsome fellow in a purple-brown suit. He said 'In my
country' quite often, in a singsong voice. The white sat away from
the Negro and turned towards him as if he were trying at once to
protect and to keep his distance from him.

D. turned up. He rang the bell and there he was, at eleven fifteen
on a weekday. 'Hullo, it's me.' He looked quite well until he had
sat down and you saw how blotchily pink his cheeks were and how
grim the flesh. He was brisk and almost gay, cracking a light laugh
as he felt for his cigarettes. He has testicular cancer. He had been
out of hospital for several days. He had not been discharged; he had
absconded. His parents did not know where he was. He had become
engaged to M., a Siamese girl whose sister, R., shared our house in
Cambridge last year. When R. first started sleeping with her English
lover, she was afraid that M. would write to their father. Instead M.
was soon following her sister's example, with less discrimination. D.
was one of her suitors and they 'became engaged to be married'.

On Thursday he heard (how?) that she was sleeping with someone
else. He got up, left the hospital and went to her flat in Fulham.

There were recriminations, and promises. She said that she loved him and belonged to him. That night she went off and slept with one of her other lovers. The next day the man came round to see M. and met D. The latter's indignation was appeased when the man, a Siamese, said that he had no idea that D. existed.

D. has now sworn never to see M. again. He is taking heavy pain-killers and walking the winter streets. I took him to lunch at Crockford's and then we went, in his car, to the O. and C., where we played snooker. He won in some comfort. Then I took him to a hotel in Bloomsbury where he had once gone with M. I felt very sorry for him and I longed to be rid of him. I shook his hand warmly and told him to phone me any time, but that I was busy for the next couple of days. I had a bridge game planned.

My first novel has been accepted for publication. It is the limit of a young writer's ambition. I am under twenty-four and I feel suddenly embarrassed by getting what I dreamed of. I was so sure of myself when I had no grounds for it, and now I am afraid that I shall be found out. But what a triumph all the same! 'This good news has quite made my day,' George Greenfield told me. Oh, and mine, and mine. Macmillan's, he assures me, have excellent relations with their authors. Jack Squire, in his reader's report, told them that they should bind me to them; they could 'expect many funny books from this chap'. Can they?

D. died.

Cefalú. We were in a *trattoria* and began talking with a solitary American. He had been in Sicily ever since the war. I imagined that he had been seduced by the myth of Aleister Crowley and his abbey of sinners. Or perhaps by Lawrencian notions of manly authenticity. Herb discovered that he was wanted for desertion by the U.S. mili-tary and was able to stay in Sicily only because he had 'friends' he did occasional jobs for. Whatever the reason, we assumed that he was happy to be in such a beautiful spot. 'Hate it,' he said.

The only copy of my new novel, *The Earlsdon Way*, has been stolen from Macmillan's office. My first reaction was to laugh. I made so many protestations before handing over the manuscript. Now not one jot remains.

1956

I finished rewriting *The Earlsdon Way*.

Dinner with Somerset Maugham at Crockford's. Guy Ramsey gave the party. Kenneth Konstam and Edward Mayer were the other guests. Afterwards we played bridge in the two-shilling room. W.S.M. clenched his cigarette-holder between his teeth in a roguish manner. He apologised for his lack of skill and increasing senility, but we had to make small allowance for them. Vivian Cox, the Pinewood producer, had asked me to remember him to the Old Party. M. said he remembered me, very well, and asked me about the trip to Spain which followed my visit to the Villa Mauresque. Mr Cox he was not able to recall. He excused himself with 'Ah well, you know, more people know Tom Fool than Tom Fool knows.'

Once I had rewritten it, Macmillans turned down *The Earlsdon Way* because it was not funny. Alan Maclean and 'Auntie Marge' took me out to lunch and, for my own good, told me that I would never make any friends if I wrote that kind of book. I said that I did not want to write books in order to make friends. I was offered fifty pounds compensation for Alan having lost my MS. I was glad to have it. It worked out at about three pounds a week for my trouble.

1957

At the BBC. B.L. is a drama producer. Recently news was brought to her that her husband had been wounded in Cyprus. She went out and bought a new hat. M. – her colleague and lover – has been married for five years. Recently, his wife called his office to find out whether he had left. His secretary was surprised. M. had been on leave for two weeks.

'This wedding ring is so tight,' she said, 'I can't imagine how I managed to get it on in the first place.'
Her husband said, 'Persistence?'

Overton's in Victoria. I happened to have lunch at the next table to Oswald Mosley. He is thick, hump-shouldered and broad. The large jutting nose is the most prominent feature in his unshapely head. The eyes are glazed; the lids and surrounding flesh carry stretched, pale freckles. He called out in a cultured voice 'Two more brandies, waiter' and then offered a clenched smile (to hide his teeth?). His conversation was about matters of high policy. He spoke of 'Hugh' and 'Nye' and 'Anthony' with contempt and envy, quite as if none of them had had his achievements. He had, it seems, all the desiderata for leadership except patience.

T.-J. told me this (they call him 'Tiddly'). The RAF bombed two ships in the bay. They could not know that they were used as prison ships and contained 'Displaced Persons'. When the ships sank, the Gestapo would not allow the DPs ashore. They shot all who survived, through the temple.
British commandos captured Schleswig-Holstein and the bodies were washed up in dozens during the early days of their occupation. The German Field-Marshal Milch surrendered to the commandos to avoid capture by the Russians. He was arrogant and bombastic: he insisted that the British and the Germans should have united to destroy the 'Bolshevik savages'.
'Savages?' said T.-J., then a brigadier. 'What about your concen-

tration camps?'

'For Slavs and such creatures,' Milch said.

After further futile conversation, T.-J. said, 'I want you to come for a walk with me.'

The Field-Marshal consented and strutted out of the mess. The Brigadier took him down to the shore where the bodies had been lugged in by the tide.

The Field-Marshal looked at them. 'Well?'

'Look closely,' T.-J. said. 'Each of these men was murdered.'

The Field-Marshal sniffed and bent to inspect the bodies. Each had a bullet wound in the temple. After he had looked at three or four, he burst into tears and sat on the wet beach.

Hugh Thomas. He has resigned from the Foreign Office and has written a novel. He is lecturing at the RMA, Sandhurst on Political Theory. He told me that the upper class young men there had lost everything in the way of intelligence, wit and the spirit of adventure which had dignified their fathers. They retained only one thing: politeness.

M. I first met him in Granada, when I was travelling with the Oppenheimers. A grey-faced man with pudgy features, he was staying at the Washington Irving and needed a fourth for bridge. When three-year-old Linda started to cry, he suggested that she be given a 'hiding'.

During the war he was a supply officer in Burma. The Chindits kept asking him for things that he couldn't provide and making him provide them. He came back to England and resumed being a stock-broker in Aylesbury. He lived with his parents. Each week he came up to London and played bridge at the Oxford and Cambridge Club, where I met him again.

One day we heard that he had been accused of assaulting a Negro soldier on the train. He was acquitted. He drank a lot. He told me that he knew exactly what he was going to do in the next war: 'I shall polish up my morse and become a wireless officer on a small merchant ship.' The other day he was killed in an accident on the promenade at Eastbourne. When one of the O. and C. judges murmured some perfunctory regret, H. T.-J. said, 'I don't know which I disliked more – the sight of him or the sound of him.'

In the Caprice bar. A humped man with fuzzy white hair on a bald pate. Black suit, stiff collar, bow-tie, gold rimmed glasses, the very type of gentleman whose word is his bond. When he went into dinner, it was clear that he had a stroke recently: they had to push him attentively into his place. His name was Holroyd Reese. He was one of the most successful swindlers in the world: 750,000 pounds embezzled, and never brought to trial.

Memories of childhood. 1943. Dad and I were at the bus stop waiting for a 37 at East Putney on the way home from the golf club. The bus came, and was full. I said, 'If this was Germany, we could chuck a couple of people off and get on ourselves.' He said, 'If this was Germany we would both be dead.'

1944. We were walking up Putney Hill when the bombs began to fall. We started running towards a shelter in Lytton Grove, a block of flats. I ran with my hand on top of my school cap. When we reached the shelter my mother said, 'Did you think that putting your hand on your head would protect you?'

'No,' I said. 'I was afraid that if my cap fell off, daddy would send me back to fetch it.'

Lee Bay in 1941. We were evacuated to a hotel with easy access to a sandy beach, badged with limpet-covered rocks. Delamain and I made elaborate towns and road systems on the long double-summer time afternoons. Mr Drake, whose own school had been closed by the war, arrived to help teach. He had a face at which sarcasm tugged like a spasm. He looked at the happy scene with disgust. 'The little girls are playing on the beach,' he said.

My father to me in the car: 'Remember, you always come third.'

The U.S. in 1935: rusting car lots on the road to Aurora, Illinois, with my grandmother in the 'rumple-seat', as we drove to New York.

The Legal Aid centre is off the Holloway Road. Two desks, one brown and old, the other treacle-coloured and new. Filing cabinets. Three black chairs for clients. A white couple sought Bernard's advice because their landlady was trying to throw them out of the flat they had occupied for fifteen years. She wanted to put Negroes into it. They will pay much higher rents.

Sir Douglas Fairbanks. He has an office overlooking Hyde Park. A door laden with plaques announcing various Fairbanks enterprises ('We have to have them for tax reasons') gives entrance to the royal apartments.

'The sun is over the yardarm, gentlemen,' he said, as K.H., the Granada producer, L.C.B. and I were shown in. 'I'm afraid I haven't any gin. I can offer you whisky, vodka and tonic...' He is fifty, with easy smile lines on the triangular face. Below the eyes there is only the smile and a scimitar of elegant moustache. 'I'm unique,' he told us, 'unique bad or unique good, depending on how you look at it.'

Two henchmen, Mr W. and Mr K., left us in no doubt how they looked at it, and how we should. Our mission was to suggest a way for him to do a TV show that would be 'different'.

F. – someone had described him to us as 'grey all over' – sat behind the wide shelf of his desk and talked about himself as about a very old friend. 'If I do what everyone does, I might as well not be on the programme.'

'What did you feel about last week's show?' I asked.

'Here's the consensus. This is of friends, you know. They thought I was nervous. That's ridiculous: I was not nervous at all. Then they thought I was condescending. Of course I'm *not* condescending, but that's what they thought. And gushing...'

'Of course that's ridiculous,' Mr. W. said. 'You're not gushing at all.'

'No, I'm not. How's the billing going to read? Could we get a lead there? Granada TV and Douglas Fairbanks...'

'We can't have that,' K.H. said. 'Granada have to be the programme contractors. That's under The Act.'

The phone rang: Selwyn Lloyd to say that, yes, he could come for cocktails on Saturday. Mrs Fairbanks had to be called, and told. It seemed that Selwyn Lloyd was filling in for some celebrity who couldn't make it.

'Now, gentlemen, a refill?'

'What about putting you in an office?' L.C.B. said.

'Too formal.'

'Or with a – '

'No props.'

'Perhaps you could do something...funny.'

'I'm not a gag man.'

'What about a backstage approach?'

'A knock on the dressing room door, "You're on, Mr Fairbanks" and all that?'

'You could try the Garroway approach,' Mr K. said.

Should we have known what that was? We didn't.

'This guy did this show on Chicago TV – this is the Chicago show I'm talking about, not the New York one. He just sort of wandered on and *announced* the next act, *casually* – he had this manner, it got to be so famous they called it the Garroway approach.'

'Casual?' Douggie said.

'Totally. Totally casual. The Chicago show this was.' Mr K. took his hat. 'Gotta go. That's just a suggestion.'

'Of course,' Douggie said, 'that's the way we do things. We just bounce an idea off the wall…'

Two hours later we were in the street, watching Sir D. being driven off in his Rolls-Bentley (sitting next to the chauffeur).

I said to K.H. 'How does he really see himself doing the show?'

'He sees himself doing it in the ambassador's room in the American Embassy against the crossed flags of Britain and America and wearing the uniform of an Admiral of the Fleet.'

'But how's he *going* to do it?' L.C.B. asked.

'That's your problem.'

We never solved it.

My grandmother's funeral. Two black-uniformed attendants, in black peak caps, watched us drive in through the cemetery gates. My great-aunt Polly was with us in the car. My mother tried to lighten the atmosphere by asking the usual question, 'Did anyone ever tell you you looked like Marie Tempest, Poll?'

'Everyone. She was an ugly old cat. But what a voice! I was going to be in the chorus of *The Geisha* with her. Had me photo taken in the costume.'

The trolley was outside the mortuary. Dad went in, alone, before they nailed the lid down. The rabbi arrived in a baby Austin, a dark, fleshy man with soft eyes. The coffin was strapped to the trolley, flowers superimposed. There was a short service and then we followed the slow cart, up the marble avenue, to the far end of the cemetery.

It was hot. Rinds of earth were piled aside for the grave. Three labourers, bare-chested and crusted with clay seemed just to have completed their work. As they lifted the coffin from the trolley, the attendant linked his hand, for balance, with one of the labourer's. Effort fattened their hands. The coffin was lowered; prayers were said. Dad was handed a narrow shovel. 'Three times, please.'

A pile of cinders had been put beside the heavy clay. Dad drove in the shovel. I put my hand on his shoulder; he seemed so near the grave that I wanted to retain his connection with life.

When it was all finished and we were back at the chapel, Dad was overcome and sat down on a varnished bench. The rabbi shook hands with all of us and went.

I drove us back to our house in Rutland Street, dropping Polly on the way. Dad lay down on the orange-skirted divan, but could not sleep.

He went to get a haircut at Harrod's. He told the barber his troubles. The barber said, 'See that bloke over there? His son came back from Cyprus with cancer of the throat. He died after a nine months' illness. He was nineteen.'

1958

Brendan Behan. I went with Tom to Blackheath to interview him. The Mill House is a large white building with a triangle of lawn. Behan, in unbuttoned shirt and trousers, no shoes, was on the telephone, talking about a lecture that Christina Foyle wanted him to do. 'What's wrong with this fuckin' thing?' Barrel-chested, curly sandy hair, fat face, sweet mouth, feet and hands small and puffy like a baby's. 'Have some whisky. It's all right, it's embassy whisky, duty-free.' Beatrice, his wife, big-eyed and freckled, brought glasses and poured with a tired hand.

At last, we shuffled off to the pub. 'We'll have a couple of drinks and then we'll do the interview.' As we left the house, he grabbed my genitals. 'Come on, boy!'

On the way he pressed half a crown into the neighbour's baby's hand as she lay in her pram. 'If she grips it, that's good luck. She's gripped it – see that? – she gripped it. That's good luck.'

When acquaintances called out 'good morning' he responded, 'Bonjour, bonjour.'

The Railway Hotel was a gloomy pub in the heart of the village. The public bar was a brown-black dust hole with sagging leather benches. A Spaniard was waiting for Brendan. 'I waited from twelve till three yesterday. You arranged to meet me.'

'Couldn't make it,' Brendan said.

'You arranged to meet me.'

'Couldn't make it. Give me a drink, Rosie.'

People came in, whiskey gents in green bowler hats, and slapped B. on the back. A stranger bumped into him and said, 'Sorry.'

'We'll excuse it this time,' B.B. said, 'but next time WATCH OUT!'

He pulled down his sagging white sweater. He was very pink and clean. He had a great loving quality. He would drivel on and then saying something perfect. We took a taxi back to do the interview which he was worried I would not get if we stayed in the pub. As we reached the Mill House, the other tenant was mowing the triangle of lawn. B. said, 'Look at that cunt.'

1959

I gave our charlady, Mrs May, a lift home. A humped over, butter-faced horse-toothed woman, moles with threads sticking out of them like threaded needles in a pin-cushion. Mother Mays they call her, old sack of potatoes, with a sick husband who used to work in the transport till he had his accident – they can't prove nothing though. She works for three sets of people, all Jewish – they're nice though, aren't they, the Jew people, nicer'n our people sometimes, I think. Stuck up, our people are, posh, they're very posh, our people; I like Jewish people myself. Course you're English really, aren't you, same as us really, Jewish people are; mother Mays coming home with a Jewboy, that's what they'll be saying, you know, oh those boys, in't it dreadful the murders, burglaries, dreadful really, in it, them burglaries; course, you've got to be careful I mean. And the women, bad women, prostitutes in'ey? I think it's dreadful them bad women, don't you? Course, my mother she brought us up very strict. She was a well-spoken woman, my mother, she brought us up to speak proper, yes. My George is nicely spoken, I'm very nervous you know; my nerves. I get very strung up. I think it was the bombs, the blitz. I think that's what did it, didn't do us no good. No. I blame myself. My Alec you know, he says to me, oh mum, why didn't you evacuate me? I kept 'im with me, my Alec. I feel guilty. Now I feel guilty. He's a nice boy, my Alec, nicely spoken boy. I suffer a lot with my nerves, you know. I take a Guinness for it, twice a week. In'it dear though? One and four now. Gone down. One and five at the posh pubs. In'it dear though? Yes, oh I like my Guinness – Bulldog Guinness, that's the best kind. I take it in two halves, you know. Yes. Course, my George, he's a nicely spoken boy. Clever. He's clever. And of course he was only young. I mean, he didn't know what he was doing really, George. Nursed him with a broken heart. Six months I nursed him with a broken heart 'cos of that girl. Course he was only young. Right after the war; he didn't know what he was doing really. I like polishing. It's hard work, mind; but I've got the muscle, see? You need muscle for polishin'. There, that's come up nicely. Yes, I nursed him with a broken heart.

Mother Mays' son married a German girl very soon after the war.
They came to England to live – George this was – and he got a job.
Her mother came over and they gave a party for her – booze, whisky
and gin and sandwiches'n'all – and she took her daughter and the
child back to Germany for a holiday. The wife never come back.
George joined the army to get out there. Signed on for seven years.

A lobster leaning on an oar.

At Lincoln, Oxford, for dinner with J.P.Sullivan, now the Dean.
W.W.Robson, at high table: 'One thing you can say for Wain and
Amis: they have got quite a good sense of humour, except for Wain.'
W.W.R. affected to despise K.A. because he kept a notebook, but
he was eager to tell us that Kingsley had used two of his, Robson's,
jokes in *Lucky Jim*.

If I am anyone to go by, a writer's notebooks grow thicker in
inverse proportion to his other work. In the years between 1960
and 1969, I scarcely had time for the kind of careful inventories
of places and people which marked my apprenticeship, still less
(happily) for sententious introspection. Beetle and I were devas-
tated when, after spending all our capital on yet more key money,
for a garden flat in Highgate where our newborn son, Paul, could
crawl among the roses, we were denied a promised new lease.
We could not afford to stay in London, but did not know where
else to go. Tom Maschler had the answer: he had an ex-girl friend
who owned a small house in Fuengirola, a remote and tiny fishing
village on the Costa del Sol. We could have it for next to nothing.
We took it; and were thus forced to a decision which shaped our
future and seems, in retropect, providential. I was given a
hundred pounds as an advance on a new novel and we left
England with our Ford Anglia heaped with everything we
owned. I began to write one novel, literally, after another. I
finished *The Trouble with England* on a Friday and began *A Wild
Surmise* on the Monday. There was almost no time at all for my
notebook. I shall make no effort here to chronicle our and our
children's lives, which were to change literally out of recognition during the 1960s. My notebooks are those of a working
writer, not of a diarist, still less of an autobiographer.

1960

'"Spend the winter in sunny Spain," that's what the advertisements said and I thought to myself, why not?' This was Miss A., a retired headmistress and president of her local Conservative Association. She was a not ill-preserved lady, pink and blonde. She had taken a flat in Fuengirola and wore espadrilles and a big straw hat and smoked Celtas. She had a brigadier and his wife for downstairs neighbours and they were 'Darlings'.

She was an embracing sort of lady. She embraced my Spanish grammar and had to be prised free of it. She came to Larry's party in the Calle Toston and thereafter always referred to him as *Mister* Larry Potter. She was determined not to be shocked, but had never expected to enjoy Bohemian company as much as she did.

Towards the end of the winter, she went on a trip to Cordoba where she met a bullfighter who escorted her to the top of the *Mezquita* tower, *after hours*. He there kissed her passionately and declared his love. He took her out and, she said, was bitterly hurt when, 'regretfully', she rejected his final gallant advances. Asked what the local Conservatives would think of her behaviour, she said, 'They would expel me.' She seemed rather to relish the idea.

In the Casino Bar. Charlie Reiter told me about this detective story writer who has taken a place in the village. Charlie said he had trouble with Negroes and Jews. He didn't like them.

A grey day with a grey sea rolling crestless waves to the beach. A man had swum out too far. Cars were parked all along the *carretera* and the beach was thick with spectators. Two rescuers reached the man with a lifebelt, laid him over it and were hauling and butting it towards safety. The man was limp; the slow, heavy water lapped over him. Busy people on shore were collecting ropes to make into a long line to throw to the men in the sea. The rescuers were tired and seemed to hang endlessly on the horizon of the waves. The busy men were barefoot, their trousers rolled over cold knees. As the rescuers worked their way in, they got the line out to them. The radio above the bar on the beach played gay music. The barman made many sales.

An ambulance came from Malaga. When the rescuers reached shallow water they were displaced by the busy men with blankets and stretching arms (Doctor Johnson's patrons). There was perfunctory applause. Admiration for the rescuers was muted by a feeling of contempt for the man who was drowning. 'He went out too far, the madman: *era loco, no?*' He was put into the ambulance like a bull who had fought badly and survives to die ignominiously elsewhere, out of sight.

O. was jealous of a painter who came into town who had already sold a hundred canvases. He was quite the Bohemian, with a beret, a bright red shirt, blue pants, 'Very West Coast,' someone told me. O. asked him which gallery he showed with and the guy said he sold his pictures through his father's furniture store. O. felt better.

Antonio, who kept the bar in Malaga, wanted to emigrate to Australia with his family. It was all agreed, with a job arranged and passages booked, when they turned him down. He had to go to Madrid with his children for the final approval. After the long train journey, they had soiled themselves and were rejected because they were smelly and dirty.

The Spaniards 'beatified' a young man who they believed had drowned after drawing a fish – symbol of his Christian faith in a better world – in the sand. He was later discovered to have faked suicide and started a new life elsewhere. He preferred to find his salvation this side of the grave.

1961

Claro? A liberal American professor, on a sabbatical, comes to Torreroja to lead the simple life. He does not mix with the tourists who despise the local people and follow their maids to market to check their change. He tells his widowed housekeeper, Salvadora, that he has better things to do than check *cuentas*. He prefers to improve his Spanish. *Claro? Claro.* He leaves cash about the house to advertise to S. that he trusts her. One day quite a large sum of money disappears. It has to be S. who has taken it. She denies and denies it. He is so frustrated that he strikes her and she confesses. He is touched, and excited. She allows, and enjoys, his conquest of her. Afterwards, he tells her he will give her anything she or her family needs.

'Why do you take everything from us?'

'Excuse me. Do what?'

'*Si, señor, todo!* You want to remove from us our last and only freedom. We do not want you to give us your money. We want to steal it from you. We do not want to feel anything for you. That is why we prefer those who cannot speak *muy bien Español* and do not try to understand us and our problems. Leave us free to hate you and to steal from you. One day we shall steal from you your life and we will live happily ever after. *Claro?*'

There is a café on the road to Malaga, a cheap *bodega* with unpainted chairs and tables. The *Guardias* were tipped off that a Red was there one night. They went to get him. He put up a fight and they killed him. It turned out that they had killed a commercial traveller from Barcelona. Since then, Bill D. likes to go down to this café, which is not convenient, and drink. He thinks it 'more real' than the Casino bar. He likes people to think that he always went drinking in this place they shot a man. When he plays poker, he plays *serious* poker. If you tease him, he says, 'Up yours with a hay-rake, Jack.' And *means it*.

Re Catullus. Romans largely vegetarians; pork only meat

commonly eaten. Grain, vegetables, cheese, herbs; loaves divided
into four. Wine or water. No beer or spirits. Best wine Greek. Local
(?) wine very cheap: six gallons for eight pence under Columella.
Water from Tivoli brought by Manlius Curius Dentatus. Q. Marcius
Rex, 144 BC, brought water from Sabine Hills, thirty-six miles
behind Tivoli; best water, last six miles abve ground. 700,000 c.m.
a day, collected in *castella* then distributed to public fountains. Piped,
later, to *insulae* and *domus*.

c. AD 200. The Octavius of Minucius Felix. Caecilius leads off against
Christianity, includes the Ritual Murder charge.

Wolf. He sits behind a steel-topped desk with a lamp on a gantry
from the wall. There are steel cabinets and African sculptures and
framed theatre bills on the walls. He is flabby, yet tough like a retired
wrestler. Inside the fat man is a thin one, struggling to stay in. He
juts his lips in an expression of contemplative, grudging agreement.
His hair, thick on chest and neck, is fine and seems to belong to a
smaller, more modest man. He confesses that he will do anything
for money. His brazenness is a shield against the contempt of those
whom he still hopes secretly to impress. When he tells you the truth
he expects you not to believe it.

1962

Mykonos. T. and M. were coming to Greece. On his advice, I booked us at the best hotel. When they arrived, they thought it too expensive and wanted to find a room in the village. After weeks of genuinely primitive life on Ios, we were glad to have a little luxury; also we had children and they did not. They immediately found 'friends'; a dress and fabric designer asked M. to model for him, in the grounds of the richest man on the island (T. saw him putting buttered toast into a bag 'for the dogs', while breakfasting at the big café). Wherever M. goes, there are famous people; if they lack fame, she bestows it on them. Anyone without a Name is dull. She told us that the fabrics which Robert and his friend were using were all the rage with top designers in Rome. We had recently spent several months in Rome, but knew nothing of the designer whose name she dropped.

At 3.30 in the morning, as we got off the steamer, I had asked to borrow *The Observer*, which was sticking out of the basket of the lady in front of me. I had been told it carried a favourable review of *The Graduate Wife*. The lady understood my impatience very well: she was Elaine Steinbeck. T. and M. were later somewhat dashed that we had met the Steinbecks before they did.

In ΑΝΤΟΝΗΝΗΣ *taverna* we saw ex-Queen Soraya. She sat sadly in her beautiful clothes and her beautiful body, like a fugitive who finds others more willing to believe in her disguise than she does herself. Two attendant women were always with her; they supported her doused queenliness with wilful affection. One of them had deserted her husband in Athens, we were told, to take care of S., who no longer (supposedly) cared for men. The Steinbecks were also there. Three young Greeks danced. They were soon joined by a young American woman, blonde, high-cheeked, prune-mouthed, high-breasted, silly-faced; like someone holding a pose in some idiot game. She breached their delicate rhythm, but she was sleeping with one of them and could not be rejected. During the dance, one of

the men bent down, put his teeth to the corner of a table decked
with glasses, fruit and bottles, and raised it. 'It's a trick,' M. said. Of
course the weight of the table was supported against his chest, but
he moved with easy lightness among the diners, in time with the
music. Steinbeck waved to me across the room. M. said, 'Who was
that?' I said, 'A friend.' 'No, who *was* that?'

At the beach. We lunched on fish, salad, *ntomates yemistes*. A bronze
and silver Englishman and his razor-faced boy-friend were next to
us. They never spoke. M. thought the young man 'very beautiful,
a wonderful body'. To me he looked as beautiful as a rubber trun-
cheon. He had a recessed navel that could have belonged to a
sixpence-in-the-slot machine.

Two years later I saw the same Englishman having lunch at *Le
Matelot*, a chic eating place between Ebury St and Eaton Square.
He was being served by a waiter in a sailor suit. He was eating
with a little old lady to whom he spoke in an affectionate,
educated voice, though his eyes were devoted to the waiter.

In the evening, at the *taverna*. A middle-aged American couple; he
admired my Greek: a pal. He admired Beetle's new *pantalonia*: a *real*
pal. He wished he could get some pants for his daughters, but
guessed they wouldn't look as good on them as hers did on B. Soon
after, T. and M. arrived, late from being important somewhere. As
the Americans were leaving, the man stopped and asked my name
and seemed embarrassed because he had seen a review of one of my
books in the US press. T. was not pleased; one of his ambitions is
to publish me. He would not like me to be famous before I had to
be grateful to him for my fame.

In Athens. A row over some sunglasses, which were supposed to
have been repaired and immediately fell apart. The bystanders
divided into non-Athenians, who supported me, and Athenians,
who took the salesman's side. I was more showily angry than the
occasion required because the non-Athenians so much appreciated
the fluency of my Greek reproaches. Later, I threw the glasses away.

We reached Skopje in the evening, across bad roads. I asked a
policeman for the Hotel Macedonia. I went down the street he indi-

cated and at the end of it we found four foreign cars and two red-starred policemen. A bronzed Englishman driving a VW minibus told me that everyone was being fined for coming down the street after 5 p.m., when it became one way. Beetle was furious; certain that this was a way of robbing foreigners. The hotel was hot, dirty, and expensive. Pictures of Tito everywhere. The mineral water tasted of drains. The whole place makes you realise the degree to which you rely on privileges. No one willingly abandons them; people always imagine they will be able to smuggle some in. A few years later the Hotel Macedonia collapsed in an earthquake.

Two Clacton landladies in the London train. One asked the other if she drove.

'No, I never have.'

'I passed my test last year. My husband went on at me, said I ought to take it, so eventually I did. I phoned to tell him I'd passed and they told me he was dead. So he never knew. Sad, really; I mean, it was his idea. I phoned his office and they told me he was dead.'

Later, the same two:

'Is your son married?'

'Robert? Not yet. He's got someone he's… interested in.'

'That red-haired girl I used to see him with last year?'

'*No*. No. She turned out to be, well, a little horror really. All she wanted was to get married. He came back from Cyprus and he had no money and all she wanted was to get married. So anyway now he's got this new girl. Margaret her name is. You know he's always gone around with these same boys – the Three Musketeers really except there's four of them – they've always gone around together; they were scouts together. All the others have married Margarets and, well, when they heard Robert was developing a Margaret as well, they roared, they shrieked.'

'What was the other one called?'

'Stella, she was.'

'Oh yes. Well, this one's better, isn't it? Margaret. Nicer name.'

In the underground: a man with his ticket tucked under his watch.

1963

'We tried being patriotic, we tried being philanthropic, we tried being everything and it didn't do us a damned bit of good. If they want to kill us, they'll kill us. What does it matter what we do? We'll do what we want to do and be damned to the lot of them. We'll be ourselves and they can do what they want to do.'

March. At *Les Darquets*. John S. came for the weekend, to see how the script is getting on. As I drove with B. to the airport to meet him, I romanced about his Caravelle crashing. Imagine the news story about the brilliant young director coming to see me. He seemed so important, so intimidating, so big. I had quite other feelings when I drove him to Nice on Monday morning. I hoped, without reserve, that he would arrive safely in Paris, where he was going to lunch with Jo and 'another writer'. Having diminished to the status of a friend, he no longer seemed very creditable to know.

He is 37, short, stout, thick-necked, almost totally bald. He likes pink, pink shirts, pink pyjamas. He lacks confidence, wonders when it's all going to go sour. Sherborne and Oxford, the son of a well-to-do doctor, who still dresses for dinner, he has the well-kept, cultured style of a man-about-Europe. He is also ill-read, limited in his interests, observant but not critical. His father has an unshakable kingdom over him; when he seeks to recount the pains of child-hood, they all come out pleasures: the big house in Hampstead, with seven servants, the country place (where, he said, they 'began to live' when the whole family, including two grandmothers, went down there during the war). He hated Sherborne, but he is in favour of boarding schools. The old family nanny is loyal, and he to her, but she is sometimes a drag: drops ash in the *soufflé*, but always comes to his first nights, travelled to his first professional appearance as an actor at Colchester Rep. He still has a place in synagogue. He cannot sever his connection with his parents' world. He has travelled but has no *knowledge* of foreign countries. He loves music (wants to direct an opera) but has little understanding of the uses of speech;

only clichés amuse him. He is eager for a script that will *explain*; he admires *and* is disappointed.

We walked from *Les Darquets* and through the gates into a huge private domain, ending in a locked up property overlooking the valley of the Loup. The turrets and outhouses (there was even a little chapel) gave the manor a seigneurial appeal, like Combray. It all appealed greatly to our little dauphin (J. reminded me of that crafty, witty, bitter, *subjugated* Shavian prince).

Those who cannot settle their emotional stomachs appease them, eagerly, with property and possessions. J. told me he was doing some advertising films in order to acquire a piece of 'early Roman sculpture' which he had seen in a friend's gallery. Even his archaeology is done in drawing rooms. He gets two hundred guineas for a day's work. He spoke of doing commercials well! Did he suspect what I sometimes think is true, that writing scripts for him and Jo is my kind of whoring? Film-making, the highest of his ambitions, is the least of mine.

Peter Churchill. His wife said he played the piano like a mixture of Billy Mayerl and Charlie Kunz. The famous wartime secret agent is now an estate agent. He moves like a cat in slippers; his narrow, grey face and his soft, explicit voice are with you before you are ready. Early on, they allowed me to make a telephone call from their place. His present wife was our dentist Gerald Lewin's old secretary; P.C.'s first was Odette. Gerald, my father's friend, was in the navy during the war. Trying on his officer's cap made me want to go to Dartmouth.

The Churchills live in an old *bergerie* tastelessly modernised, with a fine view over the olive-striped valley. He alluded to Buckmaster with a kind of velvety deference laced with malice.

I saw him one afternoon, standing by his Simca, in a grey plastic mackintosh and a Tyrolean hat. He looked the very type of his torturers. He is quite cynical, reverential about money, with no sympathy for those who lack it. He does not seem very clever, but he plays his cards with immaculate sang-froid. He is never without a handkerchief.

One can imagine a story about an 'idealistic' young journalist who cannot reconcile the wartime hero with the mercenary Riviera lightweight. Finally he asks the P.C. character to explain how he can live such a life after all the agony he had been through. Isn't it a let-down?

'Let-down? This is the only thing that makes it all worthwhile.'

June. So far J. has contributed nothing. He chides me for making
the script 'too cinematic'. He fears, I suspect, that unless it is rougher
he will get no credit for smoothing it; he is a finisher, not a beginner.
He doesn't want to know what my imagination can supply; he wants
only the opportunity to be daring in the context of his writer's
pedestrianism. His attitude is determined by concern for his own
credit; this determines every word. He is forever writing (in *Films
and Filming* etc.) of his struggles, as if until this intrepid charcoal-
burner entered the wood all had been tangled and disorderly jungle.
He battles against the yahoos, and who are they? The enemies of
his own progress. I do not trust him at all, though I like him. He is
an engine that runs smoothly when others supply the fuel. He spoke
of my eagerness to re-write a script, as if it were an automatic feature
of my participation, not a privilege to be won.

His style is documentary. He thinks that there is propriety in
giving priority to what 'really happens'. It evades the call to create.
Imagine Truffaut or Antonioni justifying a set-up by consulting 'the
facts'! Antonioni has just had to stop filming his new picture because
the money dried up. Here is the basis of J.S.'s 'artistic' scruples: if
we are *too* daring, there won't be any more money. 'Oh Lord,' is
his prayer, 'make me an artist, but not too much of one.'

Lindmann has come out. Clive D., trying to be encouraging, made
me a long speech about how I ought to be pleased at the manner
and length of my reviews. The only piece he specified, however,
was Simon Raven's: how sympathetically they all like to see you
torn to pieces! You would think that Clive was the Maestro and I
the pupil; no, *he* would. At the launch party, I was flanked by
Anthony Thwaite and ditto Curtis. I told them of Henry Treece's
grateful letter, after I praised his *Electra*. They both pulled curdled
little faces.

Raymond Stross: 'All my life I've been a pretty bad Jew, do you
know what I mean? But a few years ago I lost my mother. In a sort
of way we'd been pretty devoted. I mean, spend a week with her,
we got along fine; three weeks – I couldn't stand the sight of her.
But recently I went to Israel for the first time and I was affected –
emotionally affected – in a way I couldn't believe possible. Several
times, I broke down crying in the street, broke down and cried in
the street. So, I want to make some pictures out there. I want to
make two pictures this autumn, back to back. The lawyers are going
to be out there and I'm supposed to fly out today to sign the

contracts, only I'm not well enough. I only came out the Nursing Home yesterday, y'know? Sinus trouble. I had to have these two bones removed. Pain? I can tell you, I had to have four sleeping pills to send me off to sleep. Terrible. Anyway – I was moved to tears. So I want to make these two pictures this autumn.'

He was wearing a blue denim shirt, striped beach trousers and blue espadrilles. He sucked a cigar – 'my only vice' (not what I've heard) – and sat propped among pillows like a plump little pig in a bed of mashed potatoes. He kept telling me how he hates 'this business' and Wardour St, with its interminable talk of grosses. These films in Israel, they were going to be his way of 'giving something back'. That's why he wanted to talk to me.

The Old Boys. They go to play the school on a regular day in December. The team is composed of fairly recent old boys, though though have the accoutrements of maturity: jobs, clothes, cars and, some of them, women. They arrive in buoyant mood, glad to have left 'all this' behind them. During the day, however, the influence of the place, and the reminder of old privileges and distinctions, works on them. Those who were once allowed, by their office or colours, to sit in certain chairs, wear fancy 'haberdashery', eat standing up, become humorously scornful of those who now do what they are 'still' not entitled to do. It is suggested, 'for fun', that the old rules should always apply on this particular day.

G. demurs. The most successful in life, he was less so at school. He has travelled widely, speaks foreign languages, works for a newspaper and has even scored two goals against the school that very afternoon. 'As a joke', he is 'tried' by the rest of the team for 'festivity' (the school slang for cheek) when he sits in the head-monitor's inscribed chair. The others decide that he deserves to be bent over it and beaten. They have again become schoolboys; they are joking and they are not joking. They are somehow made more powerful, even irresistible, by virtue of their corporate decision to teach G. a lesson. Always smiling, never 'meaning anything'. The fat boy (another Jew?), G.'s friend, who – as he did at school – becomes the passive accomplice of G.'s humiliation (real or attempted). G. suddenly breaks free of them and does something 'sacrilegious': throws the House Cup through the window. The spell is broken. He goes and gets into his big car. They watch him go. 'Can't take a joke,' the fat boy says, 'some people.'

'What the Germans need is white officers for two generations.' We were on the late train to Colchester. The two men were sitting opposite us, in dinner jackets. The speaker was very bitter about the Tory government over the Galbraith affair, the Vassall tribunal and their attempts to dragoon the press. I asked if he was a journalist. He said, '*Reporter*. I'm a reporter.'

He had worked in Germany before the war. During it, he had been captured. He was a Warrant Officer but his German gave him a high place in the escape organisation. 'I had a bit of trouble with the natives,' he said. 'Disagreements with the natives.' He escaped three times, the last successfully, over the Pyrenees. Franco put him in a camp at Miranda.

He said the bravest thing he ever saw done was done by a chap called Monty Lehman. The Germans came to the p.o.w. camp (for whose commandant he had a real affection: 'I'd've contributed to his funeral any time, any time') and asked the commander of the British airmen to sort out his Jews. He refused to do so, but Monty marched forward, rags around his feet, this being a prison for hard cases, and snapped into a salute: 'Arm came up, "I'm a Jew, sir," he said.' The reporter repeated the action of the salute several times. '"I'm a Jew, sir." Am I treading on corns here?'

I said, 'On the contrary.'

'Bravest thing I ever saw. Been in England longer than I had, Monty Lehman. Since Cromwell.'

He talked about one of the guards he had 'bent' and who had later been executed. He regretted it, casually. He had killed an Austrian forest ranger whose boots he wanted. After killing him, he discovered the boots were the wrong size. On another occasion, he stole a bicycle and was caught and put in Vienna jail for a month. He said he still believed in God, and so did Monty Lehman. When you were in solitary confinement you realised – 'apologies to the lady' – that you're nothing but a tiny drop of piddle.

Wartime experiences had turned him into a pacificist, he said. Not that he held with CND. CND was as good as treason. When he produced cigarettes, the other man pointed to the NO SMOKING sign. Could fascism happen here? They both thought it could: the violence of youth alarmed them.

The second man had been to a dinner of the Society of Chartered Accountants. He had a bundle of menus with him. The *scampi bonne femme* was the most delicious thing he had ever tasted. He had said very little while the other man reminisced, but his face became more and more engorged until finally he broke out, 'Have you ever seen a man's face when he knows he's going to die? I have. And if you've

seen it once, you don't want to see it again.' He too had been in
the RAF, an observer. 'Me too,' the other man said.

The accountant had been a navigator on a Wimpey. 'Oh my god,'
said the other man, 'that was a terrible aircraft, that was a right old…'

'We got shot up and we had to land about thirty miles north of
Rome, in an area still held by the Germans.'

'Near Civitavecchia?'

'Yes. *Yes*, as a matter of fact.'

They got down on the airfield and were promptly arrested by a
couple of Germans. They knocked one out and shot the other one
with his own rifle.

I said, 'Why?'

'We wanted to get away. All we thought was we wanted to get
back to our chaps. I'll never forget the look on his face; not pretty.
When he knew we were going to kill him. You can't describe it.
It's just a thing you never forget. Thank God I wasn't the one who
had to pull the trigger. I'll never forget the shot. Loudest thing I
ever heard in my life.'

Why could they not have tied the man up, I wondered.

'He was between us and freedom. That's all there was to it.'

I did not quite understand, since he also told us that the German
had been a decent chap and shared cigarettes with the man who
killed him. He could never do it again. The episode had made him
a pacifist. 'We're both pacifists then.'

The reporter said he believed in God, but couldn't bear
Christmas. All the children gathered together made him think of
the children he had dropped bombs on. He thought of them all
burning. That said, he certainly wasn't, as he said, CND. He'd drop
the H-bomb himself if he had to. 'Oh yes,' said the other chap. 'So
would I.'

The reporter got out at Witham. The accountant said that it was
difficult for an ordinary man to make any sense of life. It was up to
the writers to show people how they ought to live.

J.J. was in partnership for years with L., a director who, when they
first knew each other, was in demand. When his latest project was
cancelled, he broke down in tears at J.J.'s house. 'It was embarrassing
like hell, I must say. I never saw a grown man in such tears.' J.J.
drove him home but he didn't dare go in to the second wife whom
J.J. had encouraged him to marry when he seemed successful. L.
walked away from his house and, so he told J.J. later, walked the
streets all night. J.J. called L.'s first wife his 'steak and kidney

pudding' because L. was always rushing off at night to get home to her. He was trying to resist the temptation of the other woman, who later became his present wife. He is sure that she will now despise him for a failure.

'No two wizout a sree.' Jo swears this is true: one of his oldest friends is a South American, R., whom he considers the luckiest man he knows. He has a beautiful, intelligent and wealthy wife ('And a mistress?' John asked), and a mistress. He was on an airliner flying from New York to Buenos Aires and got off when it stopped to refuel. R. got drunk and missed it when it took off again. It crashed and everyone was killed. Soon afterwards, in Europe, R. was booked on a Caravelle Munich to Nice and cancelled his passage half an hour before take-off because his wife begged him to join her in Milan. The Caravelle crashed and everyone was killed. R. told Jo this story at the airport in Milan. They were due to fly to London together. Jo said, 'When is it going to happpen again? There's no two wizout a sree.'

They had checked through for their flight when it was discovered that some seats had been sold twice. Six passengers would have to wait for the next flight; one of them was Jo's South American friend. He said he didn't mind waiting. '*I* mind,' Jo said. He stormed and raged in the manager's office. 'But, signor Janni, you are *on* the plane.'

'But I want *him* be on it too,' Jo said. He *knew* that if he flew without R., the plane would crash. Finally, however, he flew without him. It was the most miserable flight of his life.

Not long ago, R. had to fly to Los Angeles. They were already beyond the point of no return across the Atlantic when the pilot came through. Click: 'Ladies and gentlemen, we are going to have to make an unscheduled stop at Boston.'

R. checked the engines and the complexion of the stewardesses, who claimed not to know what the problem was. Soon there was another click on the intercom. 'We regret to inform you that we have had some extremely bad news.' No two without a three: R. was sure that disaster was imminent. All the passengers looked nervously out of their windows. Click: 'I regret to inform you that the President of the United States, John F. Kennedy was assassinated this afternoon in Dallas, Texas.'

'Thank *God*,' R. said.

1.12.63. The small house where we went to dinner with T. and M., now elevated to elegance, might have been the one in which

Hyacinth Robinson grew up: smoky Gibson Square behind a hospital with a moony clock, a shut up postal depot down the way and a high pavement where you turn in. The square is small and slummy at the corners. Grand piano (M. is a musician), Casa Pupo carpets, blue and black, very select books (T. is a publisher), excellent records in the basement of a cupboard, drinks above. M. is a fine spirit who is avid for celebrities; Carrier is a neighbour. She refers to T. as 'my man' in a tone that reminded me of Victorian ladies addressing cabbies.

The Literary Festival at Cheltenham. Gabriel Fielding laid a hand on my shoulder as we crossed the road that first night. He is, I suspect, a great *séducteur jusqu'au bord du lit*. At the bedside he would become Dr Barnsley, as he really is, and ask one exactly what the problem was. The ferocity with which he pronounces his passions ('We went to bed early because we wanted to make *love*') made me wonder if their pronunciation was not the most passionate thing about them. He told me how much he hoped we would see each other at breakfast. It is strange to agree so much with someone and yet to distrust him. How he did go on about his Catholic novelist friends, their brilliance and their appreciation of his gifts! I do lack references.

He was prison doctor at Maidstone. He is sometimes called in when a prisoner smashes his cell or goes bananas. One day he had a great row with his son and felt obliged to make a demonstration; he looked at the window and knew that he would put his fist through it. He thought if he could do it quickly enough, nothing would come of it. He cut his arm to the bone from wrist to elbow. When he next went to the prison, the word was about that he had gone berserk. 'The novelist,' he said, 'is greedy, greedy, *greedy* for experience.' Other people's particularly. Doctor, Catholic, novelist: the complete voyeur. His wife had a waxy complexion; she seemed somehow more used up than inspection proved. She was like a candle reconstituted from pious drippings. She wore shapeless dark clothes and a large metal cross studded with fruit lozenges. 'When she comes between me and a potential mistress, I *hate* her,' he told me.

On the second day he said suddenly, 'I *love* you. I love Jews.'
I said, 'I refuse to be your private ghetto.' Coquettishly, I fear.
'And when I hate them, I hate them more than anyone else.'
He told of his conversation with an ex-S.S. man and a Communist in Ireland. How guilty the S.S. man was, and how arrogant

the Communist. 'I suspect,' I said, 'that you preferred the S.S. man.'
'*Much*,' he said. 'I *much* preferred him.'

J.F. wears the beard typical of those with unpleasing teeth. His wife
has the kind of protective watchfulness of someone whose husband
has only recently become successful. He smokes cigarettes in a
fumed holder, with a curl-lipped sardony which does not hide an
anxious lisp. He and she wore a lot of woolly things. He quotes
Burke (Edmund, not Kenneth), and tells you so.

J.B. Priestley. In a red tie and blue demob suit, he looked like one
of Orwell's organising pigs. He told Ann Scott-James that he always
read her column. To me, however, he said only that he didn't want
any bloody silly *Sunday Times* intellectualism. As question master,
he hampered the expression of any opinions except his own. He
was not there to exchange ideas; who could possibly have an idea
worth exchanging for one of his? He is the man who gave wind-
baggery a bad name. Every aggressive blandness asked the question
why, since he was a great writer, he was not generally seen as such.
At dinner in the little hotel, the waitress asked if he wanted 'red or
white'. He demanded to see the bottles. He seemed disappointed
to find them perfectly acceptable. If he had the courage, he would
be a jumped up, pretentious, ex-working class Tory; cowardice
keeps him low-brow, loyal to the Labour Party and rude to waitresses.

Thea. One of the 'readers' in the Festival. Her hair hung sexily about
her sexless face; a provincial sophisticate, ignorantly knowing,
brazenly chaste. Wolf came down for the main event. He is totally
jaded, finds no point in anything, 'not even fucking'. Tom Chitty
looked as if he was meeting someone from another planet; W. rode
clumpingly all over him. Best-selling F. said to me, 'Do you really
need three thousand a year?' I said, 'Yes, to be comfortable.' Yet I
posed as the champion of value versus quantity. Three thousand a
year isn't much. Two pieces is not *that* many for one's integrity to
be in.

Harry and Charlotte were unwilling to take us to Harlem. We parked
a block from Lennox Avenue and walked past apartment blocks the
city has put up between Central Park and 5th Avenue. They were
like ships moored in a strange harbour. It was a warm September
Saturday; thousands of faces peered from the windows. Doorways

and path were equally crowded. Yet the wide street was like a pier-head, children playing and only a few people walking about.

Opposite the new apartments there were dingy tenements; a church with cough-drop windows and white lettering on the black façade. We were the only white people around. We happened on a thick gathering on Lennox Avenue. Now there were also white policemen. Malcolm X was speaking at a Black Muslim rally. Neat Negroes were selling their newspaper. They gave scrupulous change. Their good manners were implacable. *impeccable*

There was a wooden platform on which shirtsleeved Negroes fanned themselves and provided choruses of 'that's right' for Malcolm (as H. called him). The crowd picked up the slogan with a wondering kind of loudness, like people recovering, in amazement, from congenital dumbness.

Malcolm said that the Negro must learn to defend himself.'I tell you you must do what we do. You must learn judo and karate. They say we teach violence. We don't teach violence. We teach self-defence. They're not going to defend you. Are they going to defend you? They didn't defend us in Montgomery, Alabama, now did they?' He spoke with a malign, coaxing geniality. He had earnest glasses and lean, eloquent hands; he wore a neat brown suit with a white handkerchief in his top pocket. He said the whites had to be taught how to behave. 'If a snake kills your baby, if you come home and find a snake has killed your baby, you go out and you look for a snake, and if you see a snake you kill that snake, and you don't necessarily make sure that it's the *same* snake that killed your baby, because what you want to do is kill yourself a snake.'

'That's right!'

All the same, I failed to feel the deep hostility which upset H. and C. The white cops swung their clubs aimlessly. Malcolm spoke ceaselessly but unhurriedly. He was expected to go on for a long time.

After we left, carefully, we regained the car. We drove up Lennox Avenue and turned left and stopped at a light. A white Lincoln, driven by a Negro alone in the car, banged into us. No one moved. We drove another block and stopped again. He stopped short of us. Soon we lost him.

H. said that a few years ago if you had an accident in Harlem you were more likely to be given the benefit of the doubt than anywhere else in town. Negroes crowded to give evidence against their fellows. Now, H. said, he wouldn't stop if he had an accident there, for fear of the crowd.

1964

A week ago I dreamed that the same man, an Ethiopian, won the Olympic marathon as won it last time, in Rome. This evening, coming home after my anguished colloquy with the awful J. and J., I bought *Paese Sera* and discovered that my dream had come true. It was the first time in the history of the games that the same man had won two marathons. What does one make of that? Nothing. But all the same...

Cripples. G. had an excessive, aloof friendliness. At the Oxford and Cambridge club, he called those with whom he was irritated 'Old friend'. While we were playing sixpenny bridge, he told me that if I ever wanted to buy a mink coat for my wife I should buy one at auction. It was not advice which spoke to my immediate condition. He was chairman of the election committee. When they refused to elect a black Ghanaian judge as a member, I told G. that I should have to resign. Guy said, 'Freddie, you don't understand. It's got nothing to do with his being black. He's just not the kind of judge we want in the club.' I still resigned.

Another cripple who played bridge was a County Court judge. The movement of his ruined leg dragged his face down in sympathy. His brother was intact, but stammered.

I was at school with a spastic called P. I was doing stamps one day when he came in tears from the beach. I said, 'What's the *matter*?' Then I saw the brown shit leggings he wore. He went on past me without a word. I have memories of being unkind, verbally, in my childhood, but never to P.. Mrs Workman called him 'tuppenny bun'.

Mr Drake, the crippled ex-headmaster, reduced to being a humble usher, was full of scorn for those who preferred sandcastles to manly sports. For a time his system of 'houses' (a sort of miniature corporate state) was adopted. Elaborate charts depicted one's contribution to the Red or Blue total of marks. When Drake departed suddenly, his system was dismantled.

She is known as Fropax in the profession. She married a public figure who attained high office before being disgraced in a sex scandal. She announces that she is 'standing by him'. They go to live in the country. In grateful humilation, he promises her that he will never betray her again. How could he when he has never loved her so much? After a few months, she tells him that she is leaving him. His fidelity is more than she can stand. On winter evenings he can be seen crouched under the trees at the bottom of the long meadow shooting birds, with a mask over his face.

Chez D. A couple who own a gallery. She, older than he, had recently '*flambée*'d herself while cooking chicken for some friends. She had a continental accent and face, lean, gaunt cheeks, dark, dark eyes, false lashes. She spoke of Jackie Kennedy's courage. I wondered how courageous it was to act courageously in front of a mass audience. Wasn't real courage to do with how one behaved alone? She shook her head, repeatedly. She started to talk about her own bereavement. It had caused such an emptiness in their lives. They had hardly been able to face the idea of life without...*him*. Their dog had died, aged sixteen. They had not left England during his lifetime. Now they were free, but at what a price!

You imagine yourself to have burned your boats, to have behaved so scandalously as to forfeit all respect. And then you find that people haven't noticed that you were behaving at all differently.

Jo told David D. that he and Stella (!) were responsible for all the good things in the script of *Darling*. John said to *me* that he was glad that so many of *our* ideas were still in. In the film business the measure of how good a job you've done is the number of people eager to claim credit for it.

Rome. A telegram came from R.G. soon after we arrived. Sam Spiegel and Norman Panama wanted me for a script, although S.S. had doubts. They would pay me for my flight if we would return early. We did; I with a bad sore throat. S.S. had flown to Hollywood for the Oscars. I went to see N.P. who has a large office above a hairdressers' in Hanover Square. Grey trousers, tweed jacket, blue button-down shirt, knitted tie behind a gold slide; when he smiled it seemed the genuine smile of an unhappy man. He gave me the Treatment to read, a vulgar, banal story about two buddies in the USAF and the girl one did the other out of. 'Think Kirk and Burt'.

I went to see R.G. and told him I couldn't do it.

'It's the logical next step in your career,' he said. 'We're talking about ten thousand pounds for sixteen weeks' work.'

They offered eight; then eight-five; then nine. Deal.

The next day, I reported for duty. We talked about 'the characters': Tank, Mona, and Tommy. 'What makes Tommy run?' N.P. kept saying. 'What's behind his insane drives?'

Nine thousand pounds perhaps. It doesn't seem enough.

The next morning, as I set off to see N.P. again, there was an invitation from the Royal Society of Literature to become a fellow. Naïvely, I was overwhelmed, with shame. By that night, I couldn't even eat. I could not look Paul in the face when he asked me, for some reason, about money. Perhaps it explained my absence from the house all day. Was I making a lot with this film? 'Some.' 'More than ninety-nine?' 'Yes, I said, 'more than that.'

I called R.G. and told him I could not continue. He said that he had made the deal and his reputation was involved. If I wanted to get out of it, that was my problem.

I took the early morning train to London, a rainy, grim day. At ten I was at N.P.'s office. I said, 'I realise I may never work in the movies again, but I can't do this movie.'

'What do you mean not work in the movies again?'

I said, 'I can imagine the kind of things you'll be telling people.'

He said, 'Are you crazy? If you don't want to do this, why would I want you to? I'll tell you who really wants to work with you and that's Stanley Donen. I told him you weren't free. Do you want me to call him for you?'

I went to see Stanley Donen. I mentioned the idea for *Two for the Road* which Jo Janni has been sitting on for eighteen months. John was supposed to direct it. S.D. liked the idea, but I feared it had all gone too far with J., even though I have not received the option money yet, or a contract. S.D. offered me a three-picture deal; and I was to direct the third.

John admitted that *T.F.T.R.* had never been 'at the head of his priorities'. Jo, who was in Rome, was so distressed at my 'perfidy' that Stella called R.G. to say that he was going to drive straight from the airport to R.G.'s office to agree terms for my writing Byron.

A meeting with John and Jo. Jo at first, alone, smiling and financially worried. John arrived three quarters of an hour late, having had 'lunch with Columbia'. He dislikes the idea of Lawrence Harvey for *Darling*, though L. is said to be enthusiastic about the script; he doesn't want Maximilian Schell either, for Robert. He prefers to say, 'This picture will *never* be made.' He parades like an ox ready for sacrifice. He thought he and Jo should have an 'idea' credit on the script. I said that if that happened, I would stand up at the Press show and point out each 'directorial' idea of which I had thought and he would get the credit.

Richard Condon. We met in his suite at the Westbury. He was a solid man in glasses, dark lightweight glossy suit, crisp white shirt, handmade leather shoes, latched across the instep. He had just been at Forest Mere, on the total starvation diet; hot water three times a day.

He didn't start to write till he was 42 years old; now, at 49, five novels later (including *The Manchurian Candidate*), he was a best-seller.

An Infinity of Mirrors is sub-titled 'a documentary novel'. I asked if he felt any reluctance using the Nazi experience as a basis for popular fiction.

'None whatsoever.'

He told me that a friend of his, after reading the book, had to go wash his face, dunk it right under the water, to get the smell of death out of his nostrils. He had had four researchers working on the novel before he let his imagination rip. He likened himself, more than once, to 'the man squatting on his heels in a cave in the long, long ago'. To me, at times, there loomed the equally archetypal image of his agent squatting there right beside him.

I remarked that he had something in common, in terms of his selection of locales, with Ian Fleming. He went away at that point to see the photographers who had come to shoot him. I was left with *Playboy* magazine, featuring 'The Nudest Mamie van Doren'. *Playboy* supplies the modern garden of Eden: you can admire the fruit, but not touch it. The magazine is devoted to exciting desire not for women but for more magazines.

Condon came back white with anger. He resumed being furious at my having compared him with someone who 'wasn't a novelist at all'. He rewrote all his books four times. He regarded Hemingway as 'the most destructive force in modern literature'. Hemingway has misled writers into thinking that every word they put down should be *art*. Following E.H., the campus schools of Creative Writing had turned his errors into a panacea; especially his repetitiousness. People like Updike were talented, but sterile; '*Run Rabbit*' (*sic*) was all about a fouled up nobody. C. is still the front office man (he was a publicist at RKO for years) and talks about what the public wants, and what that is is 'a bigger than themselves hero and heroine, a man who screws better, eats more, gets richer'. His new book – one of his new books – is to be called '*How I defected from the Soviet Union and made* $1,432,334'.

The basis of his hostility to Hemingway came when he described a trip to Havana where he hoped to get E.H. to do the libretto of a Haitian musical he was going to produce on Broadway. E.H. received him courteously 'in the room where he had four novels going simultaneously on four typewriters' (what were all those famously sharpened pencils for, I wonder?) and seemed eager about the project. They talked for a long while, during which E.H.'s wife called 'Ernest' several times and was always ignored. E.H. much admired Condon's sports jacket. At the door he took it off and offered it to his host. 'I'd kind of like to think of Hemingway wearing my mantle.' Fearful of his wife's reaction, Hemingway handed it back. They parted amicably.

Later a story appeared in the press in which E.H. ranted about 'some two-bit Broadway producer' who came and tried to get him involved in some cuddly musical comedy. 'The idea of a great writer being interested in a scheme like that!'

'You look at page 37 of *A Moveable Feast*,' he told me, 'and see how the great writer treated the wife he loved. "We loved each other and it was good!" You look at page 37 of that book.'

The US, he said, was now a society in which a third of the population was being oppressed, as if by a Fascist party, by another third, while the third third hung about in apathetic affluence. 'It used to be that you heard about people being mugged; now it's getting so you *know* the people who are.'

The National Film Finance Company have turned down *Darling*. Rank liked the script, but they had already lost too much money on projects such as *The Wild and the Willing*. There remains British Lion, J. tells me, but the lions are five pigs all eating from the same trough. 'This film will never get made.' I'm tired of hearing about it.

Piraeus. Paul pointed out a cat swimming in the harbour, its neck stretched high and taut about the water line. It grabbed at the flat end of the gangplank but we never saw it safe.

Three Plain Women at lunch on the *Myrtidiotissa*. Suddenly one of them hunched forward over the table, sobbing. The others sat there and then ate on, admirably. She sobbed and apologised and the others understood.

One of the other girls spoke good Greek. She sat on deck till late at night talking and chaffing some fat Greeks. One of the men tittered and giggled like a huge mountain that had just given birth to the mousy transistor which gibbered and crackled in his lap. The Greek-speaker was a teacher on Cyprus. I spoke to her when we docked at Syros. She carried messages between Greeks and Turks who maintained, but dared not confess, their friendships.

10.8.64. Ios. One day it dawned fuggy and cloudy. The grey heaviness persisted all day. They waited for some disaster. The temperature reached 100 degrees without the sun breaking through. Tempers were short. They were relieved when the day ended without a murder having taken place. The next day was fine. They heard on the wireless there had been an earthquake in Persia. 10,000 people had died.

The mules and donkeys come, apparently casual, along the curve of the beach, but if you take the goat path behind R.'s house, you can see snaking tracks laid in exact meanders along the pathless sand. In the evening there are goats and sheep, sheer to their thin flanks, with long, sacrificial necks. Last year there were no birds, but now crows pace the dry field between us and the sea, black wings folded like scholars' gowns around their grey shoulders. Goats hobble and trip, their nimbleness docked.

There was once a nudist colony on Milopota. When the Frenchman who ran it died, his son jilted the daughter of G.D. and dares not return to the island. The lay-out which 'ho Gallos' made for his nudists – a flowering garden, a gazebo – is drying out. G. pillages what he wants and lets the Frenchman's rat-ridden cottage to visitors. In the well behind it, Englishmen dangle melons and beer. They stand in their underpants and their beastly socks and wash each other down like suburban motor cars.

Visitors come more thickly to the Cyclades now: provincial French, arrogant Athenians, a huge German and his neat, diminutive girl friend who waits for him as he scans the depths with his snorkel. Then there are the new barbarians: self-regarding students who study nothing. They speak no Greek and one of them asked me, on the beach, what country he was in. They sponge on anyone foolish enough to trust their word ('I'll come back and pay later,' they say, and do not). Whores and vandals, they travel without conscience, never becoming more specific (even to themselves perhaps) than 'the young'. They drop turds and tins wherever they fall, boast of the gullibility of anyone who helps them and the discomfiture of all who stand in their way.

What will follow will be worse: the transistorised termites will bore their way into every corner of the Med. The pop morons, the shouters and belters, the guffawers and ignoramuses are on the move. They will care nothing for the countries they visit. All the prejudices of the lumpen scum wll be visited on the locals. They will want cheapness above all; they will come abroad not to learn anything but because it costs less. Sausages and chips will spread to every corner of Europe; unwilling to stomach the local food, they will come Wimpey-minded and they will be served. They will care nothing – 'Eeech crap!' – for antiquities or art. Lacking the syco-phantic hypocrisy of the bourgeois, they will refuse to gaze at what means nothing to them. They will have time only for brutalisation. The English louts speak their only language in a fashion for which a foreigner would apologise. They have neither aptitude nor incli-nation to learn another.

G.D. dances lightly on Saturday nights at his *taverna*. His bare, broad feet slip and rest on the grey concrete and his face floats above them, hung on a beat of the *bouzouki*, his hands aloft as if dangling a balloon from each. He is a common, greedy Greek islander, ambitious and, no doubt, foolish in many ways, but his manhood survives, acknowledges in the gift of lightness a reverence for antique, denied gods. G. is not loud, or afraid, or cold. I fear the common crowd, but have no notion of how to keep it away.

At the *taverna*. Ronald E.; he teaches in Alexandria. Tanked up on Durrell, I envied him working in such a mysterious city. 'It's about as mysterious as Brighton,' he said. He had little time for *The Alexandria Quartet*: Durrell gave Nessim a Coptic funeral with a Mullah.

He told me how, at Christmas in Alex. the door bell rang and, when he opened it, a priest came into the flat, muttering prayers, and sprinkled holy water. 'He went quickly round and back to the door and then held out his hand. So I shook it.' He did not come back the following year.

Crickets tap out their last urgent messages before the sun sets. Chickens go neck and neck, neck and neck, into the stone house.

The sea had been stirred all day by the South wind. On the beach after the storm, fish lay drowning in the air.

D. The local rich man. He paces up and down the harbour in his yachting cap, white ducks, gold-buttoned blazer and malacca cane. He taps objects that offend him with the tip of his cane, encouraging their removal. R. went to tea with him and was offered delicious honey cakes. 'They are ordered specially from Santorini,' *ho ploosios* said. 'You can't get them here.'

Walking back through the village, R. went into the baker's. They said they could make honey cakes for him any time he wanted.

Oddly enough, R. has an air of superiority not unlike D.'s: when speaking of international politics, he never says 'France' or 'Turkey' but always 'Paris' or 'Ankara'. He likes to give the impression of being an informed circle.

'*Frederikos, pame, amesos!*' Yorgo arrived with the mules. I had been due to complete the formal purchase of the property and I had got the date wrong. I hammered my heels into the mule's sides and it set off at an urgent amble.

Flora was waiting at the *irenothike*'s office. A youngish man in a white shirt, he offered a gold-capped smile and showed me the diary, proclaiming that I had confused *tritos* – it was indeed the third day of August – with *tritee*, Tuesday, which was the next day. It was an ingenious, lawyer's excuse for my mistake, but quite beside the point: I had simply got the day wrong.

Pavlos, the hotel tout from the *Chryse Acte*, helped as interpreter. He leaned in through the office window in a macintosh hat which, he once told me, he bought in the *place Vendôme*. Afterwards he asked about a pullover (he called it a 'sway-ter') which it seems I promised him two years ago.

Flora sold us the land to pay for her daughter's schooling. Now she is leaving her husband, Paniotis. He is a small man, like a jockey, a *kakos anthropos* who often gets violent when drunk, and often drinks. I kissed Flora's hand and she mine. P. had attacked the older girl with a knife two nights before. Now he has sold his donkeys and gone off on the boat to Athens.

The trip round the island. I agreed a price with Captain Adonis: 400 drachs. When the time came, B. and I were reluctant, but it was a calm morning. How could we withdraw? We went to meet the boat at Drakos' place. They had been fishing; they were cutting off heads, excising tripes, stripping skin and then dropping raw hanks of flesh into the sea again, a derisive return. Skeins of blood floated away. Shoals of tiny phoenix fish came to feast on the flayed giants' liquor.

At last A. arrived, a small barefoot man in shirt and trousers. His steersman was nineteen or so, with a fleshy, bored face and a big lick of brown hair. I bought beer to change the sullen air; it seemed to work and off we all went. Soon we were bearing on Paros, two *caiques* stringing along behind us. They swung away finally to head for Naxos as we followed the line of the shore. Tables of rock stood out to sea, stacked cakes of grey stone which the water seemed to lift and lower. Now and again the steersman raised his arm, as if testing the wind, and you looked to see some answering movement on shore, the whisk of a donkey's tail. Otherwise motionless he stood against the yellow and whitened ladders of stone that the cliffs tipped into the sea.

Sometimes a run of goats would be sailing parallel to us, drifting like spilled ink through the low bushes. Fertile valleys were fed by good water. Then the green thinned and the gaunt mountains rose from their knees. Everywhere, signs of man, though they could dwindle to one impossible wall running against the easy axis of the land, coming down from the peak of a hill in dropping stripes of flat stone.

Some beaches were backed with careful terraces. Figs and olives and even fields of vines lent assurance to the white houses. The biggest settlement was sad with unwhitened *spitia*, though one small boat hung against the jetty.

Sarah lay on the deckhouse roof and covered herself in my striped *horiatik* shirt. The sea purpled and went white. The prow slapped spray over us. We leaned to starboard and counted the time till we landed. The pump-pump-pump of the engine was unremitting and without any prospect of acceleration. God, it was beautiful; and, God, had we had enough!

'What's yellow and dangerous?' an American student of languages asked me, as we walked back together from the village. I didn't know. He did: 'Shark-infested custard.'

The river bed goes back, widening with boulders, past fig and cactus and swaying bamboo, into the windless valley. A small barrel-vaulted church with a high palm tree before it stands on a step of earth. The vault does not meet at the top but is paved with square stones along the apex. Holy pictures on the unvarnished screen; a dish of candle ends. Outside, a huge olive tree, a mass of still strength, is encircled by a stone bench. Two legs of the tree have been cut off and lie in a stiff, amputated stride under the parent shade. You can hear people calling to each other, but cannot see them. The little church looks as if it has lived here for centuries. It was built last year, to the memory of a man's father.

The piano-teacher. She arrived with an introduction to us from H. and C. She drank *ouzo* and ate lunch and then borrowed a towel to go swimming. At lunch she had told us how she stole a towel from a hotel in Yugoslavia. She had been traced by the police and forced to open her bag in front of a silent, curious crowd. The stolen article was neatly folded on top of its contents. 'In the States,' she told us, 'the towels are included in the price of the room – they *expect* you to take them.'

When she took our towel, I said, 'Don't put it your case, willya?'

Germans on holiday seem often to fight their women (which their women seem to like) and push them into the sea. Twice the women have been very small, and the men very large.

Two attractive Greek girls on the beach, wearing bikinis of similar design. The taller, prettier girl's was a vivid orange. One could imagine the zeal with which she had encouraged her guileless sister to buy the less eye-catching model.

Autumn on the island. The sea is goosepimpled with white. Storm clouds, like reconnoitring barbarians, stand massed on the crowns of the hills. G.D. came with his folding rule and his bobbin of string to measure out our new room. He squared the corners with a medicine box.

The old kitchen door could not be padlocked. G. chipped away the concrete of the doorway, then hammered a hook into the cheap round wooden doorpost. He avoided splitting it by holding a rock against the wood while he hammered. He swept up the dust, deft as a woman, smiling shyly: '*Etsi*!'

'So at last I am alone. The wind is strong again tonight. No one will come up to the cottage. The steamer is on its way to Piraeus. They are gone. The paraffin lamp seems to make brass out of the bamboo canes which lie across the roof-tree. I sat for twenty minutes watching the sun go down over the furthest, outstretched arm of the bay.

'The sun's chariot gives a last flick of its tail-light and goes down. Sikinos is shades of grey and now, behind the point, orange embers glow. The sky is back-lighting for dark silhouettes. The blades of a rowing boat stitch the thick water. Black figures stand in its prow, ready for landing.

'There may be five days to wait. I have plenty of time to suffer, and amuse myself.'

The ring of truth? Fiction.

A black dog sprang and was still on the fawn sand. Donkeys and mules were coming back into the gale along the morning shore. The tired mule-drivers lean on the wind.

Unscheduled ships appear silently at night. They come, unnaturally large, across the bay, bearing their rows of lights slowly, evenly across the darkness, like the easy targets in a fairground. The lights *are* the ships. Once they pass beyond the limit of the bay, you are tempted to look back at the point where they entered it, expecting them to roll up again, like those very fairground targets.

At night, you can see people coming, with their bobbing, waning torches, down the road from the village. When they reach the old path down the cliff they drop down with a different rhythm. Paul and I call the old path 'the greasy pole', so steep is it. The torchlight descends like dripping candle-wax: falling, stalling, then tumbling again.

Yesterday in the height of the gale, I saw a crow flying backwards. When they start to fly upside down, you know it's time to go.

Sept 16th. We spent much of the morning in Constitution Square with P.M.G. and L. and their nine-year-old son, Timothy, who was unsociable in a grey, prep school suit and a comic. He was about to make a solo flight to England. 'My father,' he told us, 'says I shall be spoilt by the hostess.'

As we all got out of the bus at Glyfada, I realised that Peter was probably responsible for my having been made FRSL. He acknowledged, with public school embarrassment at a discovered good turn, that he – among others – had been instrumental. 'Overdue,' he murmured.

He had been involved in a correspondence in the *TLS* about John Sullivan's anthology of Roman Satire. I asked if J. had asked him to take part in the Men of Letters symposium in *Arion*. He said, 'No. I think there are two reasons: first, I don't think Johnny Sullivan knows which way up to hold me.' The second was a review (anonymous, of course) of J.P.S.'s latest, which had appeared in the *TLS*.

A prompt echo of this hit me when we arrived in Rome. A letter from J.P.S., waiting for me at American Express, referred to 'Peter's unmistakable vulgarity of style' which revealed him as the author of the *TLS* review. If P. is to be believed, and I think he is, he had nothing to do with it.

Another letter, from John Schlesinger, was in a Hassler envelope. It told of his panics over *Darling* and, parenthetically, of his and Jo's hiring of Edna O'Brien to 'rewrite certain scenes'. My first reading was superficial; I censored the painful news that I had worked for months and months, without pay, on a script which was now being altered behind my back. How gracious of J.R.S. to inform me of the treachery in his own fist!

I was told that the script would be credited to me; it was more important that it should be creditable. It arrived yesterday, the 27th, the day in which shooting began. Where it was not cheap it was incoherent; where coherent, it could be bought by the yard at Woolworth's. Every concession imaginable has been made to the demands of the actors and of the distributors, even where the latter are unvoiced and merely float to the cowering director on the general tide. I called Jo last night and he listened bleakly to my comments. I said I would rewrite the most maltreated scenes for today. He said that his secretary would call at nine-fifteen this morning and take them down.

I hope that the unit's imminent arrival in Italy will allow me to talk some sense into them. In the end, however, all directors want is to be applauded. The whole cinema gang are nothing but puff balls, tinpot admirals of a fleet of toy boats. They care for their commands, their gold braid, their salutes, *et praeterea nihil*. Yet I wait tensely for the phone to ring, *internazionale*, and I ache for news. Their virus works in my blood.

We drove to Florence in the rain. Jo told us that when you telephone Fellini his wife, Giulietta Masina, answers. The conversation goes: 'Is the maestro there?' 'No.' 'When is he coming back?' '*We* don't know.' 'Is he coming to sleep?' '*Forse!*'

Rome. Sergio, the estate agent, described the co-operative where there was a bargain flat (65,000 lire a month) as a '*casa di gran' briganti*'. It was owned mostly by senators and there was always a uniformed policeman on the door. We found a flat in the Via Francesco Ferrara, in Vigna Clara.

We had left the Vanguard station wagon with Sr. Manzo five and a half months earlier and it needed an extension of its time allowance in Italy. Paul and I drove all over Rome and out to E.U.R. in the hope of finding someone with enough authority to prevent us having to drive all the way to France in order to re-enter Italy on a new lease of time. It seemed impossible. I was told to get some *carta bollata*, explain my reasons for seeking an extension, and then apply to the Questura in the Via San Vitale. I went on Saturday morning, after we had left P. and S. at school. I climbed wide stairs to the fourth floor, whence I was sent to the fifth, from which I was returned to the ground floor.

Back in the Tourist Office, I became unwisely indignant. I was then obliged to fill in a form in order to get permission to stay in Italy myself. I demanded to speak to the *direttore*. He was a handlebar moustached charmer with an emollient air. He read my statement of claim aloud, and with interest. When he saw that I wished to remain not only for my work but also to improve my Italian, he revised the entire text for grammatical lapses. '*Sono ritornato*' he substituted for my '*ho ritornato*'. I had mentioned that I was a Fellow of the Royal Society of Literature. When I said, '*Non é di gran importanza*', he said, '*Si, si, é importante*' and stood up to prove it. As he did so, the two *carabinieri* at the door snapped to attention. I had won my case.

October. *LA GRAN BRETAGNA ALLE URNE*. Justice insists that the Tories must go, but since the socialists barely offer Socialism, the alternative scarcely excites. Ultimately Labour, whatever their incidental reforms, offer a *lesson* to the Tories, not a change; they are a threat, never a solution. Being in opposition may, however, fracture the Tories into progressives and diehards; and this could result in the emergence of an ultra-nationalist element. If the Tory party retains its cohesion, it will return to power. Meanwhile, I take the Socialists to win by 30 seats.

We bought the children two small, mouse-coloured birds – '*Bengalli*' – with orange beaks and rouged faces, as a present after their first morning of 'proper school'. P. and S. ran in eagerly and insisted on having the birds in the dining room for lunch. It was casserole of chicken.

After lunch, one of the birds escaped while being given vitamins. B. trapped it in the wastepaper basket after it dazed itself hitting the window. It sat for the rest of the day in the bottom of the cage, wearing an air of lacrimose dignity like R.A. Butler.

At the Hotel Parco dei Principi. The lounge is paved with white marble and has ice-green walls. 'You press a button if you want snow,' Jo said. We had bourbon and waited for John. There had been scenes with Julie. Presently she came in from the bar. Her eyes were diminished by her puffed lids; dark smudges under them. The trouble was about what she was to wear in her nude scene in the Florentine *palazzo*. She stood below me (she is very short) and screwed up her face as I explained the 'justification' for the scene. 'Oh, I know it's *valid*,' she said, 'it's just that I can't do it. I've got such a terrible figure. It's all *wrong*. If I had a beautiful body like Bardot or somebody, I wouldn't mind.'

She was a plain girl as she stood there, skin all corrugated with half-removed make-up, neck chicken-red and slightly ribbed; tremulously truculent. She wouldn't stop for a drink. Jo said, 'She takes her clothes off for nine out of ten men who ask her and she won't take them off to be a film star.'

Jo says that he detests producers who use their power for sexual conquests. C. used to have four girls supplied nightly to his suite at Claridge's. He told them, 'Order anything you like. I'm here to satisfy your every desire'.

John arrived after Julie had gone. He sidled up behind Beetle and kissed her, arm around her shoulder. Julie, he said, was being marvellous. Dirk thought her 'the most exciting English talent I've worked with in years.'

Dirk, to Pinter, re *The Servant*: 'Was he really a gentleman or not? I don't *know*, and I should.'
H.P.: 'I don't give a fuck, dear.'
Why can't I talk to people like that?

At Galeassi in the Piazza Santa Maria di Trastevere. We dined with

Stella and Jo. J. told us of the homosexual friend who asked him his advice about getting married. Jo said that he should think about it very carefully; he needed to be very sure about it. Both of them should have a very clear understanding of what they were doing. 'After all,' Jo went on, 'if you were to have children...' His friend blew up. 'Are you mad? Are you *mad*? I wouldn't be marrying a *woman*. It's just that I need someone to look after me. And after all, I've got a house; I could do with someone about the place.'

'He's so *vicious*,' Stella said.

Jo took us to the famous keyhole in the Piazza dei Cavalieri di Malta. We queued to peer, in the darkness, at the distant luminosity on the dome of St Peter's. J. fantasised about the disappointment of the tourists who, on looking through, were cheated of St Peter's by the interposition of a beautiful naked woman and wanted their money back. We went to the Capitol too. I quoted Stendhal on the Marcus Aurelius equine statue: it looks as if M.A. were actually speaking, whereas the Henri IV in Paris looks as if he were having trouble staying on the horse. Jo regretted not having read the Stendhal. I took it to him as a present when we went to the shooting on Capri.

After seeing *La Dolce Vita* for the third time one realises that it is a ballet. Its hero is a non-dancing maypole around which the orgiasts cluster. Fellini fills his film with dances: parties, crowds, *paparazzi*, all in constant, choreographed motion.

Capri. They had been shooting *Darling* in the Piazzetta. John procured a parade of grotesques: a man carrying a bed following two Lesbians and a side of meat intercut with the fleshy bare legs of the tourists. The mayor threatened instant expulsion.

After we arrived at the Quisisana, I called up to John's room and was favoured with 'Will you come up? We want a line from you'. I heard later that Julie had said, 'Oh no, don't let's have the author. We're just family as we are.' She was wearing the usual short, rumpled sacking dress; her hair, lank and just washed, was constantly fed back behind her raw, out-turned ear by her red, bitten fingers. Next to her sat Jose-Luis de Villalonga. ('When I first heard him mentioned,' L. said, 'I didn't know if he was a person or a place.') Later J. called him 'Villa-*longueurs*'. A lot. He also said, quietly, of Julie that she had behaved towards L. 'like the perfect little bitch'. Happy cast.

J.R.S.: You're as good as saying that we're messing it all up.

F: Since I have some regard for other people's feelings, I'll say that I'm sure you're doing an excellent job. The only question is whether I shall derive the smallest satisfaction from it.

J.J.: Look at the Keith and Villis. Those two have had contract after contract since *A Kind of Loving*.

F.: I'm not interested in success. I'm frightened to death of it. What interests me is whether I've wasted two years of my life.

When we drove back to the Parco dei Principi, there was a press conference for J. and J. J.R.S. asked me to come in with him.

'Not bloody likely,' I said. 'I'm tired of playing the elephant to your Hannibal.'

Mile End. We went to the *shiveh* for one of B.'s uncles. He had long been a stall-holder in the Mile End Road market. The terraced houses were in a row under huge tiers of modern flats. The family sat, in their hats, eating fish and chips. They wanted us to have some. Two of the old man's sons were doctors, one with a French wife. Their sister was a teacher who sat out her dutiful mourning on a hard chair. I sat on the broken-springed sofa. The widow loitered, ennobled by bereavement, with four hundred pounds in her handbag in five pound notes.

Dirk. 'His taste is between his toes' he said, of L.H. Dirk is 43, still pretty, like some neat zoologist's exhibit. Full face, he has a dreadful knowingness; in profile he retains the spent innocence of a second-hand midshipman.

A crossed line.

'I hope you enjoy yourself in Worthing.'

'Worthing?'

'Isn't it Worthing?'

'Cheltenham.'

'I thought your brother lived in Harrogate.'

'That's my other brother.'

'Oh, the one I was always trying…'

'That's right. This is the other one.'

'This is the one in Worthing.'

'Cheltenham. We're driving down – lunch in Oxford, tea in Gloucester, and stop the night in Ross-on-Wye.'

'I had a brother in Gloucester.'

'Oh yes?'

'I told you about him.'
'Oh, *yes*.'
'I wish I was going to be beside you, in the back seat. Of the car.'
'I wish you were.'
'Give Benozzo a spank for me.'
'Oh yes...'
'That's a funny kind of a greeting, isn't it? A spank?'
'Yes.'
'Well, bye-bye then.'
'Bye bye.'
'Bye bye.'
'Bye bye. I'll send you a card.'
'I should hope so. I should hope you would.'
'Oh yes. I will. Bye bye.'
'Bye bye.'
Critics will tell you that people don't really talk like that.

Eileen Ward. A trim female academic: red shoes, black and white silk dress, pretty in an underblown sort of way. She has recently published a highly praised study of Keats. She insisted that Byron was a thoroughgoing, responsible radical, a revolutionary who 'died for Greece'. I doubted if going to Greece and dying was the same as dying for Greece, but her smile was unamused. She defended the seriousness of Byron's politics with the glum steadfastness of a lover.

David Storey's *Radcliffe*. I have had words with D.S. and hence I had a certain urge to find his book chasteningly terrific. His language is inadequate to the 'Lawrencian' pretensions of his insights. Nothing *specific* is possible in a novel without natural detail or symbolic diversity. It is too much a case of *Thus Shouted Zarathustra*. He is so vulgar and so heavily shod he *will* shout at us – and this ends by being his message: he must shout at us and any failure to submit is due not to our revulsion from *him* but to our refusal to 'face life'. His imaginary landscape is not only less interesting than the world we can observe for ourselves, it is less imaginative. Clouds, rocks, torrents, mud and turds, this is the machinery of his monstrous vision: the standard furniture of drawing room romanticism. There is a certain force in the writing, but D.S.'s 'solutions' are so ludicrously melodramatic, and so noisy, as if all life's problems were 'ultimate', that he ends by seeming the kind of man who would prescribe dynamite to cure constipation. It is typical of a certain apocalyptic impatience to crave crises and dramas and never to want to beautify life by the 'illusory' delicacy of common politeness, decency or attention to detail. D.S. thinks himself the reincarnation of D.H.L., but where are his Bavarian Gentians, where his serpent at the well or his Monsieur Mosquito?

14.11.64. Stanley Donen called, last night, during a broadcast on behalf of the *Partito Socialista Italiano*. I had sent him the script on Wednesday; it was Friday. 'It's the greatest thing I ever read,' he said. 'It's so funny and so *mooving!*' He phoned again today, saying he had hardly slept and was still 'jumping with joy'. Paul Newman and Audrey Hepburn? What did I think? I have felt ever since his call exactly as if I had eaten too much.

1965

The Romans make a peculiar belching noise when they want to convey to you that something is impossible (getting a taxi, for instance).

I went to Switzerland to see Audrey Hepburn. I almost missed the coach from Termini to the airport. While the Alitalia man ran to hold the coach, I was sent to several places for bus tickets and finally ran out, forgetting my sunglasses, which Beetle brought to the coach. We barely had time to say goodbye. Later she told me she wept as she walked away in the bright cold sunshine.

I was overheated in my sheepskin coat. I got through to the Departure Lounge at Fiumicino without having my boarding card. I had to go back again and resume my course from the beginning. The flight was being called at Exit 6. I ran along the black rubber floor, toting my camera and a tartan zip-bag. A red light was flashing. Almost at once, despite the sunshine and the plane gleaming on the apron, a delay of 60 minutes was announced. We were not in the air till 12.30. Then we could not land at Zurich (fog) and had to put down at Basle.

As I was handed a first class ticket to Zurich, a girl came running after me: Monsieur Donen was landing and I was to wait for him. He came through wearing a camel hair coat and a sealskin fur hat, Russian style. It irritated his forehead. He carried a small fawn brief-case marked with darker leaves and kidney shapes. A huge suitcase of the same pattern was brought off his plane.

A large grey chauffeured Chevrolet was waiting. We drove through the efficient landscape in late sunshine and entered the obstructive fog only when we had bypassed Zurich. We stopped in the first town in the district of Lucerne to have glasses of tea and rich cakes. The chauffeur went to buy me a toothbrush and some batteries for my razor. He joined us in the first-floor tea-room, but sat at an adjacent table.

The town had the odd gingerbread building to allay the impression of modern soullessness. We headed for a new tunnel which had been opened only three days earlier. S. told me how Italians made tunnels. 'They start drilling, one party from each side and they aim to meet in the middle. And if they don't meet? Two tunnels.'

On the road to Burgenstock, we came out of the fog to see the white mountains against a yellow and black sky. The Queen Mother's trainer had invited S.D. and Adele to a weekend party. Noel and the Shawcrosses were there; Christopher and Mary came over. They all watched the special BBC nostalgia programme for Winston's ninetieth birthday, compèred by Noel. Someone sang one of the Master's songs, ineptly, and he called out 'shit' during its performace. Much merriment. S.D. was delighted by the Queen Mum, whose energy was amazing. It was difficult to find time to change one's clothes, since she always had to be the last person into the room and she was always ready to go.

Burgenstock was still and snow-lagged. The Waldheim was a small, rectilinear hotel. Previously it had been a traditional wooden building but there had been a fire; the proprietor's wife and three children had been suffocated. He lived in the new building with his new wife.

Audrey's house was a few hundred yards up the mountain. Mel took twenty minutes to explain how to get to it. It took us five minutes. Stanley had brought 'ski clothes' which he had bought in Klosters. 'Oh,' I said, 'do you ski?' 'No.'

I slept off a nervous headache and called Beetle. Then we climbed to the Ferrers', S.D. in his *après-ski* boots. The house was burnt sienna coloured; chalet roof, concrete terraces; a Swiss door that looks like the front of a safe deposit: you might have been going into a vault rather than a house.

Fretwork banisters went up, white, to the first floor. A neat hall with candles alight in green sleeves. We were shown into a waiting room with yellow dunlopillo seats on three sides. The wall with the door into the living room (where a fire burned in the raised fireplace) was filled on both sides with impressive books: *War and Peace*, *Guerre et Paix*, Avedon photographs (two vols.) etc.: literature in dinner jackets.

Audrey came in in a long green skirt and jacket top; abundant hair drawn back, with a fringe curled over her forehead. Her face was drawn back too, with the eyes burning under finely veined lids. She spoke as if she had much to say, embracing 'Stanley, darling' and seeming to find herself ahead of schedule at the end of her sentences. She opened the drinks cupboard under the shelf where a little picture of sticky mimosa leaned against the wall. Later she questioned S. about *his* pictures. He hedged (as if she had asked him 'What did *you* get for Christmas?') and said he has spent three years' salary furnishing his London apartment. I believed him.

Mel appeared, in cavalry twill trousers, beige cardigan and a full beard. 'Stanley, man, how are you?'

'Here's Melchior,' Audrey said. 'How's Melchior?'

He had been telling little Sean a story; he told wonderful stories. Before he arrived, Audrey had time to whisper that he was going to direct and produce a picture he had written himself and he was 'like a little boy', he was so excited. 'It's going to cost about $350, but he's going to do it himself, his way.'

He looked at us with his baleful, deep-set yet oddly prominent eyes, and looked anything but excited. He spoke all evening in his hip jargon. 'This is the chick,' he said, producing stills of the girl for whom he had written the script of *El Greco*. She looked to have the innocent knowingness common to sweet young starlets on the make, though she did not look as if she would make very much.

'Let's have some music there,' Audrey said. 'How about Peggaly?' While Peggy Lee sang, Audrey apologised for the lack of 'proper staff'. We were served asparagus soup with cream, roast chicken, roast potatoes, beans, salad, cheese, apple tart. Afterwards Mel, artfully primed by S.D., showed us the production stills from *El Greco*, in which he was to star, in Toledo. By bold generalship he had secured permission to film in the cathedral. The high altar had recently been cleaned for *Life* magazine, at Luce's expense ($5,000) and he got it for nothing.

Audrey said, 'I don't want to say too much about how much I like the script of *Two for the Road*, in case it embarrasses Frederico.' She could say everything she had to say about it in ten minutes: 'Now, if you like.' S.D. said 'Not now', as if it would have been absurd, as it would, to have come all this way for a conference parenthetic between dessert and coffee.

Melchior was flying to Madrid next morning. We were called to come up to the house at 11.30. As we discussed Audrey's comments, S. was tactful but not compliant: he accepted what she said about Joanna, her own character, but rejected what she said about Mark. She wore a brown jumper and brown stretch ski-pants, brown hair in a pony tail; businesslike and attractive, not sexy.

We had omelettes and cheese and salad. I drank a mug of beer. While Sean had his rest, Audrey lent me a pair of Mel's boots (I could get into them, but not zip them up) and we went for a walk with the dogs, Assam (Sammy, a Yorkshire terrier with a bow on its brow) and 'Sean's' alsatian. The dogs were not used to each other; we spent the whole time trying to reconcile them without Assam getting run over. Only in the pursuit of favours could one devote so much polite care to animal welfare.

We walked first on the snow-carpeted nine-hole golf course which Audrey's friend, a local 'property owner and industrialist' had 'blasted out of the rock'. It seemed an exaggerated exercise. We walked down the still, fir-fringed valley until the next big drama: we met another dog. First S., then I, had to go and collect our two, or one or other of them. In the next valley, whose crest we had crossed, there was a layer of cloud through which the scream of jets was suddenly audible. There was a Swiss military airstrip somewhere down there. A jet burst out of the clouds and cleared the mountain.

When we got back to the house, Sean had woken. '*Tesoro*,' Audrey said, '*mio amore, com'estai?*' We left A. to be a good mother and had tea in the hotel. We went back to supper, but stayed only briefly. In the morning, the taxi took us down into the *nebbia* and we drove through intermittent fog to Zurich, which was quite clear. S. said, 'I want to buy some watches.' We went into Turber, where they served watches on framed velvet trays. S. looked at self-winders and stop-watches and finally bought me an alarm pocket-watch ('Oh go on, have a watch,' he said, when I demurred) and another for somebody else and a wrist watch for somebody else again. He spent about $200, with enjoyment and without show. Later, buying presents at Sprüngli, he remarked that two dollars was a lot for a box of chocolates.

We set off for the airport in thickening cloud. It seemed impossible that we could fly. The concourse was swarming with disconsolate travellers. The planes on the tarmac were few, and scarcely visible. We watched one set of passengers go, and I said, 'If their plane crashes and then they call our flight, what do we do?'

'Go get right on the plane,' he said. 'Did you ever hear of two planes crashing one after the other?'

They did call our flight, which was amalgamated so that it was going to put S. (and others) down at Geneva, and fly on to Rome. Out we went. S. was first class, of course. He told me later that the Captain had refused to take off until one of the crew got out, so heavy was the pay-load. We all had to disembark at Geneva and, unexpectedly, I saw S. again; he was carrying the bag of a young woman with a small child.

We were very happy to be together again, Beetle and I. Sarah loved the rabbit I bought her in the Geneva terminal; P. the fire engine I found in Zurich.

A woman tells her husband that, after some years, she has lost interest in her lover. She belongs to him alone now. His days of jealousy and rage are over. He leaves her shortly afterwards, unconvinced that it was not her lover who lost interest in her.

The *mille feuilles* brickwork of the Capitoline hill.

Clifford: 'They were brothers and hated each other so much they paid to read each other's comic books; can you imagine?'

What destroys the Greek heroes is not *hubris* in the routine sense of pride; it is that they forget, in their individual vanity, that the hero-king owes his authority to his certain doom. He not only lives but also dies for the people; when he seeks to prolong his majesty, he must be tripped. The decline of tragedy is to do with the end of the principle of human sacrifice. Wherever a system has the strength to demand a man's life, and no one can save him except by over-throwing its gods, you have the conditions for tragedy. The tragic figure cannot suffer *tragically* unless he does so for a principle. Socrates' death has tragic elements, but when it becomes an affir-mation of personal *choice*, rather than inevitability, it becomes in a sense comic: S. could so easily have escaped; his ironic 'faith' in the *polis* is altogether too civilised for the divine machinery to stay in place. By choosing what he is, and when he dies, he mocks the gods; he dies for it, but so do they.

Ajax *means* the man who went mad and killed captured sheep in the belief that they were Trojans; Oedipus *means* the man who blinded himself because he had committed incest; these figures have no possibility of different C.V.s. Pity is recognition of who they are.

25.2.65. An evening with Monica Vitti and Antonioni. We dined at the Ristorante Bolognese in the Piazza del Popolo. Jo, B. and I arrived first and inspected the *antipasti*. Michelangelo and Monica were soon there, though Jo had said she was always late 'Not minutes or hours but, I must tell you, *days*'. She wore a light-coloured, fluffy fur over a low-cut black dress with a pleated skirt, thin-strapped shoes. The dyed blonde hair hung in two brackets about her pale, milky face. She had an almost albino appearance, especially in the rectangular and narrow smoked glasses. She spoke in a husky, almost coarse voice. Moments of slumped indifference alternated with bursts of brilliant, laughing animation. We all ate at different times, different courses. A plate of *pasta* common between three of us delighted her.

Antonioni wore a dignified grey flannel suit and dark tie. A tic tugs at his face from time to time. He lacks theatrical pretensions. There is about him a kind of grave respectability, as if he were a great specialist whose diagnoses were never good news. His face was without inner vitality; it flickered with rare reactions, sometimes creasing, *backwards* as it were, into an appearance of painful gaiety. Towards the end of dinner he told a rather banal story, about the director who goes to heaven and is offered all the facilities, unlimited budget, etc. by the archangel in charge of film production. He is amazed to be told that he can do whatever he likes. There are no restrictions *but* there is a '*piccolo angelotto* that God would be very grateful if he could find a little part for...'

Jo told a less sly story. A good and a bad brother die. The good brother gets tired of heaven and asks to see where the bad one is. They show him the bad brother sitting in hell with a blonde on his knee and a bottle in his hand. Not bad. He is seriously jealous until they tell him that the bottle has a hole in it and the blonde does not. Monica was not greatly amused, though Jo had told me, with a sad leer, that she was now 'getting interested in sex'.

After dinner, we followed M.A.'s white Giulia GT along the via Flaminia and over the Milvian bridge, under the Ponte Flaminio (where P., Sarah and I were stuck in the snow) and up a tree-lined road scored with potholes. Jo warned us that there was going to be a party and that, since this was 'the Rome of *La Dolce Vita*', it might involve the '*spogliarello* and I don't know what'.

M.A. and M.V. have two apartments, one (M.A.'s) above the other, on the top floors. We went up in a lift which had a flashing, silently urgent, light when you pressed for it. Monica's plain, dark cousin opened the door. It was her birthday, which we later celebrated with chocolate cake and bubbly wine (Beetle whispered to me, 'Is this champagne or champagne charlie?').

As soon as we arrived, Monica proposed chinese checkers, of which she had many sets. I faced her, with a man called Calderone and Suso d'Amico's daughter, Silvia, making up the four. Several big books stood upright, pages half-open, on the marble floor and ledges: décor, not reading.

Antonioni joined in no games. He sat apart, smiling from time to time. He claimed attention passively: by withdrawing and making no demands, he seemed to wish to be in demand. When I told him, in the restaurant, that he was the only reason I was interested in film, his face filled with light. I asked if we might spend a day together sometime. '*Ben volontieri*,' he said.

Later in the evening, B. and I went up the spiral staircase to M.A.'s flat. He had a collection of clouded bottles in a shelved case above the fireplace: Roman or Venetian. We talked rather gravely, the three of us, like adults who have rather shamefacedly deserted a children's party.

A woman carefully brushes together all the crumbs on the dining table, while her husband sits pompously at his place with the paper. When she has combined the crumbs in the palm of her hand, she tips them neatly into his lap.

Jack Gwillym, the Shakespearian actor. His agent arranged for him to audition for a big American spectacular. He spoke proudly of his Stratford experience. The producer said, 'That's fine. Now would you roll up your trousers, please? I'd like to see your legs.'

He got the job.

Dear God, to read of tax increases and glance anxiously at the twenty thousand a year column!

Among his forms of pastoral, did Empson include works which cover a limited span of time? *Brief Encounter* for easy instance, but also all 'romances' in which the lovers celebrate (and lament) their passion within a tight schedule. This kind of thing has elements of both contest (trial) and sporting event. It is played, to the last second, in the knowledge that the whistle will go. The return to 'reality' signals the end of the eclogue. Film often makes use of this artificial limit in order to lend pathos to the improbable. *Room at the Top* contrasts passion with opportunism and shows that passion may, in a developer's metaphor appropriate to the times, lead to the acquisition of an unrewarding property. How to exploit and explode the pastoral frame? By having a play within the play: the girl (typically) imagines herself to be enacting a true passion, but her own language (style) reveals her delusions about 'love' and its consequences. History (before and after) ruptures all idylls, kingly or otherwise.

The kind of pastoral I am talking about truncates not only sexual episodes but also social. In *On the Waterfront*, the 'optimistic', upbeat ending blinks the facts of what really happened on the New York waterfront: nothing nice (another, truthful ending was vetoed). How heroic to pretend that one man's bravery could procure a 'free enterprise' social revolution, and how fatuous! The elimination of Jocko de Paris, in *End as a Man*, has the same narcotic moral, but upside down: there is nothing wrong, we were incited to believe, with any society that the eviction of a single bad hat will not take care of. One could imagine a Sovcolor version, in which nothing was wrong with The Party which the expulsion of a Trotskyite would not remedy. It is often the case with these exposés that they are daringly truthful *up to the last reel*. Only the solution fails to solve anything.

Antonioni achieves extension in limitation by altering the tempo. Allowing 'natural time' to be longer than conventional screen time, he contrives a kind of genuine slow motion. In *L'Eclisse*, by preceding a brisk affair with a resumé of the torture which typically follows the rupture of much the same kind of 'romance', he questions the – what? – sincerity, *value* of 'that sort of thing'. Can it be that he deliberately subverts the excellence of his scheme by the inadequate individualisation of his characters? The whole film is narcissistic and loving, not of the girl and the men, but of Monica and Delon. What would a satisfactory life be for these people? We are not even given a myth of man's possible redemption. It is different in *La Notte*. In this respect at least it can be said that the three elements of the 'trilogy' are indeed related, in an order of descending prospects for the characters, and for 'us'.

Il Gattopardo. We came out with a sense of the utter deadliness of the cinema. The supposed brilliance of Visconti, the supposed stardom of Burt Lancaster. He gave a moving performance, I suppose, but who is not moved by a dose of salts? It is a tuppenny-ha'penny epic which achieved epic proportions by the most tedious means: extension.

Ios. July. Eric and Elizabeth T. had rented the Rowlands' house. When G. Galatsios came down with a message for him (he had '*ena gramma systemeno sto horio*'), I went and translated. Eric is about fifty, brown, slim, blue-eyed; khaki shorts, hairless, tanned chest with crumpled nipples, silver hair carefully brushed. The blue eyes would be polished if they could be. He says he paints. He warned me, before I met her, that his wife is an invalid; she has serious heart trouble from which she will never recover. He was very polite and proper, but when he told me this he drew down his lip, as if he had had occasion to tick me off. She came out, almost an old lady already, in a pinky rose dress which hung limply from her shoulders which huddled forwards as if to protect the source of her pain. Eric told me that he was financially 'strapped' (they had been slung out of Kenya) and that they could not afford to keep the Rowland house for August. Was there any chance of our renting them ours when we went? I said that there was none; we would let them have it for nothing. The next day, in casual conversation, he told me that they had been in Palestine at the end of British rule.

'Really?' I said. 'What were you doing there?'

'I was in the police force,' he said.

We set out to catch the boat to Santorini at six in the morning, leaving the children asleep in Joy's care. At seven thirty we were in the port. A strong wind was blowing.

Stubby waves sped across the harbour. The *Limnos* was due at eight, or nine. She arrived at eleven. We were in two minds. Suddenly we saw that the lighter going out to the *vapori* was already in the harbour; we had missed it, so had another couple, a girl called Rosemary – the brisk-skipping-freckled-ginger-mouse-haired-blue-jeaned-saucy-seeming holiday mistress of a studious-spectacled-brown-voiced-thickknit-sweatered-shambling-slow-to-smile-Oxonian. We were hustled into a *caique* which then lost its rudder. We got moving at last and pumped away down wind – oars had no effect – and reached a station near the far rocks. The sea cracked and drenched us. We began to inch back towards the *Limnos*. As we edged in, she swung away from us, until she was almost under *Aghia Irine*. She straightened and, as we came up from a fresh dousing, we saw that she was sailing out of the harbour. All that for nothing!

We landed. 'It's so bloody silly,' Rosemary said, 'it's MAD!' She instructed me to have a helluva row with the harbour-master. I said I would ask for our money back, but not have a row: the Greeks despise people who shout. How wise I've become, how *relaxed*! The others thought that someone had to be blamed. 'Never mind,' I said, 'perhaps she'll come back!'

There was black smoke behind *Aghia Irine*.

'Back in the boat,' someone called.

By God, she *was* coming back. Having just congratulated ourselves on not having to go to sea in a gale, we found ourselves back in the *caique*. A large yacht had come in for shelter; a sharp, flat boat with a busy outboard motor was scudding across our bows with a mooring rope. Yells from our crew were unheard in the gale. The yellow line lay like a long splinter under the blue skin of the harbour. After a long minute of helpless imminence, the rope ravelled around our stilled propeller.

Finally, we were on station again for our approach to the *Limnos*. As the gap closed, we were told to be quick. I grabbed bravely for the iron hand rail, thumped my head on it, lost (and regained) my sunglasses, and at last stood dripping among the apathetic officers. Everyone else came aboard and B. and I went and ate three fried eggs (two forks, one plate) and drank *koniak* out of coffee cups.

An hour later we were drying under Santorini; red, toasted cliffs above a purple sea which has been known, they say, to boil. Barrel-shaped houses are built on the shells of those ruined in the most recent earthquake. The white town sits on the husk of the old one, flesh not properly grafted on old bones. We rode up the famous, numbered *skala* on numbered mules with tourist-comforting saddles and pursued by a pallid boy calling '*Delax, delax*'. He prodded my beast's ear with his spiteful stick; it kicked and jibbed. Thanks a lot.

We took a big old Ford taxi to Old Thera. Few trees apart from eucalyptus; walls of fat, pocked stones between fields green with grapes and vegetables. The far side of the island is a long track of black beach where thunderous seas spread fans of foam. We climbed the high back of the rock through hairpin after hairpin, past slagheaps of fallen rubble. We came to the rounded end of the lumpy road. The *othigos* pointed ahead to our next guide, crouched with his black mongrel, braced with a stick, in a crack of the towering cliff. The wind was strong enough to knock us down. At the top, we tottered from guide-post to guide-post, gasping and clutching our way around the grey ruins.

The guide, in his grey sweater, island sandals and peaked cap, treated us to the full range of his set pieces. While we arched ourselves to the gale's tune, he played a sedate continuo, some of which I could never have followed and most of which was shredded into the wind. The acropolis was first settled, in historic times, by Sparta; the Dorians arrived in the seventh century, under king Theras. Their high fortress is typical of those who conquer but do not love the sea or sea-faring.

Later, Ptolemy III (?) sent an expedition and their settlement was more lavish; an excellent temple with niches marked with religious devices: a dolphin, a bird, a lion. A shallow sauce dish for sacrificial offerings in the grey stone floor and the footprints of a god's statue (Apollo?).

Beyond, the Roman town (between them a temple of Dionysos, badged with a large phallus and testicles); baths and a Hellenistic theatre with 14,000 seats. Below the far side of the mountain we had toiled up, measured, tilled fields, without green, went flat to the edge of a saucer-shaped plain where another white town glistened in the sunset.

It was dark when we returned to the modern town. We went to book tickets for the steamer the following morning, but (this week) it was not going to stop at Ios. It was too windy, they said (and we believed it) for *caiques*: we must wait till Sunday. The poor children! We could do nothing.

B. had her hair done in a green, wood and formica *koureion* while I stretched out, airless and pile-tormented, on a stiff green bench. The proprietor shouted a great deal and treasured hawked spit which he brought in from the '*Salle de dammes*' (*sic*) and spat into the basin where the assistants washed their hands hygienically.

In the late afternoon we walked out along the tar road (having renounced the road to Pyrgos when the clinkers rasped our feet), past a shuddering power station to the cemetery. On the way in, I hit my head on the cross above the gate and said, 'Jesus.' B. noted that some people lived to ninety or ninety-five; some didn't.

Rosemary and her now Greek-peak-capped lover were astride a red motorbike on the way back from the beach. He said later that it was like walking on caviare, which he had always wanted to do. At dinner in Loukas' *taverna*, he told her, in a voice as intimate as a party political broadcast on behalf of the Conservative and Unionist party, about a lift he had got into Oxford one night. The man deposited him at his college and then stole his suitcase containing the proverbial 'year's notes'. He hailed a police car (how do you do that?), but it had to stop on the city boundary. Another constabulary traced the runaway and he was charged with theft. Our friend had not wanted to prosecute, but the police were not free to desist. The man was put on probation and afterwards they shook hands: 'He said "Sorry, old chap", and so he went out of my life.' One suspected that he, in his turn, was about to subject Rosemary to the same treatment.

As we were going down the long steps to the quayside, a man heard the mules coming and, perhaps expecting someone, put his head out of a small house with cracked greeny-blue shutters. There was a look of rare apprehension on his face. It was Adolf Hitler, to the life. I rode on.

We got up at 5.45 to catch the *Despina* back to Ios. The children greeted us happily and ran to meet Yorgos, as he led the way. He gathered them up and enthroned them on his donkey. Had we had a good time? I suffered all the time from my piles and could not walk ten yards without having to stop and, as discreetly as possible, thrust my insides back into place.

1966

The creak of the pigeons in the *piazza* San Marco.

April. Leslie Bricusse called from California, at seven in the morning, to tell me that I had won the Oscar for *Darling*. I had not lain awake wondering if I would and I was not all that delighted to be woken with the news. Tony Newley and Joan Collins added their congratulations. Not a few years ago, Newley shook my unknown hand and, as he left Vivian Cox's *garconnière*, said, 'Good luck in whatever you choose to do in life.'

A few days after winning, I was at a literary party. Jack Lambert said to me, 'Well, from now on you can say goodbye to all hope of being reviewed on your merits.'

Karl Miller had just resigned from *The New Statesman*. I called Jane because Paul was ill and could not go to tea with their son, as planned. She said it was as well, since D. had been knocked unconscious in the school yard. K. was very upset. B. had cooked two ducks and a *pâté* for dinner; the Fermans were coming, why didn't I ask the Millers? Jane said she would have to ask K.; he assented.

I had opened champagne. K. wanted whisky. Before dinner, I asked concernedly about D.'s misfortune, which was the right thing to do. At the table, carving intransigent ducks, I searched for another topic and, with entirely unpremeditated tactlessness, mentioned that I had been asked to sign The Brophy Letter, to *The Times*. It was intended to repudiate The Amis Letter, which – above no-nonsensical names such as Levin, Raven and Braine – urged unequivocal, unboatrocking support for the U.S. in Vietnam. The circular with The Brophy Letter named Nick Tomalin (and J. Miller) as others who had been approached. Wrestling with the duck's unflappable wings, I let slip that I had called Nick to see what he thought about the whole thing.

'Nick who?' said Karl.

'Tomalin.'

Too late, oh much too late, I realised that Karl had far from recovered from what he felt to be the humiliation of being displaced as literary editor of the *Statesman* by N.O.T.

'After all,' I said, 'Nick knows more about Vietnam than I do.' His article 'Zapping Charlie Cong' had first alerted us to the turkey-shoot aspect of the Vietnam intervention.

'What does he know about it?' Karl said. 'He's been there for five days.'

'Five days longer than I have.'

'Five days; just time to write one piece and then fly home.'

'Well,' I said, 'I thought it was worth finding out what he thought.'

'Well, of course, if you can't make up your own mind. If you need other people to make your decisions for you.'

'I was interested to know what he thought of the whole performance. There's something to be said for listening to people with more personal experience than you've got yourself.'

'I don't think you've got any right to say that,' Karl said.

'Look, mate,' I said, clashing the carvers, 'I shall say what I bloody well like in my own house.'

The bourgeois shows his silver-plated fangs.

Jane attempted to calm things, by making an analogy between what happened between K. and Paul Johnson and what other people might imagine had happened. K. said that that was something he had *absolutely no wish* to discuss.

I wonder if there is an apocryphal version of the parable, in which The Good Samaritan receives a stinging slap on both cheeks and the advice to mind his own bloody business.

1967

Stephen's birth. The midwife, Mrs Preston, took the grey, stretched baby and held it horizontal and blew on its diaphragm. The milky-grey skin rippled like the surface of a liquid and the big-balled baby shuddered into life. He was born with the cord four times round his neck; if it had been any shorter (it was exceptionally long) he might have choked at birth. Even after the first tremulous breath it seemed to me that he found it difficult to be alive. He was put, with admirable lack of anxious display, into his cot (how quickly possessions clustered round what had been, moments earlier, a question mark!) and oxygen applied through a mask. Gradually he grew from paste into pinkness. There had, apparently, never been any problem (except with me). By the time, an hour later, Paul and Sarah came down, blinking, he was definitely sentenced to life.

Stephen at eight weeks lies in his pram and stares up at the branches. His eyes go deep blue and swallow, without the lens of words, what hangs over him. He breathes urgently and his face opens to the view as a greedy man's does to a banquet.

The family seat. 1945. 'We stood on the balcony of the Town Hall. I remember how confident daddy seemed. How could a DSO possibly lose to a man who had spent the war as a member of the local Agricultural Workers' Union? When the figures were announced, I was ready to weep. Then I saw how cruelly wounded my mother looked and I could not entirely fail to enjoy the occasion.'

Langham. August. Resuming the privacy of a notebook is like rejoining oneself at some guilty rendezvous. So much to tell oneself, so furtive an inclination to hold one's own hand! It used to be that I wondered how believers in a deterministic world found anything worth doing. Now I see that the futility of kicking against the pricks in no way stops one doing so. The patterns of my life recur again and again; to be forewarned is to be fore-disarmed. I imagined that being cured of my piles would greatly alter my life; it merely relieved my piles. Even happiness I cannot endure happily.

The phone rang. It was Monica Vitti. She was in England; she had seen *Darling*; she wanted to meet me. In fact, she had seen my article in the *S.T.* with her picture at the head which spoke of my admiration for *L'Avventura*, which she called 'The Adventure'. I reminded her of our meeting in Rome, which she scarcely recalled, but now she said she 'admired' me. 'And I admire you.' On that basis we plan to meet '*dopo il quindici Settembre.*'

I recall that Joe Losey hated her (Dirk Bogarde went around during the shooting of *Modesty Blaise* saying, 'Miss Veetee is a peetee') and that Jeanne Moreau 'loathed her more than anyone she had ever met'. How can such a woman fail to be intriguing?

Beetle said, 'Who was that?'

'Monica Vitti.'

'I bet you wish it was.'

Poor B.! If she knew the command she had of my feelings, she would be less suspicious. Her smile illuminates my day.

Publicity. I drove up to town at six in the morning to do interviews for *Two for the Road*. It is like taking exams; you assume that those who ask the questions know the answers. In fact, journalists ask you to write their articles for them. Sitting in the boardroom at Fox with my feet on the chairman's blotter, I noticed that I had lost a button on my shirt cuff. Jo W., the publicist, sent out for one and did repairs. A man from *Photoplay* suggested that I wrote novels with Jewish content 'because of a pre-sold market'.

I said, 'There are still more Christians than Jews in this country. Contrary to what you may suppose.'

'Yes,' said he, 'they are rather vociferous, aren't they?'

When vulgar people use words like 'vociferous', you may be sure that their prejudices are deeply engraved.

Lunch at *La Terrazza* and then a huge Austin hire car, driven by a man with high blood pressure, to the BBC in Maida Vale. Peter Haigh alluded much to his tin leg, as Ken Allsop does. He assumed I would soon be directing films. Did anyone guess how full of doubt and timidity I am?

Supper at J. and M.'s. M. has discovered that there are enough H-bombs in the world for one to be let off every day for the next 140 years. J. had read an article in *The Times* about a Black Power meeting which led him to believe that American Negroes would soon be literally up in arms about the racial question, nationwide, one and all. Both J. and M. agreed that catastrophe in South Africa and in the Middle East was imminent. J. had met a doctor who was doing research into rabies. There was *no cure* for those suffering from having been bitten by a mad dog. Mad dogs had come into Western Europe from Poland during the war and were now breeding in the vicinity of the Black Forest. 'Ipe!' cried M. 'We were quite near the Black Forest.' '*And*,' J. went on, 'they're coming closer all the time. It's only a matter of *when* they reach the Channel. It's absolutely *vital* that the six months quarantine period be *rigidly* observed or it'll get across the Channel. *And* there's absolutely no cure *whatever*. They can ease the pain, to some extent, but that's *all*.' He spoke so challengingly that you felt you had wasted your day not researching into rabies.

Guy Ramsey was the first person to encourage me to be a writer. He said that he would play Flaubert to my Guy de Maupassant and tell me when the moment had come for me to venture into print. If he never wrote his *Madame Bovary*, I fear I have yet to write my *Boule de Suif*, but let it pass. When he died, at the bridge table, Celia came and stayed with us in Fuengirola with their son Simon. After *Lindmann* came out, Celia wrote to me and said that I could now 'do anything I wanted' in fiction. She did not foresee *Orchestra and Beginners*. In it, I suppose it could be said that the character of Vernon Dorset is very like G.R. I thought I was paying him the best compliment I could imagine by putting him in my pages. When painters paint their friends, it is rarely considered a disservice. I never imagined that Celia might be affronted. She herself was guilty of a disdainful sketch of G. in *The Dry Land*, when he was still alive, as she confessed; she has often threatened to put *us* (B. and me) in a book, and actually did so with Dorothy Tutin (whom she hardly knew). She was keen to take it that Guy had been defamed, though I had intended only to commemorate him. The first I heard of her indignation was from Cape, enclosing a solicitor's letter demanding changes, especially to the passage about Guy's 'greatest scoop', the whereabouts of Rudolf Hess after he landed in 1941.

Did C. once fancy herself as Léah to my Chéri? She said, meaningly, that I needed 'more experience of life' and that I should not spend all my time with B. She tried to wish Simon on me as a ward in 1959; I ducked the responsibility, not being short of burdens, and being very short of resources. Now she has perfected the rhetoric of the sigh. The humourlessness of the whole business, its lack of personal contact, is the proper conclusion of something that never truly began.

My mother phoned to say that she had detected the reason for Celia's fury. 'It was nothing to do with Guy. It was because of the picture of his second wife.' Of *course*. I had made her very plain, and that was inexcusable.

For GUILT. Dilys and her husband design dresses. The first we see is a 'poster dress' of a naked woman, clinically accurate. The model shows it and then turns away to take it off, modestly (hole for navel).

O. Flush with success, the one-time artist now toys with becoming a businessman. He is the very symbol of fashion; he raises and lowers his aesthetic skirts in the prevailing style. His non-conformity is in conformance with the going eccentricity. He has the knack of suggesting that what everyone else is doing is 'last year's'. His eager acceptance of 'life', of 'what our bodies tell us' betokens his own want of assurance. He is like a commander ever alert to what his intelligence officers tell him, but without the means to collate and evaluate their data. He makes looking bright a form of illumination. Like the chameleon, he is at once colourless and highly coloured. Having no decisive shape, he can fit in anywhere. To follow fashion is his idea of being avant-garde.

Norwich. They made a little film about me for Anglia. The interviewer carried his 'duty suit' with him on a hanger, like a head in a box. 'Working' in a film panders to a vanity which is far from self-admiration. The modesty of film stars in private suddenly seems understandable, and genuine. All their narcissism is vested in the public image. One's private 'reality' carries all the burden of failings and fears; the screen face and voice, about which something can always 'be done' have a perfectibility which crass reality cannot attain. Endless revision, the excision of whatever mortifies or offends, is always possible in the shadow world (that of The Ideal). Hence screen heroes represent absolutes and the most successful films are moralities (albeit 'pastoral'). Characters are 'reversible' but not mutable. What the actor admires in his own image is that it both is and is not 'him'. The counterfeit is shit without a smell, erection without tumescence, a half truth more fetchingly real than crude, unlovely reality. Film is more complete, more *born* than one's real

self. Language retains the umbilical, binds one to messy sources; film
severs it.

McLuhan. 'A charlatan' (Muggeridge), 'one of the major intellectual influences of our time' (*Life* magazine); no contradiction there.
McL. is a parody of genius. Einstein was famous as a 'brain' when
few understood what the products of his mind meant or signified;
McL.'s fame is not a cheapening of his qualities because the vulgar-
isation of what he means *is* what he means.

The *Gutenberg Galaxy* is written in the Latinate riddling style of
professorial antiquarianism. It proclaims the end of the tyranny of
print in the dictatorial style of the tyrant. McL. would strike the
fetters from our minds the better to cram them down our throats.
He boasts that he never encounters any hostility from his students.
Why should he? He is the uncensorious censor, the self-effacing
super-ego, the Rector without rules, the grammarian without
syntax and the Father Confessor without sin-tax, the Saviour
without conditions. McL. resembles a parody of the Church to
which his work is basically committed: he has his Jesuitical and his
populist side. You may find your way to Him through the fun-
group or through cerebral means. Either way, the message is the
same and McL. is the Medium.

Lunch at the Connaught with R.G. and Natalie Wood. I sat and
talked with her in the bar while R.G. finished making my deal with
Dick Zanuck and David Brown. She showed enticing, charmingly
hairy legs under her mini-skirt. Having grown up as a child star in
Hollywood, she has no affectations of having arrived: she has been
there all the time. She has little conceit. She knows the dangers of
the business, but they are not foreign to her, so she has, it seems,
little fear of them. Her face changes from the expected, unexcep-
tional prettiness into a longer, more languidly Russian sadness;
awareness of age and time throws a tincture of shadow. She was off
afterwards to Mary Quant's. In John Frankenheimer's suite she
cadged a fiver from R.G., like any good working girl, or princess.

A meeting at the Dorchester with the Men from U.G.F.
International. They were like a trio of reformed hoodlums: dark-
suited S., monogram-shirted M. and never-lost-a-fight Irve. I was
in no hurry to sell; they were in no mood to buy. Chalk and cheese
made a meal of it.

At the Round House. Jo Strick was yelling the merits of his *Ulysses*. I said, 'Jo Strick thinks that if you take a great book and make it into a film, it will be a great film. He might as well boil it in a pot and think it'll make a great meal.'

Willie Maugham. He was so determined to allow none of his uncertainties to confuse the false calm of his style. It lured me into a belief in the happy possibility of amused aloofness. Locking the door on his private foibles, he imprisoned others in the proper bondage from which he longed to escape. His style excluded the indigestible, unaccountable elements which he thought he could purge from his system but which, in the long run, made nonsense of its civilised conceits. He elected to be a complete fraud because he could not face the shame of being an incomplete man. Working in the tradition of the very society which made homosexuality a torment to him, he accepted all the boring formalities of an audience to which, as a satirist, he might take amusing exception but to which he always hoped to appeal. Is it a sign of the homosexual in particular, or of the second-rate in general, that he cannot live without the defences of the very society which would destroy him if it were ever aware of his real feelings? One can excuse another writer almost anything, apart from having admired him.

On the day *Two for the Road* opened in London, Audrey and Mel announced that they were separating. Jo said that if they were going to do it, they could not have chosen a better day.

Mel is mentioned in Stephen Birmingham's *The Right People* as having been a member of the 'Knickerbocker Greys', a select NY cadet group of the sons of the socially acceptable. How curious that all Mel's affected sophistication turns out to have been the real thing! The well-pressed, well-tuned personality hides nothing: if it is only a front, it has no behind. No wonder Audrey imagined him to dispose of a wealth of experience (and wealth) which would provide a princess with her palace. He turned out the trickiest of all fakes to see through: the genuine article.

A woman retains her ability to cause pain long after she has lost the capacity to give pleasure.

Peter Green, in his intro. to Juvenal: 'His (Cato's) official post as censor was one to which every satirist unofficially aspired.' And aspires; his ambiguity is sustained by the tension between his desire and his fear of getting what he wants. Frustrated, he shouts for change; offered a free hand, he embraces his bonds. Oedipus: the child dreads the consummation of his guilty craving, but rails against the world which denies it to him. He looks back to a generous Golden Age (of breast-feeding). The satirist dreads 'growing up', yet he appeals to the audience to give in and give way to him. His fury is that of the battle-cruiser *Hood*; he sails to the attack with a combination of excessive firepower and very thin armour-plating. The only programme of 'reform' which really appeals to him is one which will procure him the world's love. Juvenal loved children, but not women who preferred others to him. Yet J. refers with scorn to *all* the Latin deities *except Ceres*, the quintessential Mother, to whom he dedicated a statue.

Camp depends on the existence of a square world.

The drawing room revolutionary: 'Can I help it if I have come through the bloodiest era in human history without ever seeing a drop spilt? I've waited at all the black spots I can discover but, do you realise, I've never seen anybody knocked down by a motor car? I'd like to go to Africa and see the breakdown of law and order and the collapse of all civilised values; I'd like to be penniless among the penniless, but I can't afford the fare to get to them.'

1.12.67. I went alone, by taxi, to see Fulham play Liverpool. I bought a ticket from a spiv: two pounds ten for a ten shilling ticket. I walked up and down looking for a sweetshop or a pub. Finally, I went into the ground and found a bar under the concrete shelves of the stand. I ordered a double brandy and drank it, cold, from a footed mock glass. Then I went to my seat and read *The Golden Notebook*. The stand filled slowly, regulars calling out 'All right?' to each other.

Cohen was soon hurt. 'He must've hurt himself,' someone said. When he got up, the same man said, 'He's all right now.' Eventually, however, Cohen limped to the touchline. 'He's going off, I expect.' He had done the ligaments in his knee.

Halfway through the second half, after Fulham had gone ahead through a gloriously headed goal by Clark, a Liverpool-scarved supporter leaped the barrier and began to run the full length of the pitch to where the players were. He then set about Barrett, the Fulham forward. After a few seconds, players from both sides formed a screen around him and put the boot in. A posse of policemen arrived to do together what none had had the wit to do separately. The intrepid coward was hustled into the darkness. My neighbour turned to me and said, 'I don't know why he attack Barrett. He ain't done a thing right all afternoon.'

When I told Brian Glanville this on Tuesday, after the Bill Naughton game in the park, he said, 'Barrett had quite a good game actually.'

The injury to Cohen finished his career.

Soccer violence. It is usually away crowds that cause the damage. Pre-war crowds behaved well less because they were cowed than because they were composed, with few exceptions, of home supporters. The new mobility of criminals makes criminals of the mobile. It is systematically liberating to be 'away from home'. The brothel was for years the epitome of the away fixture: nobody had to account, except by paying, for what happened there. The commercial traveller is the stock figure of the dirty joke; it is not commerce but travelling that gives him licence. Concorde is the great cooperative enterprise of the moment: it will enable a man to be out of his wife's London bed in the morning and in his mistress's, in New York, by lunchtime.

Home supporters are civilians, encumbered with wives and families and front gardens, while the visitors are the Dorians, who sweep in and retreat to distant fastnesses. Mobility transforms morality; it makes unsocial actions available at sociable prices. And away we go.

December. The wedding, and breakfast, at Mrs Fleur Cowles Meyer's (A 5) Albany flat, of Bill and Susan F. The apartment was scented with the mandatory joss sticks. The ceremony was in a large, cluttered drawing room; redoubled pictures on the walls, flowers – it was hard to distinguish real from false, and false from real – sprouted from elaborate holders, themselves floral. In the middle of the room had been placed a sort of one-sided playpen with a raspberry-coloured hassock. A grey-winged, sonorous priest, banded for action, primrose halter folded in his hand, stood in manly skirts, ready for action.

At last Susan arrived to be married; Bill to be remarried. He was tall and neutered by the occasion, in striped tie, carnation, winged coat; S. in a short white dress like a wilted doily. The priest (from St James's, Mayfair) sprinkled personalised toilet water; it was, he confessed, the first time he had performed so intimate a service. At the end, Our Man From St James's laid a hand on each of the newly-wedded heads and called down Jesus to bless the girl from Miami and the Jew.

Bill Dozier pointed out a stuffy-looking man as having been the fourth husband of Margaret Sullavan. Bill himself had been going with her while she was being courted by the other. She told him she would never have another divorce. When she committed suicide, he wondered if it had been out of morbid determination to keep to her resolve. Bill whispered to me that, despite all his compliments on the décor, the magniloquent priest would *never* be invited to Fleur's again. Why? I could see no fault in him. 'He pronounced Meyer in the Jewish way,' Bill D. explained. 'Mire. She only likes it when it sounds like a female horse. How do you feel about doing a screenplay of *The Well of Loneliness?*'

'Are you serious?'

'One thing leads to another. That's what one thing is for, right? I'm very serious. Jack Clayton wants to do it.'

Mrs Meyer announced in an invalid tone that something terrible had happened: her Chinese chef had burned two turkeys, melted their silver platters in the oven and quit in shame. Mrs Rayne told her not to worry: *her* Chinese chef had almost committed suicide after failing the driving test.

Invited to enjoy what was left, we were led through a dressing room with a Vertès screen profiling Fleur *en fleur* as a young girl, then through a flowered room and another door into a second, pastel-coloured, drawing room with a false ceiling. There was salad and brie; no wine. Nancy Wilson, editor of *Harper's Bazaar*, told me of the 'irresponsibility' of the anti-war demonstrators in NYC who gave comfort to the V-C. She told me how disappointed all the draftees were if they were *not* sent to fight in Vietnam. She and her friends had voted for Barry Goldwater.

When I left, I bumped into Terry Stamp and a mate standing in the roadway outside. He had just had lunch, *tête-à-tête* with Ted Heath, his neighbour. Terry had proposed that Piccadilly be made two way again, if Heath ever came to power. They talked about pot as well. I went back to Terry's book-filled pad and drank brandy with him until it was time to go and play tennis at four.

Peter Cook was 'beaten up' by some Manchester United supporters after the Tottenham game and phoned the *Sunday Times*, doubtless while still bleeding internally, to give them the news. He came a few days later to play in Bill Naughton's park game. He lasted only half an hour in our unflattered company before limping off. There was no report in the press.

M. said, 'Freddie, *Two for the Road* got *stinking* notices!' She had taken Mrs J., her daily help, into St Mary's to die, on the under-standing that she would do so within twenty-four hours. She lasted almost a week. M. visited her every day. The undertakers refused to move the body unless they were paid their full seventy-five pounds in advance. The burial grant (fixed in 1948) is twenty-five and takes 'weeks to come through'.

A letter came from James Kennaway, whose first book, *Paths of Glory*, was reviewed in the same batch (but more gloriously) as mine, commiserating about the press for *T.F.T.R.* He accuses me of being 'a careless bugger' but, in an honest and friendly way, invites me to write and not to 'slash around'. He promises that I am judged well by my 'peers'. I am touched and embarrassed by such simple, imag-inative decency. Like Mr Boldwood, I am 'happier now'.

She is a good woman and has adopted twins. She invited me to see them in their pram. I warned myself to be unsurprised if they turned out to be black. No; they were two pale, large-headed baby boys, one heavier than the other. She pointed out the frailer one with apprehension, fearful that it was already turning into a homosexual. She told me their behinds were almost fleshless; 'Look! They've got practically no *anus*.' An unnervingly technical term from a loving mother.

D.H. Lawrence, in his essay on *Far from the Madding Crowd*, remarks that Boldwood is the only character in the novel who has no first name. This is an error: B.'s Christian name is revealed in the scene where B. 'ambushes' Troy on his return from Bath after his secret wedding to Bathsheba. 'My name is William Boldwood,' he says.

Boldwood's relationship with Troy is one of the most subtle in the book. He is introduced as a misogynist. A whole section of rustics' gossip depicts the futility of courting his attention. What changes all this? The easy answer is Bathsheba's Valentine card, which has the effect (if never the purpose) of relieving Boldwood of the fear of rejection. But Farmer Ives' daughters made *their* availability no less clear, without exciting the smallest spark. Consider the exact location in which the scales first fall from Boldwood's eyes: the Corn Exchange. Bathsheba is the only woman there; she is, in a sense, *acting a man's part*, that of The Farmer. The female female has no charm for Boldwood, but when she plays the man, Bathsheba exerts a devastating pull on him: 'My life has not been my own since I beheld you clearly,' he tells her when he comes to propose.

The 'female side' of Boldwood's character is plainly presented by Hardy: the man's 'tidiness', his attention to details, his dour bachelorhood point to repressed homosexuality. Bathsheba is a halfway stage to Troy. Boldwood courts her in his own cause, but the disintegration of his careful personality follows Troy coming on the scene. In a sense, he is *grateful* for Troy's intrusion: violence against Troy is more satisfying to him, more passionately compulsive, than 'love' for Bathsheba. He is somehow *relieved* by his role vis-à-vis Troy, whereas he is contorted and divided by Bathsheba. His whole being is involved with the Sergeant. There is more than plot involved in announcing himself to be 'William Boldwood' and offering Troy money. When he discloses that his name is William, he reveals the 'private part' of himself to the man to whom he feels instinctively inferior. *He* then echoes Farmer Ives' daughters: devoting nights of tears and pounds of cash to the seduction of a man.

When Boldwood's 'resurrection' is occasioned by carrying Bathsheba's unconscious body, he is also in a way *impersonating* Troy. His manliness imitates (submits to) his rival's. The 'female' room which Boldwood creates 'for Bathsheba' in his own room is no less a 'legitimisation' of repressed femininity.

The consummation of Boldwood's passion for Troy, by shooting him, is the climactic tragedy. There is manifest sexual symbolism in the shotgun being fired at Troy; by killing him, Boldwood achieves total command of the beloved's life. At one stroke, Bathsheba is deprived of what she really wants and what *he really wants*. Boldwood

destroys Troy *after* saying 'Bathsheba, go with your husband'. A
curious sequence of events. Thereafter, Boldwood is purged of all
feeling, either of remorse or of interest in Bathsheba. He neither
desires nor pities her. How much did she *alone* ever matter to
William B.?

Peace such as England now enjoys is fertile with dismay for the
conventionally successful or settled. They have no commanding
brake to prevent the young getting away from them. When those
in uncertain authority wish to impose themselves, they look forward
not to a golden age but to a disaster. The generation which
commanded between 1939 and 1945 did so by the reimposition of
notions of service to king and country which had perished between
the wars but which, like perished rubber, stretched without real elas-
ticity. Confronting Nazism as a war between nations turned politics
into a matter of patriotism. The social consequences – Beveridge
etc – are more like bandages for the wounds of '14–'18 than a serious
attempt to provide a framework for the future. Postwar British
politicians have fought the last peace, just as generals often fight the
last war.

L. had been having an affair. O. rewarded her by getting involved
with a young girl whom he promised to give up, after due punish-
ment had been inflicted on L. Then he moved out. *Then* he called
to say that it was all a dreadful mistake; give him time and he would
be back. Having charged L. to 'tell the children', he now tantalises
her with hope. Poor L.! So mature, so womanly, such a parody of
the *femme du monde*! Something about her demands chastisement.
By deriding sentiment, these women (graduate wives for the most
part) render themselves ritual victims by accepting, no: *embracing*,
male standards. Men are delighted and relieved to see their femininity discounted by their wives. Having created pseudo-male
mates, they can now impose monosexuality on the whole of their
society. 'You lucky things,' L. calls us.

In all B. is good and staunch and true.

Critics. Except for the fact that he is wringing your neck, the executioner is the most boring little man alive.

Frank Wild. He was a finalist in the Wimbledon men's doubles in
1935 and played in a Davis Cup trial. He coaches at the covered

court in Hall Road. He drinks Heinz Scotch Broth out of the tin
between sessions. I suspect there is sometimes more scotch than
broth in the tin.

'We must have that weight on the front trotter,' he says. 'I want
the full performance, Mr Raphael. I want to see the full face of the
racket.' When I am leaving he says, 'Don't forget your wand.' The
lesson ends with a demand for 'Six classic forehands and then we'll
bring our volley up to the net.' When I play a bad shot, he says,
'We will eliminate that one from our repertoire.' One day he asked
me if I knew a certain Mr B. 'No, why?' 'He gave the bucket a
nudge,' he said. I said, 'I'm sorry?' 'He died.'

Stanley told me this. The telephone rang and the operator said, 'Mrs
Donen is calling you from America.' 'Darling?' 'What?' 'Darling?'
'*What*?' 'Mother!'

John Moss told the latest breathalyser joke. Barbara Castle fell down
in a dead faint at some function. George Brown gave her the kiss
of life and she turned green. Get it?

Orchestra and Beginners is *not* a failure. Tom Maschler had a letter
from the librarian of the sergeants' mess at Luchars, in Fife, thanking
Cape for all the good books – Deighton, Morris, Ballard – they have
published this year. He ended with 'my personal number one: *O
and B*'. Success without fame, the fate of the minor novelist.

I sublimate my malaise into a furious desire to travel, spiced by
Gordon Meyer's *The River and the People*. Can Paraguay be as gaudy
as he makes it? Can I, inclined to stump and stumble, make as elegant
tracks as he? I met him for lunch at Crockford's in the early summer,
B. still pregnant, heat on the city one never thinks of as warm: an
Old Etonian in his late forties, maybe fifty, in a cool suit, his face
grey-brown, blue eyes with a certain weariness in them. He disliked
England with a harsh pity; fresh from Uruguay, he was amazed that
anyone could live here. I sensed rage under his calm style, the rage
one feels at having believed past lies. The life he thinks of as *life* has
been devoted to the pursuit, misguided or successful (or both), of
an Argentinian woman and then to that of his present wife, who is,
I think, from Rio. He is a favourite of *The London Magazine*. Alan
Ross recently brought out a slim grainy volume of new stories,
which he inscribed and presented to me. He likes South America
because 'it's so peaceful'.

K.S. had a country place with a cottage in the grounds occupied by a gardener/handyman. One weekend K.S.'s wife asked the man to bring in some logs. He flew into a rage. Later he came into the kitchen, picked up a knife and said, 'If you try giving me orders again, I'll kill you.' They tried to sack him, but he had tenure of the cottage. K.S. called the local policeman and asked if charges could be brought. 'Difficult without evidence of actual violence, but I'll tell you what I'd do, get a couple of thugs to come down, beat him up and chuck him down the lane, and then turf all his stuff out of the house and lock it up. Once he's been locked out, he's got no further rights.' K.S., amazed, said that he knew no thugs. 'Ring up one of these private detectives,' he was told. 'They can always get hold of people.'

I asked K.S. if he had done as he was advised. 'No,' he said. 'I got a private detective to go and bribe the man to quit.'

Sometimes I look in the mirror and I am surprised to see what I look like. I could well imagine passing myself in the street without a second glance, quite confident that I had never seen myself before in my life.

Snow whispering in the darkness.

Last night Ian Smith hanged the three Africans 'reprieved' by the Queen. Bernard Sheridan handled their petitions. When I spoke to him this morning, he was unemotional, wondering only if he had made the right moves to save them. He does not see what more he could have done. Tomorrow, he thinks, Smith will declare a Republic. The main villain, B. says, is Beadle, the Chief Justice who could have tipped the scales justly, and in accordance with his oath, but failed to follow the course of duty, loyalty and justice. Plato justified: to ensure justice, create the just society and even the spineless will stay true; create a dishonest state and you waste your time hoping for honest functionaries.

A dream. I was involved, in some Holmesian way, in getting to the bottom of some opium smuggling in the docks. I presented myself as a customer and was taken through a warehouse to my contact, who 'marked' me as reliable by making me hold my thumbs over a naked flame until they had browned. One took a painfully long time and then 'took' only in an area which was disqualified.

In another dream, we seemed still to be living in Rutland Street, which was littered with decaying cars. The house was robbed – it was also Seymour Walk, where we now live – but I felt quite detached, almost glad, as if something had been *proved*.

Before 1961, my work was almost all fiction. Since then I have written films, and made money. Before I was indifferent to the prospect of riches. In May 1960, I had a telegram at the Calle Toston telling me that I had won the Lippincott Prize, $2,500. It seemed like the largest sum ever paid to anyone for anything. Eight years later, I am prostrate by the delay in paying me twenty times as much as the first instalment on a script. Have I become smarter or much, much more foolish?

I can see myself giving up this film business without having the smallest urge to keep even the most tenuous link with anyone I have met in it. I see us in a small cottage, with a terrace and a table, in one change of clothing. I see papers burned, luxuries abandoned and traitors eliminated. Why hesitate? Because renunciation is so complicated, so unambiguous and so final. I rely on my speed to be in two places at once. Unwise. Agility is the least reliable, or enduring, of gifts.

Another dream. A brilliantly lit Fulham Road (actually a displaced King's Road), open late at night. I was driving, then on foot, waiting for a haircutting appointment. At 5.15 the man was free, but he signalled to another customer. I went out uncut. I was in a newsagent's where there were glossy Italian and foreign papers in a horseshoe of inclined counters. A woman insulted the proprietor and I remarked '*Es loca*'. Jo Janni was there and told me that there was no such expression in Italian. I felt crushed. I kept trying to read one of the papers, to prove my linguistic ability, but the print slid.

I look into my dreams to discover my fortune like an old woman reading tea-leaves. She pours herself another cup and hurries through the real pleasure, burning for another episode of superstitious fancy.

'I am a man without argot. Most people have some rough sub-culture on which they can draw for vulgar advice. I never did. What I know I have picked up from books. I can pretend to belong, but I draw no dividend from it. I am all super-ego, alien to every natural association; I accept imposition but feel no allegiance. It is as if everything began with me. I have no culture. I feel guilty for just that reason; I have nowhere *natural* to go. Rootless? Yes. Restless? Yes. Yet rooted in guilt and resting on fearful conscience. And why do I come back here? The victim comes to his killer? The spy returns to eliminate the man who might expose him? That's more like it.'

At home. Suddenly, beginning almost wilfully as she stood in the doorway with the tea tray, the hall dark behind her, face mildly flushed by a compliment, I saw how beautiful and how gentle she was. Heart, cock and care all grew at once. I felt I loved her and had always.

Another dream. By the waterfront. On the run, as usual, from roughs. I found myself in narrow streets of houses once quite elegant. Then I was near a sewage farm. Going down an alley (I was in New York City), I saw the sea between two headlands, very calm. I admired and envied the people who lived in the brick house (behind a fence) overlooking the untroubled bay. I looked again and saw that the calm was due to the soggy turds discharged by the sewage works. The quarter, despite the elegance of individual houses, was hopelessly derelict and beyond reclaim. The landscape in general was composed in lustrous, unEuropean tones; they belonged, I think, not so much to the America of my childhood as to the toys I had in those days.

Intellectuals mourned Kennedy's death less because he was a President they admired than because he was a President who admired them.

V.E. called. He had just come back from Nepal, where he had been prospecting for locations. It was beautiful, but impossible to film there. The Minister said that the government was opposed. Furthermore, though charming, gentle people, 'They steal.' We talked about the business in general and then suddenly he said, 'I must see you.' 'Sure.' 'Nothing to do with the movies. I just have to see you. I don't know how much longer I can keep it to myself. I really can't go on any longer. I'm so unhappy I can't talk.' Somehow this man has always seemed so much older, more mature, more assured than I. His tears brought me near to tears myself. I gave him what affection I could. Yet, on putting down the phone, I found that my own malaise was entirely gone. His confession had quite set me up.

Another dream. Chicago. A line of my dialogue: 'I shall speak to my M.P.; remember this is my constituency!' We spent some time in a large public lavatory and barbershop. Deceived by the barber into thinking I should soon be served, I accepted a ticket; I waited and waited. B. and my parents were waiting for me. A boy was cleaning the latrines, on his hands and knees, with a cloth. The place was very clean, but I was ashamed at his humiliation. The morning wore on and I looked at my head in the mirror. Though I had plenty of hair, it all came from the front of my head. On lifting it clear, I saw that the whole top of my head was bald, with very few hairs growing out of it, as if from the back of one's hand. I became unwilling to have a haircut at all. Then the boy came and said they were ready for me.

I never had the haircut. I found myself sitting at a polished round table at which we were to lunch. My father, sunburned and younger, though diminutive, had a lost expression; he confessed that he had lost his wallet. I looked around and soon saw it, very flat, under a neighbouring table. I claimed it, expecting an argument. There was no trouble. I restored it, rather contemptuously, to my father.

Later, walking with Beetle, I met Hilary, fat and short, walking with a friend. We spoke for a short time and then parted, after a pale kiss, planning a meeting which we knew would not take place.

'Apes. They call them apes.' Mary McCarthy on the U.S. attitude to the Vietnamese. And what did Edmund Wilson call *her*?

V.E. He tried to buy off his wife A.'s resentment, first with gifts and a lavish establishment which he himself does not need; his work is always his ultimate home. Secondly, he tried to sacrifice himself by demeaning and debasing his own talent. When, a few years ago, A. claimed that she 'had no life', he gave her half his company. Now she is putting in lawyers to check the accounts. The proof that she has got what she wants from him is his sense that he is wasting himself. He convinces himself that he cannot owe her anything more by giving her everything he has. This capitulation convinces her that he has been holding out on her. The next step is cold hatred on both sides. A. is an ageing tapeworm who has, all her beautiful life, drawn nourishment and riches from the overstuffed entrails of society. V. remarked bitterly that she did '*nothing*' quite literally: she sleeps most of the time. 'She's asleep up there now!' he said, gesturing, stabbing, at the flat upstairs. Her latest lover is death, or rather – since she never totally commits herself to anything – she is flirting with it. She sleeps with death; her hatred of V. is that of a woman caught with a lover. Like Hephaestus, he trapped her under a web of prescriptions. Her hatred of the doctors is almost as great as that of V. She suspects everyone. Of what? Of wanting to deprive her of her lover. Can she really love him that much? If she really wanted to die, surely she could cheat the vets. Ah yes, but she is not by nature an eloper; like all women who glory in society, she is a natural adultress. A. wishes to betray V. no less than to embrace his rival. She fears sex and she fears death in parallel fashion: she wants the consequences – to be loved, to be mourned – but she does not want actually to be crumpled, consumed, destroyed. She sees age as death's minister and *almost* prefers to go the whole way immediately rather than to be won slowly. She will take to death while it still seems like a wanton fling and one which will cause pain to her husband. Deprived of her father in childhood, her polygamous frigidity is her revenge on the uncaring male. (Cf. Plath's 'I hate you, daddy', etc. If only he could hear her!) A. sacrifices the intimate for the formal; the emotional for the social life. She fastens onto the rich and the titled, who never respond as they are desired to. It is futile to crime her snobbery: she is the very impersonation of woman as social chattel: you might as well pass moral judgement on a suitcase for having a handle.

Lunch with Tom Maschler at Prunier's. Tynan came to lunch at another table. T.M. had to go over afterwards and be important. I stayed by the door, not wishing to be deferential. The lunch was amiable. Since Tom was not paying he was in expansive humour. As a guest, he was the perfect host.

As Aalvar Aalto used to say: Why not do it in alphabetical order?

Cleveland on a Sunday night in February, sifted with an icing of snow. No indication of where the city centre was. An affable, ear-muffed Negro gas station attendant directed us to the Hertz office; they recommended the Sheraton-Hilton. The lobby was covered in hundreds of yards of red and black carpet. There was room for a small aircraft to take off. Our $21 room was really a single, on the ninth floor at the end of a long, long corridor lit by glazed globes. Almost no other room was occupied. The elevators, run by bored coloured girls, descended like thunderbolts and came to sickening stops. The restaurant was closed, so we went to The Black Angus down the cold, cold street. Few diners in the big red room. We had bar–B–Q'ed chicken; scrawny, with treacle sauce. I asked for wine. Sorry: not on Sundays. 'Not,' I said, 'until they start growing grapes in this State presumably.' That made no new friends.

A loud man came in, with an embarrassed buddy, and called for Martinis, which were available. The waitress brought him a menu. 'Would you like something to eat?'

'I'd sooner have a pretty girl.'

Oh boy.

On the color TV: Ed Sullivan introducing dreadful acts with an executioner's charm.

We woke to steady snow. Where was our host from Kent State? A call came eventually from the lobby: 'This is John Beacom; I'm down here with some students.' He wore a grey suit and a grey tiredness which might have looked gallant in hero's uniform. He introduced us to Tom, Nancy, Pudge and Marge. Each of the 'panellists' was to acquire a set of acolytes who became our staff. Tom, a fair boy with large, beguiled eyes, was our driver. I was swaddled in my sheepskin in the corner of the Compact. A truck had jack-knifed in the snow and blocked the highway. During the delay, Pudge was emboldened to ask me if *Two for the Road* was based on personal experiences at all possibly. She blushed when her daring was shushed by the others. Could this be the America of revolutionary students? The difficulty, during the week, was to get any of them to express any urgent ambition or rebellious thought. They appeared willing to learn from anyone, but is *anyone* the best teacher? The classes I attended suggested they were at the mercy of any wind that blew. They had never heard of Ayer, Giedion or Kenneth Burke. Your presence lends them zeal, but they wilt as soon as the stimulus is withdrawn.

Kent is a small town; the campus is near but not dear to it. The usually empty lines of the Erie-Lackawanna railroad run through the town; nights howl with passing freight. The depot is old, rust-red, made antique by the steel trains that gabble past it. Across the valley, a white warehouse with three rows of elegant windows, like a Georgian mill. As we went into a bar by the station for our first lunch together, the kids asked me what I thought of Kent, I said, 'I like that warehouse.' They thought I was mocking the place, but Tom told me that it was the oldest building in the town. They couldn't even appreciate the anonymous strengths of America. Their education is too often for *use*; one pretty girl, Judith, was majoring in Public Relations: i.e. attending a place of truth in order to learn how to peddle lucrative lies.

Dr Beacom ordered soup, water, a glass of milk and a double martini. He spoke of 'our President' with contempt, likewise of the local community: 'They know what you're doing the minute you start, whether it's burning pancakes or making love.' His outspokenness was greeted with egalitarian 'Mr Beacom!'s. He told me he had been astonished by the speed with which I had agreed to come to Kent, about 10 seconds. He was the kind of man who suspected that there had to be something wrong with you if you had any time for him.

Stanley Kaufmann. He wore a sheepskin-lined fur coat and a Persian lamb Kremlin hat. His 'keynote' address was made to a sparse audience. He was introduced by the college vice-President for External Relations, a lustreless man in a bone-tight suit who should have been a tax-collector specialising in intimidation. He flattered K. unflatteringly with overdone praise (sprigged with a quotation from A. McLeish). By drawing attention to the fact that he was reading from notes, he proved that he had no real interest in the proceedings. Finally, he chided the students ('It must be very cold indeed today') for their lack of applause. That really provoked them to spontaneity.

S.K. was billed as 'a man who goes out to meet his time', and proceeded to overstay it. After making disclaiming noises, he read an intelligent speech too bright to engage the dim, too subtle to amuse the alert and not quite brilliant enough to justify itself. His vanity was wounded by the meagre attendance; the gallery, to which he would later prove his ability to play, was empty. The four 'artists' – Ross Lee Finney, Jean-Claude van Italie, Voulkos and I – were ranged on hard chairs, like premature main courses for a meal still at the soup stage. K., at the mercy of what he had prepared, went over-length and over the heads of his audience. We could feel ourselves getting cold on the sideboard.

In the early 1950s, S.K. wrote a novel *The Philanderer* which achieved the publisher's dream: it was arraigned for obscenity and acquitted, just. It described the compulsive infidelities of a man who really loved and wanted to be loyal to his wife. K. and his wife have been married for twenty-five years and (he told B.) 'together' for thirty. He echoes his hero's lechery in a general sauciness which, with the young, expresses itself in avuncular outspokenness. He is a careful dresser and, if shameless, he is well washed. He apes the

civilised seducer who will make all the scores he can, sexually and
intellectually, but will not be lured into any passion or caught in any
eccentricity which might threaten his public position. As if to
preserve his wicked reputation he made moves towards any attractive female. When the time came for us to leave, the students cried
to see us go and swore eternal friendship. As Tom kissed Beetle, and
gave her a clay moomintroll as a farewell present, S.K. said, 'I think
I should make it clear that Mrs Raphael belongs to Mr Raphael –
and to me.'

I had prepared nothing for my 'event', which was more crowded
than Kaufmann's. I relied on deprecating Mr Beacom's prefatory
eulogy and, after a short statement, invited questions, to which I
gave long free-associational answers. I talked for an hour and a half.
'He let himself be turned on,' van Itallie said, inevitably. I was turned
off by Mr Beacom who came onto the stage and closed the tap.

Ross Lee Finney captivated his shamefully small audience by his
innocent and expansive enthusiasm. He told how he came to write
a certain quintet. It was a comedy of interruptions: no sooner had
he started than Menuhin asked him to compose a work for solo
violin. We could 'well imagine' that this was something he 'very
much wanted to do'. He had taken time out and done it. No sooner
had he resumed the quintet than the Baltimore Symphony
Orchestra commissioned a symphony from him. We could well
imagine that *that* wasn't the sort of thing one turned down lightly,
so there was another interruption. His style of narrative was to rush
clusters of words to the edge of the stage and topple them onto us.
His eyebrows – shaggy and agile – signalled his energetic joy; piping
hot with memory, he rehearsed the numerical permutations which
had run through the three works in the sequence alluded to. 'Now
take eleven; now what can you do with eleven? You can imagine
eleven isn't the sort of number you can get very *excited* about! I have
to admit eleven isn't exactly *attractive*.' Sixty years old, he admitted
that he couldn't entirely change his whole way of musical thinking,
though he thought the future of music would have nothing to do
with traditional counterpoint; soon there would be no purpose in
teaching it. Electronic music was bound to be the thing and he had
enjoyed playing with it himself. He had such buoyancy that you felt
that even on a windless day he might sail away. He wore a wide-
skirted brown overcoat and a multi-dimpled beret. When I aimed
a cine-camera at him, he froze, as if expecting me to dive under a
black cowl and let off a magnesium flare.

At his 'demonstration' lecture, Voulkos punched and stabbed slots into the surface of his pots, a deliberate assault on form. He is a professor at Berkeley; his aesthetic vocabulary is limited to what turns him on, and off. He is big ('Very vir-ill,' Nancy said). When he worked clay he adopted the pose of heroic sculpture, one foot advanced, weight forward, jaw determined. He was like the man who baked the bread of the gods. He gagged constantly, as if to make up for keeping us waiting twenty minutes before he showed. He said he wasn't used to having even his wife present when he was working; his jokiness seemed rooted in genuine embarrassment at doing a private thing on a public stage. One laughed (he was brilliantly funny, his timing positively professional) but one was not amused; he mugged so shamelessly, forever pulling his short sweater over his crotch because, he said, the zip had gone on his pants. His work was phallic and he grinned at the obvious. He kept up a running gag – 'Is it time for the panel yet?' – which ridiculed all the pious arrangements of the organisers. He answered questions more seriously, though 'hang up' and 'turned on' kept turning up and hanging on. He told about a student who was hung up as soon as his ceramics stopped being 'pots'. To be a pot, it had to have an opening in it; it could be as unconventional as it liked, as long as there was a hole; close the hole, he seized up.

Our week at Kent State was spoiled only by Beetle having an eye infection which needed antibiotics. For the rest, it was an experience of the naïve heart, and third-rate mind, of the middle Western student body. The Sixties made them no less deferential, though they deferred to some strange ideas: the film school interpreted the *Cahiers du Cinéma* notion of the '*caméra-stylo*' to mean that you had to wave the camera around as if you were literally writing script in the air. The result was student films so hectic with unfocussed motion that I had a devastating migraine attack. We were touched by the dogged affections of the kids delegated to take care of us. They told us that they would never forget us and that they did not know what they would do without our company, Beetle's and mine. They loved us so. They *had* to see us again; would we write if they wrote? We would; they certainly would. We never heard from any of them again.

But we did about Kent State. Two years after our visit, it was world-famous. Thirteen (unarmed) students were shot dead by

the National Guard after the R.O.T.C. office had been burned
down and the Governor declared a state of emergency. Mary
Beacom, whose husband had died in the interim, wrote us a letter
in which she detailed, with moving clarity, what had happened
on 'the Commons' during that fatal day. The National
Guardsmen were hicks, some from the town of Kent itself, and
they hated the students. When we were there, we had heard as
much, but discounted it as the usual 'town and gown' antipathy.
The hatred had been real and murderous. Even now there was
no remorse. It was difficult to believe that the unchallenging kids
whom we had met had metamorphosed into dangerous revolutionaries in so short a time. Nor had they: they were children
who dreaded Vietnam.

With her permission, I sent Mary Beacom's letter to Harry
Evans at *The Sunday Times*. He published it in full. I knew him
first when he was an up-from-the-provinces producer on *A Word
in Edgeways*, a BBC radio chat-show. Sometimes when I visited
Thomson House, in Gray's Inn Road, to cadge books for review
in the *S.T.*, after he had become editor, a slight, nervous, bespectacled figure came up to me and offered his hand. When I looked
polite, but puzzled, he would say, 'Harry Evans' and I would
pretend to have recognised him, of *course*. At some stage, he was
transformed by the contact lens revolution and became handsome. Not long after that, he married Tina Brown. I have not
shaken his hand since.

At Miami airport. I had booked a Hertz car at Cleveland and was
promised it would be waiting for us. It was hot and humid at Miami,
and we were wearing sheepskin coats, ravenous for luxury. The
Hertz girl said she had no record of my reservation; she had no spare
cars either. I was instant rage, but when I had to go and get the bags,
Beetle managed to be allotted a cancellation. Then my reservation
came through on the telex. 'At least you now know I was telling
the truth,' I said.

'Oh I knew you were telling the truth,' the girl said.

We drove off in an island of pressed steel: a Ford Galaxie 500,
beige. Dusk was soon on us; the highway streamed with vacationers'
cars. 1,200 miles and 80 degrees of temperature from Ohio, there
were the same whoppers and shakes. We drove along US 1 past
Florida City. Key Largo came up; memories of Lauren Bacall and
banging shutters merged with the wayside gas stations and Funeral

Homes, the glitter of riding lights and the mute flamboyance of *retroussés* motels.

At Jewfish Creek, we settled ourselves in a restaurant promising lobsters. Then we were told there was an hour's wait. We went on and pulled in at a sign COMPLETE VACATION HOME. There was a huge car-park and a chromed restaurant, where we had daiquiris and lobster tails recommended by a couple from the state of Washington. I asked the waitress how full the place was. 'Last night we had a line outside at this time. To tell you the truth, we all need a rest right now. I need three weeks off.' The man from Washington overheard me and said that they had had to take a suite: five beds for two people! They had two separate bedrooms, entirely separate, and would be glad if we would take one of them. It began by sounding like a gift, but it became a business proposition: he would 'certainly appreciate our participation'. He was tall and outdoorsy; he might have been a Gentile Arthur Miller. Did he imagine we hesitated because we feared a sexual ambush? He assured us that he and his shapeless wife were 'old enough to be your parents'.

We drove on. NO VACANCY, NO VACANCY. We headed on down the keys across narrow bridges that puckered the air as we passed. At the Howard Johnson's at Islamorada ('Sorry, folks'), they said there was maybe room at a place called The Indies Inn. 'I hear it ain't that reasonable.' 'I haven't come to Florida to be reasonable,' I said.

We turned in through an entrance elegant with low white walls, subdued lighting, and went between palm trees with coloured spot-lights glowing at the base. A tall bellboy came with a tall trolley to load our things. *Grand luxe* at last! A girl with intelligent spectacles and hair in an elaborate asymmetrical wave offered us rooms at $36 and a suite for $45. I was a cheapskate and settled for a room.

There were two double beds bracketed together by an ornate metal bedhead exorbitant with pineapples at each end; clean, white vinyl floor, generous terrace facing the velvet night. I gave the bellboy two bucks, wondering if five might not have been a wise investment.

Morning revealed a nine-hole pitch'n'putt course on which Bermuda-shortened guests were flexing themselves. We had breakfast watching their reassuring ineptitude. The tray was adequately stocked, though without plates for spreading jelly on the butter-wet toast: a straw in the wind of incompetence to come. That night, the breakfast tray was still on the terrace; the beds were unmade. At dinner, there was no table for two. We had a big round table for six and sat like hosts whose guests have stood them up. The head-waiter tapped a rubber-ended pencil against his temple and waved with uncertain imperiousness at arriving guests whom he lacked the confidence to face. He was tall and wary and, with his pale massiveness, might have been a promising Marine officer cashiered for cowardice. His waiters rushed from one crisis to another, like Plato's barbarian boxer who put his hands to the place where he was last hit. Our waiter did not know what there was for dessert. Beetle said, 'Perhaps we should have ice-cream.'

'It would certainly make things easier.'

The previous day's breakfast tray was still on our terrace the next morning. We went to the dining room where a Greek family was complaining that they had been waiting an hour. We exchanged Greek compliments. A more distant customer came in to complain about the delay. 'If you insist on sitting outside, *sir*, we'll do the best we can and that's all I can promise.' The man and his lady waddled in and sat where there were no excuses. They waited self-righteously for what did not come.

The following morning, there was no room service nor could I make a telephone call. The waiter who took our order for breakfast, in a lounge suit, clearly cooked it himself. My tower of griddle cakes lacked butter. In the lobby, a guest was telling the desk clerk that the cigarette machine had broken down. Another lady asked when the gift shop (it had to be 'The Knotical Shop,' didn't it?) would open. 'She's gone to Miami. I don't think it'll be opening today.'

I had gone in there earlier and drifted between racks of overpriced dresses while two saleswomen talked to each other. The older was saying that she been married for twenty years. 'Quite a record these days,' the young, red-headed one said. 'Whaddyamean?' 'For a marriage to last that long. Do you know most marriages break up the eleventh year? Statistics show that. I guess you can be quite proud; most people would be divorced by now.' 'Oh, don't worry: I've filed already.' 'Oh?' 'This week. Would you go on living with a man who tried to say you were nuts? That's what he's been saying. Would you go on living with him? I certainly wouldn't.' 'Don't you have a little boy?' 'Little girl.' 'What's going to happen to her?' 'She'll come and live with me; she loves her mommy so much.' It turned out the red-head was divorced already (on entering, I had been taken to be her husband). Their joint disgust with men was uninhibited as soon as each identified the other as a sufferer from the same blight.

We went to the room and rang for someone to come and get the bags. Finally we humped them along the corridor and out to the car. A damp red-blazered boy held the door open for us but lacked the tip-cadging nous to help us over the last few yards. We realised, as we escaped, that we had come to the condemned playground itself. What could be a better parable of the West than this lavish spread, this sumptuous sponge for soaking the rich? And they, having agreed to be milked subtly, *pleasingly*, discover that are to get no such suave treatment. Yet how bemusedly they react, how docile their irritation! They had come to spend their money and, unless people made it totally *impossible*, that was what they were going to do. Bad service inconvenienced them less because they did not get what they wanted than because they could not display their wealth by overtipping for it.

'You could say,' a woman remarked to us in the parking lot, 'that we were a little disenchanted.'

That's America. It has no problem financing almost anything nor in composing slogans to advertise its qualities; it lacks only the will and the consistent tradition to make it work. The guests of the Indies Inn reacted to the breakdown of the most obvious amenities not by concerted, purposeful indignation, not by withholding cash for services not rendered, but by offering to pay more for them. Just as John Glenn and George Peppard, when I was on that TV 'discussion' with them in Chicago, told the beads of the nation's wealth when trying to pray off America's failure in Vietnam and at home, so the guests were helpless in the face of the rebellious (in fact striking) staff because they could not believe that 'an expensive place like that' could possibly be as bad, as nearly bankrupt of all reasonable expectations, as this one actually was. They tolerated ineptitude, furiously, because they dared not challenge (even in their own minds) the whole basis on which such luxury relied. They could not doubt the propriety of the gigantic establishment whose very size was (at least partly) responsible for overstretching such manpower as it had contrived, or chosen, to recruit. (There was no Negro help in all the surly crew.)

Guests and staff were at the mercy of the same delusion: that the simple satisfaction of simple needs was unworthy of them. Those who stumbled with overweight cases to oversized cars neither intended to bring less next time nor to seek a less pretentious hotel. Their greatest adjustment would be to go, next time, to a *new* milking station, bigger and more expensive, until they found somewhere that the dollar *did* bring to life, where wallets were saluted as snappily as officers. They never consider becoming more self-reliant or toning themselves up for a less indulged existence. Helplessness is their socialism; requiring assistance their only acceptable way of spreading the wealth.

Strange how the bank robber has such a symbolic claim on crime stories of capitalism. Customers and clerks risk their lives with irrational courage in order to confound crooks who, of all pests, probably do less damage to any specific human being, or fortune, than many whom none would think to challenge. Why? The hope of reward? I doubt it. I suspect it is the sense of *sacrilege*: the bank robber resembles the scoundrel who robbed the temple treasury. He transgresses the laws not only of men but also of the gods. No surprise that Greek temple architecture became the established style for the sanctuaries of Capital. I forget the name of the Canadian writer who opened his novel with a woman discovered on her knees in a banking hall which she had mistaken for a church.

Lunchtime at a single-storey EATing place set back from the Keys road. No air-conditioning; tables under a still fan, bar with wooden stools. We asked for eggs, but it was 12.30; eggs stopped at 11.00. We could have egg sandwiches. OK, with glasses of milk. The sandwichmaker rang a bell when they were ready. But each time, the sandwiches were a 'to go' order. Our waitress, heavy blonde with a bun, sat down at a table and put her head in her hands. I called out, 'Could we at least have the milk?' When our sandwiches didn't come, *again*, I asked to have them wrapped to go. I paid for them angrily and we stormed out. The blonde sang out after us, 'Hurry back.'

In the plane on the way back from America, Beetle said to me, 'I feel that I shall be saying goodbye to you at London airport.'

A. wanted only to sleep. When V. tried to rouse her, she turned on him. 'We must spend less money,' he told her. '*We?*' Their bargain had been that she could have whatever she liked; that, literally, was the price he was expected to pay. She woke him at 2.30 a.m. 'If you're leaving me, you can bloody well leave when I say so and not when it suits you.' She went on yelling at him until he packed and quit.

Athens under the Colonels was quiet and docile, like a resigned cuckold. We stayed at the *Grande Bretagne* overnight. Stee, who had been violently sick on the way from Langham to London (he shrank like a punctured balloon and we had the first *crise* of the trip), now padded energetically from room to room, while P. and S. hoarded their privacy. I went out with P. to hunt for a new bed. We had been monumentally uncomfortable when last on the island (yet the first time, we slept on boards and straw, in Niko's cottage, and never complained – much!). That first time we went to Piraeus in a *kamion* loaded with all our gear, but such means are undignified in *anastasis* Athens. Thalia had spoken to Yorgis who told her to tell us that all was in order and we were to buy *tipote*. I went and bought everything I could find.

I managed to buy an interior-sprung mattress at Piraeus, after searching for over an hour while B. and the children waited on the *Kanaris*. I ran all the way to Retsina Street, said to be a 'street of beds', but it was filled with metal-workers who could, I daresay, have riveted me a bed while I waited, but not what I wanted. A ship's chandler had folding beds but nothing *thipla*. I bought a blue-and-white striped canvas bag from high on the wall, whence it was plucked with a long stick and banged for dust. I ran back to the market, bought fruit and sought tinned butter, always being offered Bitam. In a shop stalactitic with pendant lights, I was told of a bed shop near the *eelektriko*. I ran again (having tramped almost back to Athens with my heavy fruit) towards the dingy arched temple of the station. I had twenty-five minutes before the *Kanaris* sailed. The bed shop was there, advertised by a metal frame. It was a warehouse stacked with mattresses; baled, in piles, single, double: *ola*! Doubles were only 1 metre 20 wide; standard size I was promised. I doubted it would do. '*Ti thelete, kirie*?' What did I want? '*Alla pragmata then echete*?' Did he have anything else? Twenty minutes to go. He took me upstairs and I saw a plastic-enveloped spring mattress in the gallery. That's what I want! 1,200 *drachs*. Done! But could it be got to the boat? It could. How? A calming, cooling gesture; *siga, siga*. The mattress was carried out into the street. I imagined a waiting van. We went up to a hack stand where an old horse stood between the shafts. The driver and the boy with the mattress folded down the creaking black leather hood (shades of my London boyhood) and I was sat with the sagging mattress screening me from the driver, and from whatever lay ahead. Ting! Off we went, swaying gently, creaking, myself blinded, high above the cars and pedestrians who came into my view after the tinging of our bell had claimed a way

through them. He took a different course, my Jehu, from that
followed by the motorised traffic. It was as if, sidling, plodding,
lurching in the liquid continuum of his progress, he were following
a path entrenched in the hidden sands of the foreshore, like the
meandering tracks stamped into the beach of Milopota. We went
diagonally across towards the docks and rode into the quayside in
good time. '*Trianta drachmes.*'

Ios for Easter. Paul and Sarah walked up through the village while
we came round in the boat with the luggage. Yorgis has handed
over his donkeys to Yanni, his step-son. The white-haired man's
boat slapped through the low waves, sea the colour of bruised flesh,
and tied up at the Drakos landing stage. Yorgis was looking glum.
Heavy rains had drilled through the floor of the old house and
flushed through it, ruining most of what we had left there. The force
of the water had also undermined the new room; there was a crack
in the concrete floor. '*Ochi kalo.*' Indeed not. Under a grey sky, we
appraised the damage. It was not *so* bad; the old *spiti* was unusable,
but we had not intended to use it. The new room was breached,
but not ruinously. At least there was no shortage of water in the
sterna. A new tap lay on the hood of the pipe-stem, but had not been
attached in the nineteen months of our absence. The terrace was
littered with fat crumbs of dust and fronds of dried palm blown down
from the sunshade. We worked all day setting up house, B. in her
usual state of vexation with Yorgis, who sat about or interfered
abruptly, undeniably, with what was already being taken care of. I
considered borrowing the deserted cottage above us for P. and S.,
but B. suggested putting up the tent. I did so; childishly proud of
my skill in assembling so practically what was already practically
assembled. I oiled rusty joints with olive oil and scoured rust with
an old tin opener.

Yorgis had had Yanni plough the soil on our terraces, though
nothing had been planted. The tent-pegs were all too easy to
hammer in. Only the main pins, for the guy-ropes, had to be driven
into stiff soil. We now had only to wait for the sun; there was no
wind, at least; yet.

After a couple of heavy days, we had a wholly magnificent day;
it seemed set fair. We lazed, we swam while the old handmade
umbrella (which I repaired with clothes-line) shaded the sleeping
Stee. The next day was less good, though the sun bored a hole in
the cloud. We never saw it again. The wind came up. P. and S.
were alarmed: it was very dark and the gale howled and prowled

round the tent which they had previously enjoyed. I hammered the pegs again into the unresisting soil and laid rocks on their heads. At 5 a.m., P. appeared at our door: the tent was blowing away. I went out into a grey tunnel of light in which, it seemed, a yellow wind was blowing the skirts of the tent up over its steel knees. Sarah lay like a spoon, asleep on her bed; I picked her up and carried her into the house. The wind blew incessantly; the children's beds never left our room; the holiday was over. No peace; no sex; no sun. The terrace, dusty and cold, was our only walk. P. and S. entertained themselves gallantly; Stee had always to be held, fed, watched. He climbed over the old mattress which barricaded the end of the terrace and fell with a cement thud, luckily without damage. We had to eat indoors; all day we moved our unsteady furniture, shook out the rug, prevented disasters. By the Thursday we were minded to go. When Friday was no better, we decided to return to Athens. Yorgis said there was a '*megalee fortuna*' and we should sit it out. We were determined to catch the *Kanaris*, due that afternoon. We packed what we had so recently unpacked and – the final betrayal! – headed across the heavy sands to Paniotis Drakos' place, where the infamous taxi (the first mechanised wheels on the island) was to collect us. Sarah rode, happy, on a little grey donkey.

The *Kanaris* lay at anchor, *mesa*, waiting to sail for Santorini. We were soon told that she would not leave till next morning. The HOTEL DENAXAS was full of old Ios hands who had come for Easter and with disembarked steamer passengers, either bored or displeased by the price of victuals on board. Kosta, the small, square owner of a stale shop in the village, had rooms in his new hotel, a three-storey tower with cells on the middle floor, next to the *Teloneion*. Black Japanesey chairs and table on the mock-marble landing. Every door was at first difficult and then only too easy to open; running water. The wind clapped like a first night audience. What could be done but to sit it out?

Kanaris was still at uneasy anchor next morning; no plans to sail. We went to the white-haired man to order lunch. The previous night we had been cheered with mullet and salad and cold apples and retsina. Lunch was *langosta*, the best we ever tasted. At the big table, loud French-speaking Athenians leaned over a huge lobster. Their hostess owned a commanding three-decker tower on the slope across the harbour which did not exist when we first came, in 1962. We drank retsina and found life not so bad.

I was in and out of the Denaxas Hotel with Stee's tins to be heated and the thermos to be refilled. Marooned passengers sat in their best suiting, juggled their beads, played backgammon, waited on by their women. The sly-faced, baggy capped man with blue eyes and wide cheekbones which recalled 'John Brickell' (the landlord of 5, Jordan's Yard, Cambridge) came down from the village with new blankets, so we slept warm on the narrow beds in the ice-chest of a new room. Yorgis arrived with red eggs and baked biscuit-men from *Kiria Maroussa*; P. and S. drew pictures and spread crumbs and made expeditions. 'Brickell' had brought us ashore, a young man, on our first visit. Six years later he was lined and sunken, eyes alone still youthful, though he remained jaunty and appeared subtly humorous in a way beyond his likely capacity. It is tempting to credit physical lookalikes with similar mental qualities.

We would have to stay another night. Lamb after the *langosta* had been enough for the others for the day, but P. and I went back for more fish. Ten-year-old P. was delighted to be alone with me, and I with him. He is tall and slim and physically assured, his face splen-didly lidded in repose, slanting bones, classic, steady profile.

Frank came in, another 'double', of Chuck, the monopulmonary pensioner of Fuengirola who married a Spanish whore and died of single pneumonia. Frank came from California and had a wooden leg, from an aircrash; civil or military we were not told. He was one of those apparently self-sufficient people who attach themselves to you like burrs. Parading independence, they will accept any alliance. His face was pale, circles under vacant light brown eyes, Gothic head: pointed yet not narrow, crispy fair hair. He threw his wooden leg ahead of him and stalked like a ghost through the crowd. He had spent two years, off and on, in Ios. He said he had been travel-ling round Sicily and I asked Yorgis, quietly, if he were a writer. Y. put his thumb to his mouth and tipped his hand upwards. 'A drinker,' he said.

He threw himself — brown woollen shirt, dark grey slacks — into a chair by where P. and I were eating and began a conversation from which I couldn't extricate myself. P. became glummer and glummer, though I talked to him as much as I could. Frank was garrulous, but impersonal: his politics and his intelligence were taken, one guessed, from some magazine. He had the resident's fund of stories of island passions and rivalries. Greeks who came back to visit their birthplace began with sentimental tears and ended in furious denunciation. One American Greek was afraid that if he stayed much longer his wife would 'revert'. Frank said that they all spent hours on the verge of passionate violence; they would be 'better off if they went away and practised mutual masturbation'.

The expression coming from those cold lips, under vacant eyes, made you wonder whether a spot of m.m. might not be agreeable to the speaker. Ours took the form of conversation about Keynes and the world economy. The more we talked, the more I felt I had let Pau down, but what was I to do?

The next morning was Easter Sunday. The *Kanaris* blew her hooter at midnight to celebrate the resurrection. At 6 a.m., she sailed for Santorini; she should be back by eleven. I was met, coming back with the thermos, by the 'customs officer', a young man with the commanding servility of a minor official. He wanted to get onto our balcony in order to put up a flag. He was in a state of nerves as he returned, with a crowned flagstaff displaying the royal standard. Pau watched him lash it with wire to one of the lights which, come summer, would illuminate the roof garden. This same man, now lavish with thanks, had scowled at our arrival and disapproved of our going round to Milopota in the same boat as our luggage. '*Ya tee*?' Why? '*Apagorevete*,' Y. told us: it's forbidden. '*Ya tee*?' '*Apa-gor-ev-ete*.' I said we would take two boats, after which we went in one.

We were hopeful of the *Kanaris* not making too heavy weather. On board at last, we ate lunch with a good appetite, though Sarah removed to the deck halfway through. On the way to Melos, the bows rose, the stern dawdled and came up and spray slashed across the wet deck, down and up swung the bows again, salt whiteness boiling on either hand, the quick spray and the sidling ship in one-sided conflict. S. deposited her lunch in a neat patty over the grill covering the scuppers and fell asleep, her head on my knees on a bench in front of the saloon doors. I had jerked my lunch overboard in two brown spouts while on the way to rescue S. from the stinking GUNAIKES. B. and Stee sat in the saloon while P. went and fetched cereal and brown sugar from the cabin and was impertinently hungry.

We rounded Melos and were sheltered from the north wind. *Kanaris* yawned and sidled and finally we were at the dock where, 2,400 years ago, the Athenians delivered their hubristic ultimatum. *Kanaris* leaned on her cushioning tyres for a breather, then we were off to Siphnos. A woman who had just embarked was green before we left the harbour and briskly, uninhibitedly, sprayed the passageway with vomit. The disgusted steward was slow with card-board boxes (wimpled for splashes) and slower still to clear up the puke with sawdust, broom and bin.

Siphnos was a long time coming. Reluctant with tea, the steward urged us to go below, to our tiny cabin. The sea roughened. S. and I went out on deck again. She had nothing left to vomit. I comforted her as best I could, casually cardboard-boxing my tea the while.

Siphnos is mountainous, cleft by its harbour. A few houses hang along the hillside. Boats come out, as at Ios. Cases of fish were swung inboard and chests lowered into lighters, a lot of business for a small place. We went to the cabin and everyone fell asleep. At Piraeus, we were the last to leave the ship. A taxi took us to the Hilton. ZETO 21H APRILIOU placarded everywhere; buses wth slogans, taxis with flags. We had arrived on the anniversary of the *Anastasis*, the so-called resurrection of the nation. There was the ubiquitous image of Greece rising like a phoenix from the flames, a soldier as wick or firelighter. This Easter was the celebration of *two* resurrections; the daily paper's cartoon showed Greece's resurrection taking precedence over Christ's. ELLAS ELLENON CHRISTIANON.

In Syntagmatos Square, a booth exhibited the régime's achievement in photographs of regeneration and heroic posturing. The alternative to the Colonels was depicted in horror pictures of the Communist revolution of '44–'47. A loudspeaker yelled martial music. The similarity with Franco's Spain and its *tranquilidad* was obvious: in a year Papadop had turned Greece into a banana republic.

Our dear friend Thalia Taga had spoken enthusiastically about the new régime: they worked hard, they had shortened the bureaucratic delays and curbed official insolence. They had broken the tradition of rural peonage by rescinding debts (a Solonian recipe) and they had cut the inflated salaries of politicians. Order had been restored. (On Ios, we had been told of the new *eesichia* (calm) in Athens.) People were indeed sparse in the street, and so silent.

The Hilton paraded a huge Easter egg. Sniffing proved it to be made of real chocolate. As Byron did on the temple at Sounion, adventurous travellers had scratched their names. The last time we stayed at the Hilton, before Stee was born, B. and I left P. and S. in the room, with a new book of push-outs, while we went to a museum. We returned to emptiness. I shall never forget going onto the terrace and forcing myself to look down at the flat roof nine storeys below. Nothing, thank God. P. and S. had become bored with rebuilding Olympia and were looking for us in the foyer. How can a couple sustain the burden of guilt if 'something happens' to their children? How can they stay together?

Nikos. He is the proprietor of our favourite clothes shop in Syntagma and the one educated Greek we know. He speaks the slurred, meaning Greek of the metropolis, and excellent English. He has given me generous advice about ikons (*and* an ikon). He sits behind his desk and watches rather than serves the customers. His pleasure is to tell tourists that the antique knick-knacks which decorate the shop, and which they are eager to buy, are not for sale. He is a master mariner and became accustomed (just) to dry land only after his marriage, and children. ('*Pethiah, pethiah,*' the Greeks say, resigned to the sweet dutifulness of parenthood.) N. seems jaundiced, but not jaded. When I explained that we wanted to buy some dresses but had no cash left, he said it gave him an idea. He reached for the telephone, first saying, 'I take it you are not with *them*?' It was the first contemptuous reference to the Colonels we had heard.

He gave me the chance to declare my anti-fascism and my willingness to evade currency regulations in the same breath. The wife of an exiled journalist was coming round. She was in her late thirties, with a strong, anguished, brave face. She showed us photographs of her children. Sixty pounds was all she could afford to pass to her exiled husband through the straw of my mediation. She gave me his address but no message. She did not like to think that I should soon see him and she would not.

Asteris came round to Seymour Walk on the Thursday after our return, a thickly bespectacled, slim man with thinning grey hair; he seemed old at first but warmed to alert, virile middle age. He asked no questions about his wife, though both had spoken of a plan for her and the children to come to London in July. He agreed to give me Greek lessons twice a week, but has been ill and is yet to come.

She gives the impression of someone so afraid of missing a chance to shine that she leaves her lights burning day and night.

13.5.68. Asteris came, frail after fever, in a taxi. He is more correct than the Greeks on Ios, almost pedantic. He asked me to talk so that he could gauge my competence. I paraded banalities about our purchase of the land on Milopota. He explained the difference between demotic and *katharevousa*, then about the regional sentiment in Greece: Mani had always been independent; the Italians had dominated the south; Turks the north. Who are the Greeks? Indefinable, like the Jews. In a foreign language one becomes a schoolboy again. Was Cato boyish when he started Greek at eighty?

In the car, as I took him home, we were back in England. How were things in Greece? Nasty; a friend of A.'s, from an old family in the Cyclades (he spoke of them, and others, having a 'personal fief') was head of a leftist party and had been 'electrocuted' for forty-eight hours. He was a slight man, but had not broken as easily as they hoped.

A. said that until 1952 he had been unable to speak to a German. During the war, he was captured and tortured for a month. The Greek collaborators had been assimilated into the forces in the Civil War. He did not specify on which side. Anyway they had not been brought to justice. The rain fell in explosive torrents as I dropped him at Hyde Park Corner.

As the hot smack of reluctantly parting flesh slapped the silence, A. wondered how any force in the world, other than their own dissidence, could possibly come between them.

C. restored to B. the sense of her own individuality. He forced upon her an awareness of his potential indifference. She was excited to think that the time might come when she would, once again, if she ever had, have to look after herself. She knew that C. might cause her pain; in that possibility, she embraced him.

Looking across at some windows in a grim building, with much distortion of light and puzzling perspective, C. sees a girl in ballet clothes, hair up. She wears a light blue tutu, white tights and ballet shoes. She leans lightly on a mahogany piano and takes pins from her mouth and slips them under her hair; a short girl with muscular legs, breast obscured by the tilt of her body. Surprising, this vision of a stripped, yet fully clothed, figure on a Tuesday afternoon. C. wonders, as he grows aware of his own excitement, if he *should* be excited: she might be a woman, she might be a child. What if she were seven years old? There she is, in that tight room, all shades of brown, in a building marked for demolition, a young female. Another girl approaches her, in red, with gawky but mature shoulders. The first girl – inexhaustibly supplied with pins – changes her pose and steps out from behind ambiguity: she is a stocky, none-too-well-proportioned girl of about twenty; her flesh grey in the uncurtained light from the dusty window. Now C. almost wishes that he *had* been spying on a delicious child rather than this heavy adult.

John van Eyssen called and asked if I would consider writing and directing a film for Barbra. Ray Stark, her producer, was at the Dorchester. He was in his early fifties; tight slacks, a deep cadmium yellow turtle-neck; the carefully shaven, chin up face of a jockey turned trainer, sudden (false) teeth and a blue stare that was levelled like a threat. He made an elaborate show of cancelling all calls (except, I thought, any that happened to come in) and made his play. He had his star all sewn up and he could impose his will on her. What was she like? 'She is,' he said, 'a *cunt*.' He said that he liked disasters; he fights best when he is on the floor. I took this to mean he liked hiring and firing. It was difficult to listen with both ears to so negligible a man. I noted the cluttered suite (gramophone open), effusive flowers perched on narrow spaces, tea or coffee already set up, fat envelopes of scripts and stills. As I tried to prove myself intelligent and commercial movie-minded, I knew I could not possibly work with such a man. John van E. (long-pointed blue shirt, diagonal tie, blue Huntsman suit) arrived in a whiff of powdered manliness and was eager chorus to R.S.'s theme. Stark said everything had been just fine until 1965 or so and then along came this picture called *Darling* and loused everything up (big grin) and now the old things wouldn't work any more. Luckily, he considered himself 'a pretty hip guy'; he could handle changes. He gave me a 'novel' which, he said, he wanted to be the basis of 'our movie'; there were five stories and B. wanted to play the girl in all five. It was a terrific opportunity for virtuoso writing, and directing. Directing was the lure. I had a strong suspicion that they would depress the price of the script with the 'promise' of my directing it and that, after I had delivered, I would be dumped. The stories were trash. When I opened the luridly covered book, the text smelled like unwashed underwear.

I drove to London to play tennis and then to Columbia to a screening of *Funny Girl*. I was a little late for the reception committee; at my important entrance, J. van E. signalled to the projectionist to start. The picture was old-fashioned, garter-sleeved showbiz narcissism. B. was ugly and talented; talent implying a kind of impersonal personality: light without source shone from her. Showbiz as a vocation has called her, as it had Fanny Brice, and she gave it everything. Nothing existed beyond it; war, pestilence, famine were unknowns. Her eyes were only for the meretricious. The Columbians laughed when she was funny, sighed when she was pathetic. They sure did their stuff. When the lights came on, there wasn't a dry glass eye in the house. In the street, we all took sepa-

rate taxis. On the way to Liverpool Street, I started to rehearse my
excuses to Ray. Saturday, transatlantic, I gave them.

Forgiving and forgetting. But forgiving *is* forgetting; what is
forgiven is lost. Every act of forgiveness involves a remission of
awareness, a small death. A writer must not forget, hence cannot
forgive; his memory preserves the vitality of those who cannot be
let off.

The essence of the machine which Andy Warhol dreams of being
is that it has no memory (and no hopes?), no consciousness of the
past or dread of the future. To this extent, his idea may be out of
date: the modern machine *does* have a memory. Its psychological
problems will arise from its inability to repress (or jettison) memories; they will all weigh the same. The consequence will be witlessly
determined responses. Incapable of inconsistency, a society based
on machines will be ritualistic in the extreme.

The French revolution broke out about two weeks ago. The
assumption is that it will subside, since it is not 'going anywhere'.
But that is why it may *not* subside. The same could have been
assumed after the first meeting of the Estates General. Then (too?)
failure to disperse amounted in itself to continuing the struggle. The
presence of the discontented in each other's sight developed the critical mass to become a dynamic force. The established order is like
the old language in a metaphysical dispute: it cannot, by the logic
of its structure, fail to be wrong, or right. Any argument which
accepts its preconceptions must allow it to be right; the argument
is not about facts, but systems. The students are said to have (and
acknowledge) 'leaders'; what is this but a penetration of the new
order by the (logic of the) old? (By the middle of June, the leaders,
conscious of the contradictions in their position, sought to
anonymise themselves.)

The 'problem of violence' relates to what happens when we
'know' that our opponents are wrong. In philosophy we were
taught to work to 'unpack' a situation so that the holder of metaphysical views could purge his own errors, willingly. One discovers,
of course, that this humane method does not work. Even intelligent disputants can rarely be lured onto neutral ground where
agreement need not entail surrender. The mere presence of 'the
reasonable man' often excites a violent reaction. 'The patient'
prefers to lose his temper rather than his prejudices.

I spent the night at the Mortimers' cottage after the 'coffee-party' at Dunhurst. John and Penelope sat either side of a log fire in the scrappy sitting room and talked to each other with an infinity of weariness. J. was to do a film, *The Love Department*, by William Trevor, with Silvio Narizzano, whose *Georgy Girl* was surely one of most improbable successes of all time, but Fox had gone cold on the script. J., the Q.C. with judgement given against him, did not question his own performance but doubted the validity of the court. Between them, my hosts scanned the arts scene and found nothing good, except for a play of Jennifer Dawson's, *The Ha-Ha*, which they had thought of buying for a film. They might have been partners in some creaking business rather than husband and wife. J. said that he went again and again to see *Belle de Jour*. 'Do you?' P. said. 'Yes.' 'I didn't know that.' 'Yes, I do. Yes.' When we dined with her and C.D., P. told us that she thought *B. de J.* was 'a joke'; she didn't see how anyone could take it seriously.

I drank Chablis and talked and talked, postponing my appointment with a single bed. J. and P. spoke of dreary parties at the Tynans'. Kathleen went recently to a private dinner party at the Bruces', the American ambassador's house, and began to stick anti-Vietnam war slogans on the walls. To make a party, the Tynans asked the Pinters to dinner with the Snowdons. Vivien Merchant asked Margaret whether she wasn't ashamed of being in the Royal Family. Apparently she wasn't.

H.P. sat silent throughout. My only experience of his losing his famous cool was when I asked him about the Arab-Israeli war. He grew excited and said that the Arabs had asked for a bloody good thrashing and had got one.

The Tynans asked the Mortimers to a Christmas Eve party. P. took this to be a spontaneous whim, but the next day she looked in the *Evening Standard* and saw Mrs K.T. billed as one of London's top hostesses. (Recalling Adele's tenancy of that role, it seemed to me a poor augury for the Tynans.) The Mortimers had arrived to find 'the most boring people in the world' and spent a miserable evening. K. was eventually heard to call for dice (P.'s heart sank, she said, and then rose when Kathleen brought *ice*, only to sink again when K. repeated the dental prefix). He proposed to shake numbers to decide which of the women should remove a garment. All protested that they were covered with surgical scars and could not possibly reveal their hideousness. 'Most of them,' P. said, 'were held together by elastic.' In the end, the only person to undress was George Melly.

Q. maintains his present stature by inflating his own life-jacket with frequent puffs of self-administered hot air. He has neither brains nor force; if he supposes that success and compromise have been wished on him by the vulgarities of others, he will have a rude awakening on finding that, with every opportunity offered him, he is still as limited as ever. The best he can hope is to be the next David Lean, unless David Lean is.

In Bond Street I was flagged down by a passing Jonathan Miller and walked with him to the underground station. He wore a khaki overcoat and seemed like a man designed by Gaudí and claiming, despite all the asymmetrical discrepancies, to be rationally put together. We talked (again) about a film about Wittgenstein. He was on his way to the BBC and promised to raise the idea with S. Hurst. He was confident we should be able to do something.

I mentioned the curious influence of Vienna in shaping minds at once revolutionary and yet which promised that when the dust settled, everything would be undisturbed. Freud may have changed our attitude to neurosis and sexuality, yet he insisted that the will, once all was acknowledged, could control behaviour; he continued to look to marriage to provide the matrix for 'mature' sexuality. Wittgenstein challenged the utility of metaphysics, yet his method came to be, in a sense, conservative: philosophy, he warned (or promised), leaves everything as it is. Which did not mean that it left *philosophy* as it was, but the style was close to that kind of *salon* brilliance that outrages only those who are eager for safe outrageousness. There was, I suggested, something profoundly superficial in the Viennese passion for reshuffling; the cards might never be in the same order again, but the pack remained unaltered. J.'s topaz eyes lit at my words and he came towards me as if more surely to unload the cargo of my idea. 'I never thought of that,' he said. You will, Jonathan, you will.

When I mentioned this to Tony Becher, he pointed out the influence of music on 'systems' in Vienna. Now I wish I'd thought of that.

Another Viennese obsession: bridge. I play perhaps for two hours a week these days, only when I am jaded and usually when tired. What smoking was to Svevo, cards – bridgecards – are to me. I can neither enjoy the game nor renounce it. I lose sullenly and I win, despite a measure of skill, only rarely. I should give it up but, dammit, I *want* to play. Yet I find my fellow-members of the club as obnoxious as they probably find me. They admire Ian Smith. The food is now lamentable and there is little cachet in membership. Even the bridge is of poor standard; yet I have the feeling that I should be amputated from something I really desire if I were to give up what I also believe I do not want.

J. and M. The beginning of the end of the affair. Cooking for him, she chopped some parsley on a board near the cooker, which she took to be appropriate. M. 'nearly went berserk'; it was handpainted, valuable or decorative or both. On another occasion, J. heard that an Oxford friend of hers had been killed in a mountaineering accident. M. was sympathetic with her tears for a while and then became impatient: she was spoiling the weekend. He had not asked her down to be wet. She would have married him, but when he ended the affair, she decided that she had not been in love with him because she got over it so quickly. She found him 'set in his ways', like an old man. When they went to parties, he sat in the corner and yawned. He is a mean and unimaginative lover who seeks the maximum return for the smallest outlay. He once told me that he would never demean himself by going with a whore; he would sooner make whores of his girlfriends and get their services on the house.

Those encased in ideology are the most inhumane of all. Who are these people? The standard example of a doctrine that endures no contradiction is Nazism, whose iron 'logic' condemned millions to death. The Nazi example (and that of Stalinism) has made cowards of us all. We concluded that arguments should not be taken too far, lest bad consequences follow. But this is itself a bad consequence. The young – who are not haunted by the Nazi experience – are now pointing out what capital the old order has made out of our squeamishness. The new students are conscientiously impolite: the system which they reject offers a 'dialogue' which is chillingly repudiated. They know that this is going to be slanted towards the victory of those (the established order) in whose terms it is conducted. We have heard this version of 'dialogue' over and again: the march around the walls of Jericho takes place daily, but they never come tumbling down. Violence then! The success of the French students is remarkable; if we – owners of houses and cars – shake, we should also applaud. The refusal to play the old order's game has cost remarkably little in heads. A student is knifed (horrible); a police inspector is crushed (abominable); but how much worse is such violence than the aggressivity of an impatient driver or the hazard of an unprotected machine? Rhetoric! Indeed; but doesn't there come a time when the heads of *argument* must be broken, when you have to look at what is lived behind words?

Violence follows the inability of established society to see any reason but its own. Its leaders' position is entirely understandable; that is why they do not need to be hated, but attacked. The best guarantee of the students' good faith is their lack of an integrated plan or firm proposals. The new charm of Trotsky is that he was a victim of the *apparat*, a believer in non-stop revolution. This is the political counterpart of the 'metaphysics' of inconclusive reasoning.

Don't feel obliged to editorialise.

De Gaulle's latest decision – to remain in power and dissolve the Assembly – has been received by those sympathetic to the students as an example of bad losing. In fact, it is better that the Emperor be defeated in some conclusive way than that he withdraw or 'scratch'. Had he retreated to Colombey, he might have been resurrected on the third day. Better if he is discredited by the very machinery which was designed to favour him. In that way, France may have done with him for good; no later claims of treason or subversion can form a 'legitimate' basis for reaction.

In fact, his 'party' (he affects, as president, to have none) looks certain to improve its position and impose itself on the country. The People wish it! The strength (and bigotry) of the middle class has been increased, if anything, by the brazenness of a revolution which has been more trailer than finished production. Now the students concede that they were a minority, even at the Sorbonne. But then *all* revolutions are the actions of minorities. As Bismarck realised, majorities accept more than they initiate. The French might have accepted the revolution, if it had seemed inevitable enough; as soon as resistance solidified, it was instantly irresistible. Once the bluff was called, the game was over. It could only be by the subversion of the police and the armed forces that serious change could follow. These things were never on the cards. After the sincere performance comes the rueful, almost amused, reading of the notices.

S. has been here half a dozen times now. A man past fifty, mixture of determined resource and almost passive resignation. He supports old Papandreou. He flinches from association with the extreme left

EDA, but I suspect him to be further to the left than prudence admits. There is a kind of slow amusement in his eye that hints at 'things we both know'. He complains at the denial of a passport to his children in Athens and threatens the Colonels with 'strong measures' if their rights continue to be ignored. Who blames him? Yet there is a kind of inconsistency in an opposition which expects the enemy to play the game. The Colonels want to silence him, but what is he saying? He tells me weekly of new cases of torture: this week in Thessaloniki. There is something curious in the manner of his telling. He seems to be confirming something and it almost entertains him to do it, as if some long-delayed investment was paying off, after everyone had scoffed at it. There is vanity in his attitude which amounts almost to satisfaction. You see? You see?

We set off for Cambridge to go to the King's May Ball, at John Sullivan's suggestion. The drive was often over roads which had not existed the last time I went up from London. In Trumpington, we wriggled between suburban houses to Luard Road, where the Bambroughs live. A beige Mercedes 200 with German plates stood in the deeply gravelled drive: the Sullivans'! The door of the grey stucco house was opened by a red-haired pretty eight-year-old in a nylon nightie and big blue slippers: Annabelle, with Moira's white skin and Renford's precisely humorous mouth. M. came to meet us, confident in her own house, surrounded by her four children. Richard, the only boy, seemed withdrawn, nervous, secret. Renford himself was absent.

The furniture was grey and black and rectilinear. Two of Pamela Wisdom's paintings hung in tandem. The children were excited by the visitors; Beetle rewarded them with generous attention. We changed in Renford's rooms. Judy Sullivan, with her good jaw and neat head, looked pretty and pale, dark eyes and hair set off by trim shoulders and a red floral dress. B. glittered in sequins. P. looked puffy, as if everything about her had lost focus; the minutest adjustment might seem able to pull her together, but could not be made.

J.P.S. had bought the Mercedes in Germany and was to ship it back to the States. 'It's worth two hundred pounds, isn't it?' Moira knew. Consciousness of money was a feature of the occasion. J.P.S. told us later how difficult life in Oxford had been on a thousand a year; now he was making $21,000. Gigi Lloyd said that she and Geoffrey could not afford both the S.T. and The Observer. Yet tickets to the Ball had cost a tenner a pair.

I was at Charterhouse with Geoffrey Lloyd; he came into the

Classical Sixth in my last quarter. He was waiting at the locked Backs entrance to King's. I parked in Queen's Road. Tony took a broken-backed tartan suitcase from the boot. J.P.S. was carrying a fat briefcase: 'Three bottles of *Scotch*.' He has a way of biting off the last word as if it were the cue for a laugh, or a rebuke. All his actions have an element of cheeky challenge. He wears a trimmed beard, shaved below the sideboards, and thick-rimmed glasses; he has the appearance of a middle-European emigré who has picked up the English sense of humour by osmotic assimilation and can scarcely believe his own fluency. His pretty wife, who taught for a time along the Philadelphia mainline (and has the vowel sounds to prove it), and his own published affluence give him the air of a successful emigré revisiting the old country.

G.E.R.L. has assurance, but not confidence. He is short and hirsute, large head dramatic with bushy black hair, dark complexion shadowed by the heavy threat of beard. Orthodox Carthusian accent and donnish civilities come surprisingly from the shaggy personality. Modestly delighted with himself, he disclaims sporting facility, though he was in the first eleven soccer at C'house. His self-satis-faction comes from his academic connections: Moses (Finley) and Edmund (Leach) are his stars.

We sat down in Geoffrey's rooms to resilient melon, casserole of duck, boiled potatoes, cauliflower, undressed salad, then strawber-ries, which R.A.B. called 'strawbs'. We were an ill-assorted group. Showbiz has spoilt our taste for junkets and provides company too interesting and attractive for the competition.

We watched the fireworks, standing near a brazier of roasting coals, without excitement. We were (as so often) ready to go before we had fully arrived. Gigi L. wore a straight, candy-striped evening skirt and a lacy white shirt. Her earrings almost filled the pit of her ears; a certain splendid sexiness in that: you could imagine undressing her ears. Her interest seemed to be in public pleasures: she liked so many people ('Why is it Classicists are so sexy?'), but her boldness was of ambition not desire. There was no private fire between the couples. 'Thank you for the *cigarette*' was Gigi's way of asking for a light from her husband. Even J.P.S., while glad to display a pretty new young wife, seemed not to delight in her *personally*: she keeps house for him and is content to do so. How willingly women accept their men's world!

G.E.R.L. was shocked, deeply and without doubt, when Beetle said that she hoped the young ball-partners would end up in bed as a reward for their exertions. This now traditional reward struck him as highly irregular. G.'s older brother (whom I remember as being a hairy *man* at Charterhouse) has been brain-drained and lives in California. He is a pathologist. G. said that he preferred analysing the cause of death to being called in to observe its onset.

In early 1950, when I was working on the *Sunday Express*, there was a great hoo-ha about a Jewish man who snatched up his daughter (?) and took her to Paris to get her out of the hands of his wife and in-laws. They lived in Golder's Green (Rivermede Court, I think, though no river was evident). A crowd of reporters was in attendance. I recall the bloody relish in being one of the jackals. The family was barricaded in its high apartment. Perhaps because I looked too young to be a jackal, they confused me with an errand boy they were expecting. I squeezed into the flat and found myself a kind of free and invisible presence within the household. I combined the policeman, the burglar, the spy, the hunted and the hunter. I had power, but I was vulnerable; I had the run of the place but might at any moment be run out of it. I was a Jew and an anti-Semite: I felt contemptuous of the beleaguered family, and confident that society would be indifferent to anything I might do precisely because they were already victims. Once the hooks of publicity were deeply enough attached, the public appetite for having the prey dragged into view and feasted upon would kill pity and sanction malice. The family were now common property, its rights forfeit. Any fresh incision which might spill new innards was in the public interest. Once destruction has gone far enough, the 'humane' response is always: 'Finish him off.' No one is more dangerously placed than the deeply wounded man; he provokes miracles of revulsion. So I stood inside the guarded door and looked into the sunny kitchen where, in the late morning, dismay and inertia had left used cups, jagged cereal packets, spilled sugar, crumby plates: a scene of Pompeian poignancy: these doomed folks had had the same breakfast that I had!

Behind me, the brother-in-law – broad, undefeated, belligerent – was upbraiding a margin of excluded heads (my journalistic colleagues). On the inside, I could appreciate the force of his indignation. This was a scene of rape: unwanted men forcing the thin membrane between themselves and another's privacy, determined not to be refused, furious at denial. There was no sign of either the police or common decency (I was fresh from school and still a virgin). Publicity was rupturing privacy. It was exhilarating and appalling. No hypocrisy was needed to round off the twofacedness

of my reaction: I exulted in my guile and my power. I was an
inverted Odysseus who had ridden *into* the cave over the heads of
the sheep. I was genuinely sympathetic to the family even as I took
inventory of every detail. I could imagine how my master, the News
Editor, would smile as he read: 'There was an empty place at breakfast this morning. On the cream plastic tablecloth…' etc. I was truly
disgusted by the callous greed of the jackals. Now that I was this
incongruous stowaway, I felt ready to lend a hand to repel the
boarders. Yet I had grown up with the belief that Golders Green
Jews were the last people I wanted to be associated with. I doubt if
the crudeness of my aversion can be blamed entirely on my parents.
But there it was: these people seemed to me born victims just as
they were born inferiors. Their role as characters in a story (precisely
what the News Editor called them) took away their last claim to
consideration. I had become a storm trooper, grimly uniform with
my fellows, though in this case a shade more resourceful. I was
responsible only to Stanley Head; entirely immune to the pain, guilt,
confusion of suburban civilians ill-advised enough to let their problems become public knowledge. I was nobody in particular: a
Barbarian with my notebook as shield, my pencil as sword. I was
shot of educated scruple, grey and merciless. How had I actually
pierced that virgin door and entered the secret passage? I have
already forgotten exactly; I have the idea, Freudianly fraught, that I
came in somehow through the back way, which had been left open
for the laundryman. Yes, I think that's it: familiarity with my parents'
middle-class flat in Manor Fields gave me the insight that there had
to be a back way.

In those days, there was still a preponderance of working class
reporters, private detectives with endless persistence and some
cunning, but less intelligence. Their grey greed made everything
conform to whatever their papers required. Their dream of that
golden by-line was made more pathetic by the fact that, however
large the print in which their names might figure, they would always
remain anonymous to the public to whose appetites they pandered.
Even the idea of missing a scoop, that fear which never let them go
home while a colleague remained on the scene, was a delusion: only
The Street took scoops seriously. Did any readers ever switch papers
because they thought one more alert than another? Most circula-
tion was gained by features which had little to do with the
foot-soldiers: series about prostitution or crime which required
more premeditation than detective work.

The professional diligence of us Expressmen was like the bull of guardsmen: related more to discipline than to efficiency. Those who gave themselves ulcers in the service of the – often spiked – interview were not bettering the competition but avoiding the sack. The myth of the great story which would stand up forever and make a man's career was a fantastic fake, like the corporal's dream of winning a great battle.

What was I doing in that flat, and what should I do? Having executed an outflanking movement, where did I go from there? Imagine if the missing baby and the fugitive husband were, in reality, happily concealed in the bosom of the family. Could that be why the thick young accountant at the front door was pleading for them to be left alone? Could I bring off a noble synthesis: at the same time achieving a notable scoop and, because I revealed that harmony had been restored, proving myself the defender of decency? I recalled the Norwood builder, whom Sherlock Holmes had flushed out with a cry of 'Fire, fire!' If I did the same, would a panel burst from the passage wall and the secret reunion of the family be disclosed? No, sir.

How had nobody noticed me? I was like an actor who enters the stage dramatically but finds that he has no part in the play. Unless I was challenged, I might as well not be there. Only as I was being bundled out could I throw the provoking questions which might goad the family into revelations. Once manhandled, I could legitimately strike back. Nothing made me more of a prisoner than my present freedom. Accordingly, I coughed, shuffled, muttered until, when all the other reporters had been excluded, I could attract the attention of the doorkeeper. If I had been a brownshirt before, I now reverted to being a Jew: I wanted to side with the young man against the bullies outside. Yet I had to confess my association with them, lest he betray himself in confidence and so embargo my using what I had discovered.

My eyes offered sympathy and I told him that if he had any statement to offer me, I would do my best, on my honour, to make it say what he wanted, but I could not, in the nature of things, keep it to myself. I so wanted to betray this family painlessly that I never considered doubting the value of the whole shabby subterfuge, still less of The Press itself. I was so sure that something important was involved; it had all been in the papers so it *had* to be of consequence. What the hell was I doing in this suburban flat, in the bosom of this family, unless something that The People had a Right to Know was being enacted?

The sturdy doorman refused me the smallest quotable revelation.

As soon I disclosed myself, I was ordered out, and out I went. The door was banged in my face and I was relieved. Once the barrier was back in place, it became worth beating on. Suddenly there was a whisper among the reporters. A car had been hired; perhaps an AIRPORT DASH was imminent. These were the days when the dream headline read: ROYAL DOG IN MERCY DASH. We all raced along the road to a garage whose name was arched over the alley that led to it. Yes, the family *had* commissioned a car. They did so every Saturday afternoon (curious for a Jewish family). A routine drive to a grandparent. It all went down in a dozen notebooks, but it was not much of a story.

June 1967. How impossibly long ago it seems! The closing of the Straits of Akaba created a situation so emotionally riveting that there seemed no other place to look. Could the giant-killer do it again? The gloating statistics hardly endorsed optimism; it looked grim, and so did Israel's representatives. The hurried meetings of Jewish writers and intellectuals were impressed by their own importance. The publication of denunciations and exhortations became a dramatic matter of reopening deadlines and bringing influence to bear. The text of group letters was urgently composed; all qualifying phrases were ferociously disdained: this was no time for legalistic niceties or for showing any understanding of the other side. The Arabs threatened extermination and all means to repudiate and blacken them were authorised. The meetings of the writers' committee were dominated by those who claimed political experience as the justification of their formulae (and primacy). Someone claimed that the Communist Party of Great Britain *might* be persuaded, under subtle circumstances, to reject or sidestep the Moscow line; it was agreed that such a recruit to 'our' side could be of vital importance. (*How* could it?)

Not many writers found time to attend the hurried conferences, but certain strands could be distinguished among those roped in to be the scourge of English indifference. The most uncompromising were the television writers, and re-writers; they seemed glad of any opportunity to impose their worldliness (which passed for wisdom) on those more fortunate or 'rarefied' than they. There was no want of hectoring and ill-natured tirades. One came away thinking how absurdly unlikely was any prospect of Arab-Israeli reconciliation when so much enmity and so little resilient affection existed among supposedly kindred spirits and unanimous ambitions. The smallest deviation from chauvinist enthusiasm, the vaguest allusion to objec-

tive truth was shouted down. By the time events proved how irrelevant we were, the contradictions implicit in the notion of Jewish
solidarity were clearly and painfully apparent. What the *purs et durs*
wanted was an abdication of fine scruples and the petty egotism of
personal considerations. The movement was always towards
imposed solidarity, a repression of individual conscience in favour
of monolithic centralism: we might debate the 'line' freely, but we
were then obliged to it without deviation. The most fervently political was Lew Griefer, the least 'creative' person present. As a script
editor (when vexed I once called him, a 'script-griefer') he was in
the habit of tailoring everything to the shape required by the
machine. The committee gave him a chance for moral commissar-
ship: he revised us until we conformed to Israeli purposes.

With what elements of myself was I party to these proceedings?
I am a victim of vanity and of modesty; they are the muscles of a
single limb: when one stretches, the other contracts, but both are
simultaneously in play. Lured by vanity into the company of these
writers, I was impelled by modesty – and by the belief that the lives
of actual people, 'my' people, might in some way be affected – into
acting the role of a docile and uncontentious underling. What did
I know of the actual military or diplomatic situation? Like an elected
civilian confronted by a permanent staff, I was disposed, by the very
doubts I had of their intellectual or moral qualities, to accept the
validity of their opinions. Could there be malice or opportunism in
their assertiveness? The fault had to be in me, who lacked practical
knowledge. How could a mere writer brandish his naïve views in
the cannon's mouth?

There was something deeply affecting and reassuring in the solidarity of those June days. I discovered, at last, that there really were
other Jews. To submerge oneself and one's private problems in
loyalty to the cause was a relief; there was luxury in having common
anxieties. I left the very pregnant Beetle to go up to Downing Street
where, under a hot sky, indifferent tourists were observing Number
10, in very small quantities. We paced, pondered and posed, like
statesmen, or statesmen's stand-ins, within the fenced area. Finally,
on cue, we handed in a letter and, under the camera's eye, were
interviewed, or at least auditioned – somebody would have to go –
for the BBC News. How did we do? We did at least do something.
At nine o'clock, I saw myself speaking, briefly and unbrilliantly, for
British Jewry and their hope that Mr Wilson would not 'sell Israel
down the river'. It was not the kind of phrase I should choose to use
again, but there it was. How useful was our *démarche*? *Parlons pas.*

That same evening, Michael Elkins' report from Jerusalem announced, with almost drunken confidence, that the war was already won. All our pale vigil, and our passionately composed text, had no relevance whatever to the outcome. Underdog was now *ubermensch*: we could put away our dignified pleading. The writers' committee clung together for a while (perhaps it still exists), but the dummy rifles with which we had so touchingly armed ourselves were hastily dumped.

It was now suggested that the cost of the war would prove heavy; money would have to be raised. With this reversion to the financial standard, we all felt much more British again; the issue was domesticated. A few brave spirits were said to be flying to Israel to compile a selfless film; others, less gallant, were standing by to cash in, through the same medium, as soon as deals were closed. *Viva la normalità!* The cement which had held us together soon flaked. What substance had there ever been in it? Except in a specifically geographic compass, the idea of a Jewish community is meaningless without a synagogue (and unattractive, to me, with one). Racially, we may take our Jewishness to be inescapable, but what sense (i.e. *use*) can it have unless it is linked with some common religious belief, or practice? The piety of those who mumble but do not believe is as understandable, but as insignificant, as the loyalty of Old Boys. Since religious belief is unattractive to me, what other solidarity remains? Obsession with the horrors of the Final Solution makes it distasteful to admit the perfectly unshameful fact that the enclosed style of most of Europe's disappeared Jewish communities would render them, if they still existed, uncongenial and restrictive to most of the writers who imagine that their brutal destruction is an *argument* against any criticism of Israel or Israeli policy.

Do I lament the fracture of Jewish culture or do I condemn the murder of Jews? The latter. Such a condemnation, felt with all the nerves of 'racial' connection, is all that can be expected of me. Why should I pretend to an appetite for doctrinal disputations, for ritual purity or endogamy *because* of the destruction of European Jewry? I do *not* feel guilty; I am merely appalled and degraded, as much by the conduct of the 'civilised world' as by the murders it condoned or ignored. To enclose oneself in the position of the Jews and to deny any external allegiance was a temporary exercise in Johnsonian concentration, even if it was others who (for the moment) seemed to face imminent death. The sudden commuting of the sentence, followed by the execution of it upon the putative executioners, reveals the unreliability of a 'philosophy' concluded under duress.

Behind all the anxious, intelligent or bellicose responses was the basic curse: Fuck the Arabs. Very well, the Arabs were fucked. *Et alors*? Having cried 'Rape', we observed a potent riposte. The obscenity of Nasser's threats was answered by deeds, not words. Sheepishly, we accepted congratulations, quite as if we had done something. Commander Cresswell, of *de Laune Antiques* in the Fulham Road, showered me with strategic accolades; generals at the Royal Hospital, where he does charity work, saluted my father. 'We' had showed those woggies a thing or two. We had, as it were, had a successful *baptême de feu* and everyone was warmed by it.

Those who had always believed (or now said that they had) in an Israeli victory were unembarrassed by earlier appeals to human, or humane, decency made during the blockade of the straits. They had not flinched from the brutal prospect because their nerve was steady. Israel would take care of herself, so there was no call to get involved. We, who had somewhat panicked, were tripped by all the strings which we had tried to pull; yes, and by those which had made one a puppet but which, operated from above, had been so artfully manipulated as to create the illusion of free and considered action. We were back to another Johnsonian maxim: having been neither soldier nor sailor, we thought meanly of ourselves. Our urgent deputation to Number Ten was the bravest expedition we could mount. (I had expected a mob of furious Arabs at Downing Street, where Diane Cilento had been slated to hand in our petition. She was in her Sauna and could not be disturbed.)

As soon as the Israelis vanished over the horizon ahead of us, our war cries became bathetic and we disengaged. The ease of the victory embarrassed those who were loyally prepared to squat together in the last ditch. Suddenly our redoubt was miles behind the lines. Such a speedy triumph smacked of a fixed fight; partisans became apologists. How could one account for so comprehensive a knockout when our man had never, supposedly, trained for or wanted a fight?

I have been asked to a number of Israeli functions since last June and I have been warmly and generously greeted, when I went. Yet I do not much want to go to them. What has it all got to do with me? One such occasion was the screening of John's unimpressive film, where we were trodden on and disturbed, in our unobtrusive seats, so that it seemed that the whole audience had gone out of its way to step on our toes. What a petty response! Yet how I hate to be recruited! The assumptions of the Zionists need more reliable arguments than coercive 'nationalism'. We shall be treated to military bands next. The film was banal. The best sequences were from old newsreels. For the rest, this act of charity reeked of patronising haste. It will appeal only to the converted. In this, it is another instance of the Schlesinger method of seeming to be concerned with uncompromising truth while really caring only for the approval of his audience. He has no wish to change anything; his intellect is as narrow as his experience. A sequence he had thought 'riveting', a row between an Israeli and an American, was messy and inconsequential. His idea of drama is of suddenly erupting malice which reveals the pettiness under 'everything' and emphasises the dotty eccentricity of apparently sane human beings.

The poet. B.G. brought him round to see us. He is said to have been a successful satyr in his younger days. Now he is large, inflated rather than fat, and wore a dark suit, voluminous white shirt, tie with slide. His face is colourless, eyes prune-dark and heavily lidded, a touch exophthalmic, mouth dainty, hair in horizontal curls up from a high forehead, in the manner typical of certain Jews. He is a poet (winner of a recent prize) and a dealer, in NYC, in Old Masters and Young.

In the sitting room, he stood very close to our Klee prints. He told a story: ten years ago, a certain man, very unhappy with his wife and desperately in love with another woman, went to a psychiatrist and explained his dilemma. The psychiatrist was tough: he said that in ten years' time the man would look back on this love as a frivolity and realise that his real life lay with his wife and children. It was his duty, and his best policy, to return to his family and make his life with them. The man went back to his wife and had a perfectly miserable ten years. Then, once more in despair, he returned to the psychiatrist and told him of his suffering. 'You told me ten years ago,' he said, 'to go back to my family and now look at me. What do I do now?' The psychiatrist said, 'I told you to do that?' 'That's what you told me.' The psychiatrist shook his head. 'I must have been out of my mind.'

'I am thirty-five years old. I have been married for thirteen years. I have never committed adultery. I have never shot anyone and I have made a great deal of money by my own efforts. How do you think it feels to be that kind of a failure? Are you surprised that I'm tortured by guilt?'

After a week of rain and closeness, the clouds lifted. Sarah and I went into the garden and played 'pardners' on the range, weaving a fantasy of the Wyoming territory around the necessary job of cutting back good old English overgrown lilac. Phil Barry phoned at seven to announce his arrival; I am to meet him and Mark Robson at the Carlton Towers tomorrow to talk about resuscitating *The Loved and the Lost*. The last time he called The Wick, about the same project, I fell out of a tree in my haste to answer his call. Now I turn over schemes for getting out of a job ten times as well paid as the one I was so keen to hang onto six years ago. We had no central heating and one car, the old Vanguard. We thought ourselves very comfortable.

It was a hot, brilliant Sunday morning. Driving through the City, I noticed a splendid Balkan moustache among the passengers in an adjacent Ford Anglia. One of them called 'Gloucester Road?' And another said, 'Are you Grick?' I aired my Greek a little and told them to follow me. As we went along the Embankment and through the park, I rehearsed Greek idioms and, at Gloucester Road, I pulled in and signalled them to stop. '*Aftos o dromos einai o* Gloucester Road,' I said, *ktl.* They laughed, and the driver, with a comradely, even Epirot gesture, clapped me on the arm, grinning. 'We don't speak any Greek,' he said. 'We are all Yugoslavs.'

Y.'s young daughter, L., wrote and asked if she could talk to me. We went for a walk in the park. She said that she had 'lost her language' and had no words for anything any more. The wind blew boisterously. A girl in a mini-dress was wrapping a towel around herself and changing her clothes. To our right, a young man in a dark suit, with tousled hair, watched her with frank attention. L. has had an unhappy attempt at an affair. Sex was not at all as it had been advertised. L. is not short of culture, but of life. What should/could she do now? I advised against falling back on the family. Whatever parents said, they could not help a measure of relief at hearing that their daughter had not been able to make a prompt exit from their world. Men, I told her, often blamed their sexual failures on women. God, I was mature! I told her that, whatever her rebellious ideas at the moment, her upbringing would probably lead her, in the end, to a happy marriage. I was *extremely* cautious. I told her that her experience, however sad, had improved her looks.

The wind was chilly. She wore a blue mackintosh, light and

crinkly; her close-growing hair made a brown/gold helmet for her head. I was stirred by the force which her weakness had given me. She did not attract me, but I put an arm around her shoulder, comfortingly; made bold by want of desire. At a coffee kiosk, a bearded tramp, too far gone to be romantic, and too shabby even for a hippie, with gaping trousers and a brown aura about him, his sign a toadstool, came up and asked, 'Do you know anyone interested in making films at all?'

At the bus stop, I kissed L. nicely and said, 'If in doubt, behave badly.' I fear that she will ignore the advice and pay attention only to me.

If a man must choose, he will always prefer deceiving two women to loving one. Intrigue flatters the vanity more than conquest. It is more pleasing to deceive with success than to love wholeheartedly. A woman gives herself to her lover, but what caps her pleasure is the thought of her husband. She is fucked by one man, and she is fucking another.

At the M.s' for dinner. The other guests were the novelist N.B. and her husband, C., a BBC executive. Her father was a senior officer in the merchant marine. His parents are Jewish, but he has a very British style. Despite a public school minor scholarship, he preferred Pangbourne. At the age of seventeen, in 1943, he went to sea. He resigned from the navy after the war, having realised that 'There simply weren't enough ships to go round.' Beetle said that someone must once have told him that he had a good profile; when you talk to him, it is like having a conversation with a highly animated two-headed penny. He has the pipe-in-mouth cragginess of a naval officer combined with the dubious teeth and straying silver hair of the Oxford socialite. He and Jack Lambert and Gordon Meyer all commanded small boats and all have a diffident, anxiously intimate manner, while remaining isolated and self-centred. Because such a man encourages you to smile at his foibles, it does not follow that he can endure your being as deprecating about him as he is.

The Lady Novelist is plumpish and her floral dress was disposed to show her armpits often enough for you to conclude that someone once told her that they were her best point. In fact, with her reddish hair and goodish complexion (nothing quite ten out of ten), she glittered but failed to sparkle. She is a magistrate, so C. has to drive at 30 mph, at least within her fief. When she told me that her husband had two Jewish parents, I remarked, 'But he's not Jewish',

with the hint of a question. She looked at him with fresh eyes. 'Well,
I suppose he must be,' she said. It did not seem to add to his charms.
She told me that she had asked her tutor at Oxford about
Wittgenstein, whose name she had heard at parties. Lindsay replied,
'Wittgenstein does not exist.' She believed him.

She had once captured a pygmy shrew, which had run up her
shoulder in a field. People said that they could not survive in
captivity. The smallest native mammals, they ate so much they could
not be caged. Determined to disprove the story, she collected a huge
stock of worms, snails and other edibles, and put them in a big box
with the tiny creature. Exhausted by foraging, she went to bed. In
the morning, the shrew was dead. The vet said that it had died of
starvation.

I called Jack Lambert about doing an appreciation of Gordon Meyer.
It was not *news*, he said; death was not the kind of thing they were
keen on. He told me that I really ought to write a play. The new
John Osborne was so ghastly. So why had it had such good notices?
Who could say why Harold (Hobson) had to go quite so far? Jack
supposed because the latest Osborne was so much better than the
previous one. Whenever I speak to Jack he harps on the low level
of Osborne's abuse: 'all false teeth and sagging breasts'. You would
think J. suffered from these misfortunes himself.

They meet at a hole which has suddenly opened in the pavement.
He does not find her attractive, nor does he want to have a mistress.
He has come to the meeting at her request, *because* he feels emotionally remote from her. He is trying to help her face the realities of
adult life. When she tells him that she has met a young man of her
own age, the man is relieved. Then she is humiliated yet again and
threatens a breakdown. He is again 'the only person I can talk to'.
He remains aloof, but what harm can it do to indulge her a little?
He meets her for tea now and again, without telling his wife (why
ever should he, since their meetings are entirely innocent?). The girl
has been somewhat changed by the pain she has endured; she has
'realised a lot of things'. Her love for the man is openly declared.
But if he is flattered, he is not excited; what entertains him in her
absence is abated by her presence. He agrees, with a clear
conscience, and therapeutic altruism, to see her again, and again.
The girl has never been punctual, but one day she is extremely late.
He has been waiting in a public place and has time to fear that
someone will see him meeting a girl, *if she comes*, and 'draw the

wrong conclusion'. He looks at pretty girls coming up from the tube and begins to think that he is a fool for not meeting one of *them*. Callow devices occur to him, reminiscent of his adolescent passions. Perhaps he talks to a couple of girls, one of whom seems quite interested. At last, angry and humiliated, he phones the girl's home; no one there. Now he becomes anxious. Is not coming something she is doing to him? What if she does something desperate? He cannot simply be angry, if she turns up; after all, they are not lovers. At last she comes; terribly sorry, she has mistaken the place – or the hour. She is late because she did not like to leave an old lady who was nervously awaiting a different bus. A likely story, but what's the point of quizzing her? What do her fears or fantasies matter to him? If he analyses the situation as they have tea, it is only to try and help her to understand herself. She begs him humbly for another meeting; generously, he agrees.

The next time, to his furious astonishment, she is even later. He is maddened and, of course, emotionally stirred. He spares her nothing of his anger this time; and so involves himself further. She is now inclined to make light of her fault: 'So I'm late sometimes.' When he threatens not to see her again, she is tormented; which give his threat a certain piquancy. He asks her why she thinks he should bother with her. She cannot imagine, she says: if he wants to be a coward, why shouldn't he be? *Coward*? Provoked, he is hooked. He still feels no attraction to her, but he would like to get his hands on her. By threats to call him at home, and talk to his wife (why shouldn't she?), she obtains power over him. She is quite revived by his apprehension; his weakness strengthens her. Their positions begin to be reversed; she becomes more stable, and he vertiginised. He is at the mercy of a passion which is pitiless because it has no foundation in desire; even when he cannot think of anything but this girl, and what to do with her, he considers her without appetite. He goes through all the hell of a love affair, without love.

'He's on his third wife.' Overheard at San Lorenzo. An academic lady was told that the collection for her leaving present had come to 120 pounds. What did she want? A gun, she said. Why? She had been to Egypt and had an audience with President Nasser, who had much impressed her. He suggested that she come and lecture in Egypt after retirement. She said she would like to, but was deterred by the absence of fresh meat. Ah, he said, that can be remedied by hunting. She therefore required a gun. It was pointed out that it might be a little awkward to present a gun to a 69-year-old retiring lecturer. She saw the point and 'compromised with a double bed'. This came from a table of four junior academics putting on a high quality performance of simulated maturity. One of them made frequent use of the phrase 'Before I had a family...'

Lipstick on their hairy mouths.

S. told me that K. had 'refused to help him'. I called K. who said that when S. first came to London, he had indeed used him quite a lot on the radio. He even had a regular office in the Greek department. Then K's assistant gave him some assignment and he simply did not do it. Later he was contacted and said, 'There was nothing in it.' They got the impression that he was not happy working for the BBC and 'tactfully' did not ask him again. K. told me that he would get in touch with S. again. The curious thing was that S. never indicated to me that he had done any work at all for K.

Seymour Walk. In the middle of the night, about three, a terrible screaming, and then a thump, and resumed screaming. I stumbled out of sleep to confront the bright street and the shrill noise. A man: 'You bitch, you bloody bitch.' More thumps and screams and the door of a house for sale is flung open and a girl in a gold mini-dress runs out, shrieking and cowers, in a helmet of blonde hair, against the shining next door wall. 'Mrs Baker? Mrs Baker, are you all right? Shall I call the police? Do you want me to call the police?' Lit windows on the first floor and light spilling from the open front door make a false dawn. Soon the police (one uniformed, one in plain clothes); a muttered conversation, the husband's head in the dark hood of the doorway. 'This is my house. You can go to Chelsea Town Hall or Kensington Town Hall if you don't believe me.' The truculence of a man who stakes everything on the one thing about which he is certainly right. 'This is my house. I own this house.' Through the half-open door next to the house, the girl, legs up on a sofa, listens with the neighbours.

Tynan made a name for himself by his precociousness, and maintains it by being even more juvenile now that he is older. With this upside down performance, he succeeds in towering feet and ankles above his contemporaries.

Tolstoy, when he married, made his wife read his notebooks. It is assumed that he wanted her to know him properly, faults and all. What if he had less candid motives, that he was less anxious to purge himself than contaminate her? When, forty years later, he stormed out, he played the last act in a tragi-comedy whose course he laid down, with those opened notebooks, in the first days of the marriage. He may have imagined that he was putting debauch behind him; in fact he was introducing it to his wife.

Paul this evening: 'I've got good news. I'm a swimmer.'

A dream (28.6.68): driving in a small car past lights along a narrow coast road, not alone but in company I cannot recall. We came up a steep road and were suddenly in an afflicted, sick area. Shellfish, as if driven by frenzy out of the sea, were heaped, blackened and scrabbling, by the roadside, alive, pulsing but so far gone as to be beyond help. Eyes and mouths caked with fungoid whiteness. Further on there were large fish and then lambs, in similar case, muzzles rimed with beastly whiteness. We were safe in the car and drove through to an uncontaminated area.

The AGM of the Royal Society of Literature. A sparse company waited for Lord Butler to descend from Cambridge. It might have been any AGM: there were the usual apologies for absence (Lord Birkenhead) and the usual hopes for swift recovery; there was gratitude for exceptional devotion to duty (by the secretary and her daughter), the usual treasurer's report and the usual jokes about his honorary status, the usual endorsement of the accounts, the usual unopposed election, or re-election, of the committee. The only mildly unexpected moment was when Butler, in half-spectacles and full face, swollen deformed hand clutched against his old-fashioned double-breasted brown suit, asked whether the society's investments were satisfactorily lodged. The Hon. Treasurer rehearsed the happy rise in their value during the last eighteen months. 'Ah yes,' said the ex-Chancellor, 'but aren't equities rather high just now?' If they were, it seemed that there was nothing anyone could think to do about it.

In company with Constance Babington-Smith and Michael Holroyd, I signed my name with Byron's ivory pen in the red-bound register. As tea was served, there was an influx of newcomers who had come to hear George Steiner lecture on 'Eros and the Imagination'. Among them, Tom Maschler, Ed Victor and his purple-trousered and pretty American wife. Steiner introduced me as a 'Jewish English' – or was it 'English Jewish' – writer to Rabbi Finkelstein, head of the American Theological College. Like so many academic adminstrators, he had an extremely spiritual air; those who are *not* bureaucrats like to appear businesslike. F. had a trimmed full beard and smiling, dreamy eyes. I asked whether he wanted some tea. No; there were times when he did not drink it for religious reasons and times when he did not do so for health reasons. 'Does one gather that you don't drink tea very often?' 'Never.'

A crumb of wiry fruit cake lodged between two of my molars, which provided food for thought during Steiner's lecture. This was delivered from a high, narrow dais, which was occupied by Butler, Steiner and an ornate lectern. B. introduced the lecturer with that same wistfulness with which he alluded to finance (what actually *was* his domain?). His knowledge of S. seemed to derive from a fortuitous cutting from *The Times* which, he frowned to tell us, referred to S. as 'an élitist – whatever that means'. From an ex-candidate for the leadership of the Tory party this was a pretty piece of agnosticism. He referred to S. as 'Mister', which provoked a mutter of 'Doctor' from Tom. That old German respect for honours dies hard, especially if the honours are German.

S. began with a truncheoning violence of delivery. After Butler's ingratiating mumble, the panzers moved in. The lectern might have been a music stand on which the score was marked *fff*. S.'s audience might have been thousands; his voice was calculated to carry to the furthest recesses of the great hall; it was our fate that this calculation took place in quite a small room. The Germanic inability to cope with the English 'th' sreatened sometimes to srow the sing into seatrical absurdity. Such passionate espousal of great English values by a man who had difficulty getting his tongue around English syllables could not but arouse the Amis in one. Yet his thesis was powerful and urgent: he claimed that the cult of the specific (genital) description, the elimination of metaphor and the contempt for tact were leading to a collapse of the central mystery of Western life and literature. He referred to George Eliot as the supreme instance of subtle clarity, instancing the frozen marriage in *Middlemarch* (which sits fat and virgin on my shelf) as a case where all, yet nothing, is revealed. He doubted Flaubert's creed and despised the vulgarity with which Zola had, like the Goncourts, put the clinical in the place of the imaginative. (Of course the Goncourts accused F. of mugging up his books from museums and sources and failing to observe life.) Tolstoy and Proust were lined up against the modern trend; Lawrence, if alluded to, was neither attacked nor recruited. The conclusion was that modern literalists, cynical or misguided, had wetted on the sacred flame; by publicising the physical components of passion, they had diminished and degraded it. The novel, by consequence, had lost its ability to group sexual, social and metaphysical insights into an imaginative constellation.

This seems to imply (1) that once upon a time sexual relations had a 'purity' or 'thickness', a *meaning*, which they have now lost. Did they? (2) That tact is more 'civilised' and more 'cultural' than explicitness. But what are the metaphysical and political implications of this advertisement for obscurantism? (3) That the centrality of marriage is beyond question. All of S.'s approved authors took marriage to be the proper consummation and proving ground of a relationship: moral qualities entailed worthy, and happy, desires. Do they?

Blown off course, the boat is forced to put in at an island where political prisoners are living in freezing conditions, in tents and old shacks. The polite attentions of the governor; he has them to dine in his quarters and emphasises the concern with which he guards 'his children'. The sense of liberation when visiting a prison. A free society demands excellence; only giants are tall in a place where all stand upright. Even a pygmy towers among the prostrate.

Another dream, involving a rather routine gangster plot. I was to expose a gang by forcing the leader to admit his guilt in one of those stock 'But you'll never manage to prove it' speeches to which police officers were secretly listening. After successfully provoking the confession, the door opened and my two detectives appeared. The first toppled forward into the room, revealing a dagger in his back. Around the blade there had erupted a terrible tangled bubble of what looked to be strangulated intestine. The wound was purple and red and the dagger emerged from beside it. Then came the last hope, the only man left who could make the arrest and tie up the plot. He seemed uninjured, though his ox-like face was stripped of skin, like a raw, peeled tomato. He was able to speak and I seemed to be saved. Then he too fell forward and showed the same terrible eruption on his back. There was no salvation. The villain was triumphant and I was clearly for it. I elected, with suicidal resignation, to wake up. Were those scissors he was waving at me?

S. on Helen Vlachou. Her real quarrel with the Colonels was that they were '*agnostoi*'; she did not know them, and she was accustomed to having all the members of the government on her personal acquaintance list. Her own position is on 'the extreme right'; she is used to thinking of Greece as hers and her friends'. While the Colonels are seeking to impose *katharevousa* on the people, her quarrel with Papad. is that he doesn't speak her language.

The attraction of S.; he is, whatever else he is, undoubtedly an adult. Yet he has this imploring declarativeness. '*Ti tha kanome?*' he asks, after telling of the Authorities' refusal to give his children their passports. '*Ti tha kanome?*' He threatens 'action', but for moment '*Perimeno*' takes precedence.

J.R.S. A letter, in reply to mine, puts a polite close to our collaboration, not without pious hopes of some distant rendezvous. I suppose he takes me for an impertinent underling. He has never offered one word of appreciation, one hint that I have opened his eyes to any new possibilities. What emerges is the acccuracy of my first impression: he will never escape from the limitations of wishing to be admired, if not by the public, then by other parishioners of the Biz. He does not want to spend 'several years' on Byron, after the disappointments of *Far from the Madding Crowd*. He prefers, he says, to do smaller films; he has a couple lined up. Modesty? He would sooner take regular curtain calls, and cull regular cuttings, than risk obscurity for a long time in order to produce something monumental. The decision is not, he says, 'personal'. Of course not; it is totally egocentric.

I asked him, very early on, if he was a Socialist. I imagined that having done a film set in the North betokened political extremism. There was a quick, guilty smile, eyes down, 'No, I'm afraid not.' His politics are to do with his convenience; what he dislikes about returning to England is the tendency of porters to go off shift when they should be toting his bags. Yet he seemed to promise – and procure – entry to some large world from which I am barred. He has access to actors and executives, a call on the famous and the useful secured by a careful apprenticeship and the determination to lose no one who might serve his ends. He manages to be both iconoclast and devout; he may knock, but he never knocks down. What keeps him on course are his homosexuality and his lack of brains. Small achievements are wholly satisfying to him; he has none of the doubts and ambitions of those who can see over the garden wall. The praise of the present banishes all thought of the future. At our very first meeting on *Darling*, he was dressed as the Pope. ('Yerss, and *vide* the ring!')

Beetle has just come in: 'Bobby Kennedy has been shot.'

Christine, the nanny, took a guest – male? female? – to her room (two loud rings announced the arrival). It introduced something new and uncertain in the house. We returned early from the cinema (*Closely Watched Trains*) and found him/her still *in situ* and not easy to dislodge, despite greetings, artificially matey, and banged doors. Yet the night proved well; we woke very early, tired and in good humour. Today Pau came home; tall and self-confident; he has had an excellent term so far, fat with activities: last week he organised a fair for the Save The Children Fund. He found nine people to help him. They netted a pound. Our children are well, we are well and all is well. Yesterday Robert Kennedy died of the bullet in his head.

In the autumn of 1968, armed with fortunate money from a Hollywood commission, Beetle, Sarah and our small son, Stephen and T. set off for South America. My recently dead friend, Gordon Meyer had convinced me that Argentina, and its winter refuge, Punta del Este, across the River Plate in Uruguay, was the perfect place for escape from European turmoil. I can find no notes from the trip, and may well have taken none. The unfamiliarity of long-distance travel (our first experience of jet-lag, in Buenos Aires, took us by surprise) and the plethora of impressions and experiences, added to family obligations, left little time for sage reflection. We flew from B.A. to Montevideo, a gaunt city, sullen with apprehension of the *Tupamaros*, a left-wing terrorist organisation which had reduced 'the Switzerland of South America' to a land of dread. A taxi took us up the long coast to Punta del Este, where we expected a kind of unspoiled Cannes. Unfortunately, in our naïveté we had not verified the season and arrived as the place was closing for the winter. We tried to rent a villa, but found nothing to our taste. We put up in a huge barracks-like block of holiday flats, in which we were, it seemed, the only tenants. It was run by a German who might have skipped ship from the *Graf Spee*. When, after several days of depressing search, we asked the lady from the Real Estate office where she would go, if she had the choice, as we did. She looked at us with hoarded appetite and said, '*Europe!*'

We went first to Peru, and up to Cuzco and along the high railway to Macchu Picchu, and then to Jamaica. I needed some-where to write the screenplay which was paying for all this. First, we rented a modest house in 'Gibraltar Estates'. When it proved to have a very unreliable water supply, we moved to a mansion belonging to the Earl of Mansfield, above Ocho Rios. There we lived in Sixtiesish luxury which we have never enjoyed since, and did not wholly enjoy then. The swimming pool was huge, but we shared it with a variety of fauna. One had to take care when opening drawers in the bedroom to make enough noise for the rats to make themselves scarcer. Thanks to Maud, our cook, we ate well but so did she, and the other servants and their families.

I worked on a huge terrace overlooking the wide property and pretended that this was the life. It almost was; we did not miss England, but we were only pretending to be at home in luxury. The screenplay was, I thought, original and daring, but I had no sense of being the writer I wanted to be. I knew that Dick Zanuck and David Brown were interested in what I was doing; the Muses were not. In a decade when privilege and bourgeois self-indulgence were supposedly under attack, we lived in a way of which we had never dreamed. I had stocks and shares and cars in distant garages; a house in London and in North Essex and a place in Greece. I was, I suppose, somewhat famous but I was conscious of the vanity of what was assumed to make me happy (and what I wanted, very much, to make the family happy). There was a kind of emptiness in what used to be called my inner life, which is reflected, perhaps, in my failure to annotate our journey. I did, however, later write a number of short stories about it, and it continued to bear fruit when, in the early 1990s, I used our experience in B.A. to furnish the life of Guy de Roumegouse in my novel *A Double Life*.

Our ten-year-old son Paul – a boarder at Bedales – flew out, alone, to join us for his holidays. We drove to the airport to collect him. His VC10 swooped down on Montego Bay just as a torrential thunderstorm broke. Its wheels almost touched the ground and then it surged into the air again, circled the bay and came in for another attempt. Innocent of apprehension, we had no notion that landing was dangerous. The pilot managed it second time around and an older-seeming Paul was soon with us. We drove off in our hired Ford to return to Ocho Rios, unaware that the rains were already flooding the roads. Callow vanity led me to believe, for a while, that we were exempt from nature. We passed cars stalled by the roadside and never wondered whether we might share their fate. We did. At the bottom of a slight hill, water filled the exhaust and the engine cut out. I stepped out into shin-deep warm water, oiled by moonlight. I felt more annoyance than fear. But we had three children, and luggage, and we were in the middle of rising waters. With authoritative panic, I flagged down a huge Esso tanker truck whose shoulder-high wheels made mere puddles of the flood-water. Its crew of three Jamaicans made generous space for us in the cab. One of them hung out on the running-board, his arm bracketed through the wing mirror. The driver parted the waves easily and we had no difficulty in driving up to the front of the Hilton. The tanker *just* passed under the roof of the *porte-cochère*. I insisted on taking the driver and his mates into the bar for a drink, where we were not regarded with much sympathy. It was the most enjoyable experience of our entire time in Jamaica.

We flew, via Miami, to Yucatan for Christmas. We went to Chichen-Itza (where we had turkey and chestnut stuffing) and to Uxmal and then, in a defective Chevvy, we drove to Palenque, which was in those days almost inaccessible, even in a reliable car. Palenque had not yet become an easy tourist attraction; unkempt jungle encroached on the ruins. We ate only boiled eggs and whatever Beetle had brought with us for the children.

We returned to Harold Wilson's England in early 1969 and resumed our town-and-country life. Just before Easter, Beetle read out an ad in *The Times* for a farmhouse in the Dordogne, with white shutters. How about it? In the Easter holidays, we drove down to see Lagardelle. It was a wet April, with grim skies. We stayed in Beynac and we were not happy, I least of all. The house was less enchanting than its advertisement, but it was not very expensive. In a time of affluence (my script, *Guilt*, had been well-received), its purchase would make no great hole in our fortunes. I craved somewhere where I could work as I had in the days of our poverty, on a terrace in France, far from the envy and glitter of London life. On 16 June 1969, Lagardelle was ours. Once the money was irretrievably in their pockets, I asked the English couple who had sold it to us to tell us frankly what was wrong with it. The most pressing problem was woodworm; the oak beams were a foot thick but the deathwatch beetle had a busy appetite. The fumigation of the entire house was only the beginning of the taxes which the house has brought us, but I felt at home in it at once. We have done a good deal to the place over the years, but the room in which I work for almost half the year is (apart from the bookshelves and the pictures) as it was when I first put a table and a typewriter into it and, as soon as Paul and

Sarah were back at school, began a new novel, *Like Men Betrayed*, my first for three years. It is set in 'a' Greece, though the country is never specified. Despite lame sales and small recognition, it remains my favourite. Self-consciously literary, it makes none of the concessions to public taste which the cinema had required during the vacuous years of my putative fame. Lagardelle has become the place where I can write unintimidated by fashion and uncorrupted by the desire for applause or approval. In the autumn of 1969, I resumed, and have never lost, the habit of making notes.

1969

For *The triangle ABC*. A knows that the house he has built, for all his ingenuity and the purity of his effort, lacks what even a competent builder, let alone an architect, would have supplied. For all the satisfaction of practical accomplishment, he has done something unremarkable, perhaps ugly. Even as he and B are spending their first night under the shelter they have made together, he suspects her of sharing his doubts. He would accuse her of them, but if his insight is to be trusted, he guesses that she has no such feelings. With a desolate sense of the rolling wave of his past thundering after him (or of his future recoiling towards him), he has to despise her for not harbouring the criticisms which would have entitled him to hate her.

Later, he is joined in a corrupt, perverse alliance with C, an undeclared pact, he imagines it, to exclude B. He thinks that C, with all the choices available to money, must have the good taste to see the ineptitudes of the cottage. And so he is powerless when C takes B, whom his glance has (at first) declared negligible, without apology. A is left theoretically (the theory being his own) liberated, disembarrassed. Poor A! He finds that he needs the love of both B and C, but he discovers this only when he no longer has either. His tears oblige him to believe that he has been faithful to both and that both have been unfaithful to him. Now he has the opportunity he has secretly craved: he can be free, inflict pain, release his powers from domestic constraint. He has no obligations. But now he needs B; oh he needs her, he wants her! On whom else can be practise his cruelty and before whom else can he dance the triumph of liberty?

B, with her cheerful blonde energy, how could she be his wife? The fullness of her smile, the easy dawn of happiness in her great cornflower eyes, her joy in simple achievements (food on the table!), these things delighted him to tears, and confirmed the dread that what was enough for her would never be the same for him. 'Look,' she would say, 'you're happy!' And immediately he was filled with foreboding. If she could cause him pain, and meant to, then she

might convince him of having achieved his destiny. But happiness!
He searched for some corrupt, some less or more than physical pleasure to which he might seduce her, something literally unspeakable
whose recipe could not be repeated to anyone else, so that he would
have that hold over her, of being the unique procurer of her inad-
missible joy. Later he would find such a pleasure and imagine,
assume, that no one else could do as much for her. At least, he
consoled himself (and reminded her), C didn't know about *that*. 'Oh
yes,' she says, with an uncruel smile (as if to reassure him), 'we do
that sometimes.' 'How did he know – how did he – ?' 'He asked
me,' she smiles, 'and I told him. Do you mind?' A is shaken, not so
much (perhaps) by what she has admitted as by the small importance she attaches to it. She has not even bothered to take pleasure
in betraying their secret. She is now in a different world from him.
She has abandoned a reticence which he thought was typical of her,
but which, he now realises, was actually his.

Again and again we say
He revealed himself,
Revealed himself to a stranger;
We say it again and again.
But who ever gave himself
To anyone but a stranger?

We speak of the past as years;
Of the future as 'one day'.
The past is infinity;
The future a comfortable speck,
Promising unity:
One day.

The plan is to shoot the African sections of *Guilt* in Ghana. I went
to the Mayfair Cinema to see some footage. Afterwards, on the
pavement, I bumped into Clive R. who had a tall, smooth, dark-
suited young man with him, Bernard B., who was in Saunderites in
our day at Charterhouse. We had coffee (tea for me) at the Coffee
Shop adjacent to the Mayfair Hotel. C.R. and B.B. had a girl, Polly,
in common in their past. C.R.: 'You never married, did you,
Bernard?' 'No.' 'I don't know how you manage it, rich, handsome
young man, and still a bachelor. You must be almost safe by now;
what are you, thirty-eight? I envy you, I must say.' How did C.
sound? Like a doting mother; of the outspoken but only-kidding

kind. C.R. preserved a polite, polished reticence. He praised Polly, with whom he had stayed in a friend's house, a man he didn't, presumably, know very well and who had given him the use of his house and car and – could it be? – Polly, when he left the following day. Polly kept house. C.R.: 'Did she do it well? I should think she did, didn't she? I should think she did it *very* well, didn't she?' 'Yes,' Bernard B. said, with the smallest compression of the lips, as if to suggest that Polly's dusting was not his keenest memory of her.

'We have something in common anyway,' Clive said. His attitude was one of assault on B.B. who seemed to sense the other's intrusive curiosity and to resist it with cool, but not ungirlish pride. Oh, nothing *queer* about Bernard, but a decided intimacy between the two men, enough for B. to apologise for leaving me out of the conversation. I shrugged my complaisance: the revelations were, in truth, more entertaining than small talk. To exclude me is always to make me feel at home, especially among Carthusians.

The brown interior of the tea shop, in which my previous visits seemed to hang like stale credentials, entitled me to a sort of proprietorial mandate, although no one knew of them. I was neither stranger nor habitué; appropriate to the adjacent hotel of which it was not quite a part (it seemed better to enter from the street than from the lobby) the place combined the dreary and the swank, a facsimile of luxury – the fat teapot – without elegance: the creased waitresses, the want of freshness (the cakes were stale).

Considering that all three of us must have known the brazen and unrepressed anti-Semitism of C'house, it was a tribute to the spurious loyalty which the public schools can generate that our first topic of conversation was Peter Yates, the film director (*Bullitt* etc.). I had failed to connect him with the handsome, dark Hotspur who was our contemporary at Pageites. Admiration for his success was mixed with surprise: he had been so unremarkable at school. The very standards against which I suppose myself to be in rebellion are those which I continue to apply.

As we left, Clive and Bernard exchanged phone numbers. There was something somehow incestuous between these two men who were so alike, and such unspoken rivals. They shared the guilty smugness of successful homosexuals who have the air of having outflanked the normal limits of their kind.

A looks at himself in the mirror of the bathroom cabinet and then opens it, as if in search of what lies behind his image. He finds the usual paraphernalia: razor, toothpaste, Inter-Dens, contraceptive jelly (B's). He opens and sniffs the last, even licks it. (Perhaps he does not open the cabinet but smashes through it with his fist.) He wishes to do somebody violence. C? B? Himself?

A dreams of being his own executioner. We see him in his own pyjamas (stained at the front?) with a black hood over his head. The executioner's hand is on the lever. He pulls it. The trap opens. The hanged man's feet come through. It is A; the stocking peels slowly back, like ill-attached wallpaper, from his face. The executioner, in a white coat, walks away like an umpire to square leg, after giving somebody out. It is A, chucking a pebble from hand to hand.

On a ship. A rather decrepit, lifeless man in late middle age whom B recognises as the central figure in an old scandal. She is depressed at seeing so famous a lecher (an old film star perhaps) in such a low state. She wishes that she could revive him and seeks his attention. He is embarrassed by her interest, and humiliated. He dreads derision. 'What makes you think I'm D?' he says. He wishes he could say that he was somebody else. Or that she would.

I walked to Jo Janni's office in Bruton Street. *Guilt* is taking shape, though Julie has receded as a likely Sylvia. She thinks the colour question 'old-fashioned', though I do not think that I am asking it. Odd how seriously one takes the comments of those with whom there is no discussion. The Delphic oracle would not have lasted ten years if it had given reasons for its utterances. I am wounded by Julie's lack of interest, but not interested by it. Now Carol White becomes a sudden likelihood; I am to see her new film (Mark Robson's!) tomorrow. Afterwards we are to meet William Marlowe, whom J.J. thinks the perfect Nick. The script has gone to Judi Dench for Dilys. The shadows of possibility crowd over the project. I think of my ignorances and tremble. A recce to Ghana is planned for October. I boast to Bernard Sheridan that we are promised a luxury hotel in Accra. 'Terrible place,' he says.

Upon hearing of the ceasefire, the general ordered an advance along the entire front.

The doorman at Fox denied that Robson's film was being shown. I was about to leave when Jo arrived and said that of *course* the movie was being shown. The doorman said 'Fox don't tell me anything', as if he were an aggrieved majority shareholder. *Daddy's Gone a-Hunting* was bad even by the most ordinary standards. Carol White looked fat and ridiculous, at times so resembling Julie that they might both have gone to the same, disastrous, acting academy. Peter Wood came in and joined us. J.J. is trying to sell him C.W. for some Drabble novel they have bought. P.W. sat mocking the script and the director with the accusing relish typical of Jo's directors.

A secretary came and whispered that Stuart Lyons wanted to see Jo upstairs. He came back after ten minutes and we sat a while longer, staring at the ill-chosen absurdities on the screen. Jo said, 'I think I'll be going back. I've seen it already once. Do you want to stay, because…? I'd like to see you a minute.'

We all three left and walked through nudest Soho to Berwick Street where Jo swerved towards British Lion, where his lawyer's office is. 'We'll just go up and see Anticoni a minute.' P. Wood peeled off, after arranging lunch with Jo the next day. As we went into British Lion, Jo said, 'I wanted to tell you, Fox have cancelled *Guilt*.' I felt no surprise, not even much disappointment; I understood how condemned men 'showed no emotion'. The sentence was never unexpected. The grey day, a Monday, when I was never normally in London, contributed glumness, but no credibility, no weight, no conviction, to the occasion. The unchanging, teasing vulgarity of Soho, promise without fulfilment, cheat without thrills, could not furnish the background for a tragedy. The poker school was out; *ecco tutto*. My toe, which I had picked like a fool while watching *Match of the Day*, hurt more than the news which, delivered on a dull Monday when I had come up especially for the dreary vigils of preparation, had no more definition than a shadow on a sunless day. Films, even when successful directors are involved, get cancelled every day. I had survived like some berserk infantryman who continues to charge forward while warier companions fall all around him. So I had finally got mine; the wonder was that I had survived so long.

The nullity I felt was not of personal rejection. It might have belonged to some distant sharecropper who finds himself dispossessed by the contraction of a money market which he never knew existed. The portents had been there for months. I had assumed that my talents, or at least my good fortune, would save me and now I had got my comeuppance, even though it was 'nothing personal': Fox was virtually bankrupt. My fears about directing, simple doubts about competence, eased the pain. The man who is not picked cannot be expected to score goals. Still, in one day I had lost $125,000, plus the $250,000 which was to have been paid for the script of *Orchestra and Beginners*.

A producer at the end of his comfortable tether (made rich, maybe, by some profitable failure) arrives on a journey in a distant country, such as Argentina, in order to visit a writer whose book he wants to make into a film. He calls the writer's number (they have corresponded) and is told, by a woman he suspects to be the writer's wife, that Mr and Mrs Y. have gone to Punta del Este. He catches a plane to Montevideo. His neighbour is the rehearsal pianist of the State Opera, which is about to visit M-V, in a private guise, since formal exchanges between the two countries are economically unviable. By 'chance', therefore, the whole opera company is on the same plane. The rehearsal pianist is a Czech who escaped the Germans in 1938. He tells the producer about a German settlement in the Argentine hinterland which is completely rectilinear and where only German is spoken.

The loneliness of the Uruguayan coast, its lack not only of inhabitants but also of amenities, fills the traveller with sharp dismay. The chauffeur is tubercular; his cough provokes the producer to sympathetic irritation. Why make this hectic dash through a deserted landscape to what turns out to be a no less deserted P. del E.? He feels powerless, except for his money which, to his shame, can be flourished to extract a few words from the skeletal staff of the resort. In his state of – *what*? – superfluousness he feels an increasing dependence on – and resentment of – the unseen woman (the writer's wife?) who has primed a trail of bemusing clues. There is a broken, rusting wreck on the rough beach, with the ocean working over it. He keeps going to see it, although he comes away demeaned and depressed. He thinks of taking a place in the resort and looks over several villas, accompanied by a shabby-elegant lady agent whose fervent dream is of a trip to Europe. Somewhere out in the estuary is the scuttled wreck of the German pocket battleship whose defeat, by three smaller English ships, once seemed so heroic. The person who answers the writer's number continually tells him to call again in a day or two, when she may have heard something. The woman from the agency tries to make herself attractive to him. He knows that he could take her away and, if he wanted to, kill her and *nothing would happen to him*. He is a man to whom nothing can happen. He begins to hate the writer for his dependence on him. He wishes that he was able to make a movie without anyone's help. The city draws him back, but he cannot accept the 'defeat' which would leave him free to do what he wanted. He begins to be sure that the writer is dying, or dead. The woman whom he has not yet met has plans for him. In a resort without charm, in the dead season, he goes every morning to watch the sea scourging the lolling wreck.

A short film. Two babies struggling for a toy; replaced by toddlers; by children; by adolescents; etcetera. Finally two old people, who cannot even reach each other, sit glaring at each other in chairs, with nervous fingers.

They have made S. a bishop. When he was a Fellow of King's, Princess Margaret and the Queen Mum had tea in his rooms. He told us that when Margaret went to the loo, they could hear the royal tinkle. Ah, privilege!

I took Paul and Sarah to The Hamilton for lunch with my parents. A dark young man, with the air of tarnished athleticism you might find in someone who reached the last 32 at Wimbledon eight years ago, and a butch lady, close-cropped and thick, were milking the One-armed Bandit of yesterday's sixpences. They tipped them into a machine which spilled them neatly into the five pound bags the woman held to its lips. She might have been cupping a charity patient. I felt aggressive disgust with these two plumbers so boldly carrying out their rodding in front of us. My parents gave P. and S. some sixpences and seemed to delight in my children's corruption. After so many years, how is it that I am still adjacent to their world? I condescend to it, but lack the confident cruelty to break with it.

Mrs Baggs came into the bar, a collapsed balloon of a face above a violet-blue body, greedy to lose money in the machine which gaped for its diet of fools' silver. She hurried Sarah aside ('Finished?') and began to feed the beast like a favourite poodle just starting to take nourishment again after a long illness; tender greed forced cash into its tight mouth. She did not wait for the tumblers to stop at the losing place, but thrust in sixpence after sixpence, yanking down the arm, sweeping up any regurgitations, all with an air of discharging imperious duties.

When her cache of goodies was spent, she produced two ten-shilling notes and flagged the old, linen-jacketed barman: 'Sixpences.' She might have been a nurse or surgeon lacking an instrument at a critical moment. The old chap tottered round the bar with two surgical packs of coins and she ripped into them with expert fingers.

Sarah had deferred to her, unaware of how long the Baggs lady intended to exercise her monopoly. Now Sarah wanted another turn. This was strictly improper, since children are legally barred from gambling, but in the unofficial light of a deserted club, it might have seemed irrelevant. Not to Mrs Baggs. My mother said, 'Can my granddaughter have one go?' 'Not while I'm having my turn.' Mrs Baggs was as indignant as an old gentleman pulled from a urinal before he had shaken off the last drop. The act of pouring coins into the ugly chromium and plastic console had something excretory about it. She seemed to mix brazenness with a demand for modest seclusion. Her stance to the machine suggested that she was fulfilling an obligation: doing her duty, in the old nursery jargon. She had the flushed face of someone who both expects congratulations and has done something one does not usually talk about. When my mother repeated her grandmotherly plea, my father, sitting behind me in the corner of the bar, put his head in his hands and murmured, 'Oh Reen!'

My mother was not even a member of the club, so he was right: she should not have been so obtrusive, but I saw in that dropped head the fear that he had small rights in this country. He lacks the sense of belonging which allows a man to express desires or opinions simply because he has them. He thinks that correct behaviour will protect him. He and my mother carry with them the image, like that of St Christopher, of the British Bobby, to whom one may appeal as long as one has done nothing wrong. Just to be safe, it is best to do nothing at all. A clean record, like a no-claims bonus, entitles one to preferment. The corollary is stronger than the theory: uncivil conduct leads to outer darkness. They disapprove less of what a dissident may say than of his nerve in saying it. If the non-conformist gets away with his impudence, the polite are put in danger.

My father is unnerved by the Arab guerilla activitity in Western cities. Understandably enough, he finds it nasty (glass splinters in one's lungs are not pretty to think about), but it is nastier because it deranges the categories in which normality is packaged. If it is indeed terrifying and cowardly, I cannot think it 'unreasonable', since it does damage Israel; so does the use of children to throw bombs. How relevant is 'reason' to war? The second world war begins to take on an almost sentimental aspect: despite the anti-Nazi parade, it was an old style national conflict, a fight to restore a fancied equilibrium and the rule of law (capitalism in its best suit).

The dubious consequences of cartographic piety are horribly clear in the pious elimination of Biafra, because its boundaries were not sanctioned in Berlin in 1882. Asiatic and African nationalism continues to be defined by European geographers. The Arabs accept no image of Israeli survival; Israel is not one of the facts of their geography, as Germany was of ours during the war. The Palestinians find allies in the New Left, for whom a disreputable cause is one supported by the US. The Jews are yet again involuntary determinants of the political frontiers of various factions. Once more, they are more likely to be isolated than aided; even their supporters cannot forget how quiet life was before all this.

At lunch, my parents looked back with a certain nostalgia to when Oswald Mosley could be dismissed because he was anti-Semitic; his general wickedness followed from his 'prejudices'. On account of them, his social ideas, not always negligible, could also be dismissed. My mother was indignant at the suggestion that M. was not an ingrained but an opportunistic anti-Semite. She likes to imagine a time when it was not merely impolite but positively unpatriotic to be hostile to Jews. The beastliness of the Arabs is abhorrent not only in itself but also because it emphasises the mutability of her own allegiance. 'I'm a chameleon, you know,' she says.

How confident is she of her self-protective coloration? She relies also on an assumption of the underlying banality of human sentiments. People can, she wants to think, be reproved into propriety. The cold and greedy Mrs Baggs really should have been corrected to geniality by the code-word 'grand-daughter'. My father, head in hands, showed that he knew better, but not much: he has a nostalgic faith in the goodheartedness of the English-speaking peoples. How good was it, or will it be, for the Jews?

When I presented Mosley as a cynic or a wily dupe, my mother was as outraged as Mrs Baggs. I recalled how familiarly I had heard him speak of Hugh and Harold and Anthony. He had been to school with them, so to say, and his potted biog. was hardly less illustrious than theirs. He shared with the Tory radicals a visceral hatred of the interests responsible for the slaughter in the trenches. He became the kind of élitist – how different from Churchill or Macmillan? – who wished to evict the old gang without any serious social dislocation. How much more disreputable was his ambition than theirs? It is a measure as much of his naïveté as of his cynicism that 'Tom' never doubted his welcome as a celebrity, or a lover, even where he was detested as a politician. The upper class embargo on politics and religion at the dinner table confirms their sense of underlying solidarity. Why quarrel about the fluff when we are all sitting on the same kind of cushion?

The discussion of Mosley began with the arrival of Sir Guy

Domville, a courtly habitué of the five-bob room. He is in his late sixties, a man given to phantom intimacies, all winks and whispers, bending to confide banalities with cautious roguishness, one arm slung out in front of him: an unbandaged Nelson. He has a stripped look, skin tight over his head as if his skull were a darning egg. A single mild blow might fell him; he is discreetly crouched against its delivery. When asked if he was going to play bridge, he answered, 'I'm still going to a lot of cricket.' He might be a detective keeping an eye on a suspect as elderly as himself. He doesn't want to talk about it, but he is confident of an early arrest. This man, so ceaselessly fostering a popularity no one bothers to deny him, is the son of Admiral Sir Barry Domville who was one of the founders of 'the Link' and was imprisoned, under 18b, for codifying the prejudices which the rest of his class preferred should remain unwritten. He began as a cabin boy and ended by endorsing the validity of the Protocols of the Elders of Zion. On the way, he was Director of Naval Intelligence. At a by-election, he supported the candidature of H. St John Philby, the right-wing Arabist whose son also had an ingratiating duplicity. Just as Kim and his Communist friends attached no serious importance to the fate of their underlings, so Mosley could not believe that his peers would hold against him what his rabble happened to do, in some backstreet, to some other rabble. The lives and deaths of ordinary people were Noises Off; so were their silly scruples and loyalties. 'Don't be so bloody suburban' was the common cry of the uncommon.

In the five shilling room:
   'I suppose you're going to get smoked salmon all over the cards.'
   'Since this is a tongue sandwich, it's going to be difficult. Unless you'd like to order me a smoked salmon one.'
   'Oh I say. Oh.'
   'Yes, well, there it is.'

J.D. He was in a restaurant in a small French village. A woman burst in, convulsed by tears and was barely consoled by the *patron* and his wife. Her husband, a lorry-driver, had been killed in an accident in some distant town. They tried to calm her, but she refused to abate her grief. When he was killed, he had another woman with him in the cab.

The trial: a man is brought in and accused of being innocent. He is asked very sternly whether he has anything to say for himself.

'You know what I want to read some day? Tolstoy's *David Copperfield*.'

A naval officer is accused of homosexual acts and dismissed the service. He fights for years to 'clear his name'. He begins by asking for nothing better than reinstatement. At first, he believes in the 'values' which the Service embodies. However, he starts to despise its self-righteousness. He realises the strain of the years of furtive celibacy. The innocence on which he prided himself becomes ridiculous, and repulsive. He comes to see that his innocence is the real charge against him, and the real source of his bitterness. If he had only been guilty as charged, he would have no regrets. When, after many many years, they come to tell him that the findings of the court have been rescinded and his dismisssal reversed, they find him hanging in a cupboard, dressed in female clothing, with his naval officer's cap on his head, and a banner sellotaped across his chest, like an order. On it are the words 'Gentlemen, the Queen.'

Childlessness has narrowed her face, drawn it in with the suction of that vacuum in her womb. The lines contract and shrivel the flesh on the wide, handsome cheekbones. Mindless resentment cheapens the natural charm. She dreams of money and intrigue, the comforts of those whom happiness has failed. Cheated, it amuses her to see cheats everywhere. Once she depended on the happy marriages of her friends to convince her that happiness was possible. Now she relies on their infidelities and kinks to reassure her of the delusiveness of normality. Having betrayed C. out of vanity, she stays with him out of fear. To have slept with R. seemed like social elevation; he might be a common little toad, but his wife had been a duke's daughter. It was not R. who attracted her but the idea of intrigue. Today, Emma Bovary's cry 'I have a lover' is a boast replaced by 'I am a bitch'.

I am helping to buy my parents' flat for them. It is like contributing to having them buried alive. To this day I cannot visit Manor Fields without nausea. Nothing but cowardice was at home there. Its decorum was stifling and inescapable. Loneliness deprived me of vulgar experience, if not of vulgar appetite. The massacre of Jews in Europe, regarded with general horror but no particular concern, was a warning to us rather than a charge against the Gentiles. It was more like a previous conviction than a wrong. Not having suffered, one was more intimidated than those who, having known the worst, came out, if they did, careless of petty snubs and abuse. The immunity of the English Jew preserved his life, and his anxieties. My whole life has been compromised by my Carthusian experiences. It is always supposed that T.E. Lawrence acquired, or discovered, an appetite for pain after what he endured from the Turks who captured him. Did he not also discover the utter loneliness of human existence, the futility of hope and of doctrine, the thin tent of flesh which covers the bones of life and which, flayed by the cruel, the callous and the merely contemptuous, rips off to reveal the senseless blood beneath? It was not the taste for pain which became obvious; it was its ubiquity. Any time not spent in suffering was a kind of hypocrisy, a funking of the facts. Even the most trusted of companions, the simple and the loved, had to be made the instruments of further agony, if only to confirm that naked pain is the underlying substance of human reality. T.E.L., whom I have never regarded as sympathetic or significant, was a bastard whose sinister origins gave him something of the resentful ambition I notice in myself. It leads to a stupendous and provocative insolence, as if one were in a hurry to prove that one never had a chance and the world is a false and ungrateful place. T.E.L. acquired the reputation of a legendary English patriot, yet it could be said that his operations were directed as much against British as against Turkish interests. His indignation at the Sykes–Picot agreement was that of a man who sees his deep-laid plan undermined by one laid even deeper. Nothing amused him so much as the discomfiture of officialdom. His insolence infuriated the brass: what right had the little bastard to behave like that? If he imagined, later, that he had betrayed the Arabs, it was the British who never recovered from the effect of licensing, and funding, Arab nationalism.

Lawrence's dissidence went much further than mere cheek. There was something camp in his willingness to see the whole polite world shaken to pieces. He sought to protect Feisal not against some FO clique but against Britain itself. The collapse which followed his return to the UK and the regression to the role of a despised Other Rank are generally ascribed to a sense of guilt and failure in Arabia, but perhaps they were due also to his apprehension of having succeeded: he had betrayed the British no less than Feisal. Bursting out of his bondage, the bastard escaped his sense of shame and inferiority by identifying with an alien world.

The 'egotism' of the dissident, the want of team spirit which so offends the housemasters of the old school, is highly volatile: it seeks at once to rise as high as possible (to make the biggest stink it can) and to dissipate itself. It seeks both individual fame and assimilation, absorption in some generality. Such a man dreams of domination, of avenging himself on the society which gave him birth but no place (Hitler). If he cannot master his environment, and make the world his own, then he must become its slave. Superhuman energy and will are released so long as circumstances (and youth) suggest the possibility of an impossible revolution, in which he will be 'recognised'. Disillusion and self-hatred follow even achievements which seem quite remarkable to others. Wit is often the playful gunpowder with which the solitary bastard hopes to blast entrenched defences. It is a weapon as ambivalent as himself: to be effective it must give pleasure to those it is aimed to explode. The more the wit is admitted to have made his point, the more established, and impotent, he becomes. The breach in the walls becomes the niche he has made for himself; he comes to belong to what he intended to subvert. His solitude, the loneliness of a particular case not the alienation of a class, fails to gain him the confidence or support of other 'revolutionaries'; he is marooned in cleverness. If he has no time for the established order, his wit makes no sense without it. Distrusted by the political opponents of society, because he refuses their 'discipline', he finds no comradeship there.

When Lawrence sought to be absorbed in the anonymity of the oppressed, he chose the Forces, whose Other Ranks are obliged to the defence of a realm which promises them subjection. In an emergency, the underpaid mercenaries of Authority may be called upon to repress a revolution with which, from a class point of view, they may sympathise but which will regard them with even more hatred than their officers.

For T.E.L., the complexities of British society had been happily obscured by the sentimental and alien harshness of desert life. He sought in the ranks the saddest of all answers to his mental anguish: the duty not to think. The renunciation of intelligence was a condition of service. Maybe his Arabian experiences more postponed his despair than caused it. Perhaps orgasm, if it occurred when he was whipped and raped (T.C. Worsley's experience suggests it did), at least provided a paragraph, a break, in the surge of neurosis.

T.E.L.'s death on the motorcycle is perfect. He could no longer find his quietus in an ordered world. He could not sit still, but he was as alone as ever; motion took the place of action. Having lost faith in any Movement, he took his place astride a powerful machine which gave him the illusion of purposeful speed. Speed is abstract revolution; revs per minute take the place of social change.

Acceleration overtakes argument; the speed fiend anticipates the future by getting there first. But he no sooner stops than he finds the world unchanged; the pedestrian catches up with him. Those who crave speed come to crave nothing else. Yet it is the systematically futile escape of those who are prisoners of themselves: the more successful their escape from others, the more surely they end up alone with themselves. For the solipsist, speed is both the prison and the tunnel. T.E.L. could never go fast enough to escape himself.

The most sweetly suggestive rumour about T.E.L.'s death is about the Big Black Car seen on the usually deserted road where he died. Were Foreign Agents involved? Did They (whoever they were) come to avenge themselves on the bastard who had screwed them? The truth is probably simpler and more mundane. Given the chance a man will die appropriately, T.E.L. must have known that he had to go. He had blown his own road to public advancement and was committed to a plunge into a private inferno. He resembled the man in *The Killers* who was waiting for them to show up; except that he was waiting for himself. He was the only executioner who knew where to find him. With what contentment, what final peacefulness he must have enjoyed those split seconds when something, at last, was more inevitable than pain: extinction. Before the astonished, indifferent eyes of a party of racegoers who had lost their way (in their big, black car), he took his medicine and made his final statement, at 7000 revs per minute. They most likely greeted his self-destruction, as did the British in general, with 'What was that all about?'

Like the Arabists in the F.O., but for different reasons, he wished pastoral simplicity on the Arabs. He was not like them, but wished that he might be; he would then have been without his inner demons. More than their virility he admired their mindlessness. He envied not only their nomadic confidence but also their divine venality; they were exquisitely shameless.

I was playing bridge with my father when I was called to the phone. P.R. of C.M.A.: would I be interested in doing Henry James's *Portrait of a Lady*, with Faye Dunaway and – wait for it! – Jonathan Miller? I said I liked James and I liked Faye. It would depend on the deal. 'I presume you'd want $250,000.' He was putting the film together; no deal yet, but he was sure he could get one.

W. and P. invited us to meet Jim and Nancy Dine. P. said, 'It's time I cooked for you.' But then Lee Friedlander arived, P. had a cold and she asked if we'd like to go to a Japanese restaurant. They had these private rooms for six, she would ask the guy if we could have one for seven. Turned out he was upset because they were specially designed for six; seven big Westerners would unbalance things. *Sukyaki* (sp.?) had to be cooked at the table. 'I know,' I said, 'you're asking me if I'd mind eating alone someplace else.' 'Oh Freddie, don't be silly. You're kidding.'

I went to meet the others at W. and P.'s flat. It seemed fuller, hence smaller, than before. W.'s studio is now cluttered, with rolls of paper under the piano, which had been moved against the wall from the bay. An extra, make-shift leaf of his desk, supported on a pair of kitchen steps and a polystyrene box, has a movieola screwed to it. On the walls are more photographs, one of a very pregnant naked woman (P.?), backlit to the point of abstraction, and memorable. The rootless conceptions of his paintings hung clean among the conspicuous clutter. Only the plaster reliefs, with their tumorous colours, fail to convince or charm. P.'s white plastic forms, idealised male genitals, have lost their pristine tumescence. They hang like wrinkled, bled lights in a butcher's window. The sound equipment walled the room with music. W. was behind his desk, a cat curled on the typewriter at his elbow, warming the cold hammers.

Lee, hair brushed straight back and dark with fixative, stood against a high stool. Appetisers on the work table: cheap *pâtés*, cheese, butter, biscuits. Pale grey eyes framed in tiredness, Lee carries a defiant New York air, without the aggression. He takes no pride in it, but he has turned down more work than W. has ever been offered. W. affects the jargon of the kids (motherfucker, etc.), where Lee simply uses it, where he wants to.

B., bare-armed in her short (Israeli) leather skirt, sat on a low leather chair, at an angle unfamiliar to me. She looked up almost shyly, but shamelessly, caught at something she was enjoying: the attention of two men. I was alarmed not so much by jealousy as by the unmistakable evidence that she could live apart from me. The brightness in her eyes did not need me to turn it on.

Had I had a good day? I was reticent about P.R.'s (bogus?) offer, as if to harbour a secret from (and against) these people who had not needed my company. The enclosed warmth of the evening had been punctured, not seasoned, by my arrival. A woman creates her own history, the history of sex itself, and I was not a part of it. Migraine threatened, the hammer of irretrievable isolation. I despised quickly these easy riders on the tide of the modern, W. and Lee. I envied their familiarity with the vocabulary I lacked, though it was, of course, none of their invention. B. fell outside all that: she never affects any modishness of speech. What she says is never trite but never calculated to shock, impress or conform. She has an obstinate, classical un-datedness. She seemed grown up when I met her; and she has not aged since. When she is excited, unexaggerated naïveté bubbles from her. Her humility is arrogant enough to disdain modishness. She has instinctive dress-sense and a trained intelligence. Pre-dating cynicism, she remains fresh because she is capable of joy. She would be ill-suited to the motherfucking contingent, were they as revolutionary in fact as in their chat, but they like her very much. They appreciate her personality: she does her own thing without (thank God) ever calling it that. Neither opinionated nor aggressive, she has opinions and knows how to attack. There is no one quite like her. Why do I feel, at times, such frustration and resentment? Because she lacks not faults but vices. I resent her discontent, when it shows itself, because her happiness is the reward I expect for spending my life with her.

Her completeness, the ease with which she turned from one man to another, smiling, left me alone. My own need for her seemed vulgar, and childish, but there it was, and is. My hold on her becomes strangely tenuous, given that we are two people in a conventional relationship. We do not explore the vanities of 'freedom' or grant each other licence to fish in unterritorial waters. We are possessive, both of us. Was the not undiluted sorrow she showed at the cancellation of *Guilt* due, maybe, to allayed anxiety about what I might get up to if my ambitions were realised? Did my own strange lack of deep regret derive from some similar relief?

B. believes that W. is very ill. He is convinced that he will die young. Few males in his family pass sixty. He likes to think that he is very hip, in the fashion of the unillusioned 'kids', but he employs the courtship tactics of the eternal ailing boy. He tells B. that he has a lump on his back, which *moves* (fatal sign) as well as piles, or at least an irritated anus. The wonder is that he survives at all. He is, as Gene Massin said brutally (responding to brutality) years ago, a talented *designer*. He has burdened himself, irrelevantly, with an artist's aesthetic baggage. He cannot help equating himself with the great masters (and the great frauds) and calls them all by their Christian names, 'Andy' *en tête*. He succeeds only in making a phoney of himself, despite his skills. He cannot accept the image of himself as a hired hand, with the flag down and the meter ticking; no, he says that he is more than that. He would like to believe that he is a potted 'Bucky' Fuller, inspiredly patronising his patrons. They are less than generous to him. He is to fly to New York on a charter flight from Gatwick which takes eleven hours. ('Bloody reliable though, those old bi-planes,' I managed to say.) 'Sixty quid return. And there should be some funny people.' Who laughs at an eleven-hour joke?

We went to collect the Dines in Chester Square, where, W. told me, they had been 'given' a house, while the owners are in the US; in fact they have rented it, perhaps at cost. I was reminded of the days when Al Kaplan gave a party in his swankily decorated house. The square was full of big cars and Eatonian assurance. Now it seems cramped, almost seedy. I went there a year ago to look at Cyril Lord's house. He was still a ranking tycoon, but a suspicious eye might have seen, in the extravagant entrails of the place, the symptoms of coming bankruptcy. Why should he be selling somewhere so sumptuously carpentered with ingenious built-in fittings, so tailored to the specific needs of a (very small) man that no incoming tenant would want to keep any of them?

Nancy D. is quite a tall, good-looking girl. She wore a long floral, cherry-coloured cotton dress, black tights. Like all slaves of fashion, she has a tense watchfulness which makes you think that she is judging you when she is actually trying to see if you are one of the jury. Dine, irreversibly bald above and wilfully hirsute at the cheeks, wore check slacks and a white sweater. Short and neat, he is like a man in light training, bobbing about but avoiding any heavy encounter. We talked about fighting. W. alone admitted to a pugnacious past; baffled by the variety and complexity of the intellectual, he clings to memories of physical solutions. His manual dexterity gives him a link with the working man. Quick fists encourage him to believe that there can be an alternative to quick thinking.

Lee, whom you might think addicted to honest American brawn, is absolutely unwilling to get into anything physical. In Cheyenne, Wyoming, he went to a dance full of cowboys. He asked a girl to dance and suddenly found himself grabbed from behind and warned: 'No fighting in here.' He couldn't imagine what they were talking about until he saw another man being held back on the far side of the floor. It was the girl's beau, a big cowboy with the reputation of being 'the town fighter'. He was always looking for fights and now he had seen good reason. Lee said, 'Man, I'm not fighting anybody.' It took some time, and no little self-abasement, to avoid being dragged outside to his fate. Lee said that he put on his 'white-trash look', and showed us what it was: he was transformed into a goofy, slack-jawed hick. In fact he is Odyssean, evasively clever without being cowardly; he will go in anywhere, but can always escape by riding out under the sheep, or pretending to be one. His gormlessness becomes a kind of wit, a joke that only he can see, and allows him, as a photographer, to report more inside information that anyone with evident signs of astuteness could ever hope to get away with. The camera may report, but it does not report *back*: it has a vigilant neutrality. Lee is a spy without a spymaster; an assassin who leaves no wound. He is amused by the contrast between his apparent aimlessness and the furtive accuracy of his marksmanship.

We smoked some pot, passing around the joint with dutiful, baleful, watchful nonchalance. I hadn't smoked in years. I would have felt no less strange if the joint had been an ordinary cigarette. Nancy handed me the wet butt with the usual air of conspiratorial banality. B. refused it after me; unashamed, as usual, by being exactly who she was. Perhaps my sense of loneliness was increased by the smoke, as it was years ago in Fuengirola. I have never been comforted by drugs. Can it really be that the most exciting things in life involve self-destruction? Is it anything but contemptible to foist addiction (for *Christ's* sake) on one's children as R.F., one of their idols, is said to have done?

What is it about photographers that make them the totems of the time? Photography is the art-form of the eye/I-generation; it sees but it does not penetrate; photographers miss nothing but do not create anything either. They *take* photographs; not even the most transcriptive painter *takes* his landscapes. Camera Man shoots pictures as someone with fleas scratches, without thought but not without purpose.

Lee put on a purple, almost fluorescent shirt with chromium poppers in order to go out to dinner, a narrow green waistcoat over it. We went, in the end, to San Frediano. My only common ground among the company was with Nancy Dine: we discussed migraine like old campaigners. San Frediano was expensive and busy. When Lee called for pepper, he was ignored, until a waiter hurriedly passed him a huge mill from an adjacent table. With something of the same hick look that had baffled the Cheyenne fighter, he slid it immediately into his camera bag and then, with an air of increased irritation, asked the original waiter when he was going to get his pepper. I was not sure whether I was impressed by Lee's cool or squarely shocked by it. A joke was a joke, but it was also a theft. The restaurant was, I daresay, robbing us, but casuistry could not quite allay my feeling that it would have been better to complete the send-up by returning the mill rather than making off with it.

That dinner at the San Frediano, to which I made such small contribution, came at the height of 'the Sixties', a late-starting, prolonged decade which did not really come to an end until the Arab oil embargo after the 1973 Yom Kippur war. I was never part of the swinging world, but I had a fairly successful time on the roundabouts. Having had four feature films made in three years, I had the illusion that screenwriting was easy, enjoyable enough and highly lucrative. I saw no reason why, despite hiccups of disappointment, I should not get better, and even more successful, at it. Imagining my recent movies to have been apprentice pieces, I looked forward to earned opportunities for innovation and, maybe, mature masterpieces. In short, I had little idea of the movie business, of the fragility of fame or of the ironies of fate. I knew they affected other people's lives; I was not ready to experience them myself. But I did. The cancellation of *Guilt* was evidence that the era of what my friend David Deutsch called, with tactless accuracy, 'luxury pictures' was over. The movies went into a recession which seemed irretrievable. 20th Century Fox was obliged, by the catastrophe of *Cleopatra*, to sell many acres of its back lot for, it was said, some $10,000,000. On them was built what is now Century City, a modern suburb of shining, soaring offices, hotels, theaters and malls. Spiro Skouras, who presided over Fox during those lean years, probably concluded the worst deal a Greek has ever made: a Greek gift that *was* a gift.

In the Sixties, I used sometimes to meet Peter Sellers. We shared a tailor, in Douggie Hayward, whose shop in Mount Street turned into a club for wasp-waisted, well-heeled clients. Peter used to wink at me and say, 'They haven't found us out yet then, Fred.' I was fascinated and flattered by the movies, while they lasted, but I was aware – and never more than on that night at the San Frediano – that they were turning me into a writer with more credits than achievements. I had not written a book in three years. What I wrote was in response to what other people wanted of me. I was neither really in the movies nor did I belong to the hip world of which Jimmy Dine was a privileged star (he was about to have a retrospective at the Whitney) and in which Lee slouched with such noncommittal elegance. W. talked about 'my friend Paul McCartney' and seemed, after only a few months in London, to know all the people worth knowing. I was utterly superfluous. It is not an unfamiliar, or always uncongenial, role for the writer, but I was aware that I was not really writing: I was waiting for hire while pretending to be above that kind of thing, the mark of the gigolo down the ages. Not only did I fear that I was losing the love of my wife; I was not even sure that I deserved it. I did not find it easy to love myself.

In the October of 1969, after Paul and Sarah had gone back to Bedales, B. and I returned to our recently acquired house in the Perigord. I was determined to write a novel, but I had lost the confidence, and the aptitude, to begin. We had invited Clive Donner, who directed *Nothing but the Best*, my first movie, to come and stay in our new house, but I was in such a turmoil of creative impotence that I called and asked him not to come. I had written the first page of my new novel seventeen times. There was no second. I promised him lousy company. He said he would come anyway; he needed a holiday (after directing a movie for Charlie Feldman) and would stay at a nearby hotel. By the time he arrived, I had recovered my fictional fluency. Clive and I no longer communicate, for reasons which have nothing to do directly with him, but I shall never cease to be grateful for his company in those autumn days.

One afternoon, he and I went for a walk among the many walnut trees which, as the rain began to fall, dropped their heavy freight of nuts in our path. It seemed a shame to leave them lying where they were, so we went back and collected two baskets, which we filled as we strolled through the unfenced fields and woods. We returned for tea in the kitchen with B.

Not long afterwards, there was a knock. Our neighbour, Mme Barat, wanted to know if we had seen any strangers in the area. She had lost two baskets of walnuts. I said, with candid naïveté, that we should certainly have spotted anyone carrying baskets. A moment later, I realised that, whether she knew it or not (hindsight promises that she did), she had come to the culprits' house. In my innocence, I had no idea that walnuts were not common property and that the peasants knew *exactly* how fruitful the crop was. I made no secret of my embarrassment and immediately, apologetically, gave Christiane what was hers. Later that evening, her husband, Norbert, came down with a bottle of his home-distilled *eau de vie*, 100% proof that there were no hard feelings about the involuntary theft.

After dinner that night, Clive, B. and I drank most of the unlabelled bottle. I do not recall what the joke was, but we laughed more that night, more uninhibitedly, than I had for years. It was, it seemed, the end of some kind of pretence (of mine) that I was exempt from common stupidity, and simple pleasure. The purity of the alcohol left no trace. The next morning I resumed my novel with a furious vigour which I never lost.

Like Men Betrayed took place in a Greece which was like, but was never said to be identical with, the Greece which the Colonels had appropriated. I was so thoroughly lost in my creation that, when the village postman, in uniform and peaked cap, appeared at my work-room door with a telegram, I thanked him, with flourished fluency, in Greek.

The telegram, from Jo Janni, confirmed that the small hope that Warner Brothers were going to do *Guilt* had been extinguished. I did not feel the smallest regret. From time to time, hope was rekindled. On one occasion, Faye Dunaway asked me to call her in New York. We had no telephone at the house and I made the (then very expensive) call, after a long delay, from a nearby hotel. We talked for a while and then Faye asked if I could hang on while she went to get a cigarette. Of course. Fifteen minutes later, she picked up the phone again. She had had to go down to the corner. Was I still there? I was, but it didn't do me much good.

Like Men Betrayed did not find favour with my publishers. Tom Maschler said that he admired it but that he did not know quite what to do with it. Finally, he suggested that, since he did not want to insult me with a smaller advance than he had given me for *Orchestra and Beginners*, I be given no advance at all. Somehow I was persuaded that this was a mark of particular favour. There was, I suppose, something wilfully solemn about *Like Men Betrayed*; I was not only determined to make no concessions to commercialism, I had been horrified by what happened to Greece. I was painfully gratified when one of the critics, imagining that he was being savage, remarked that the book 'shows no sign whatever that the author has a sense of humour'. During the Sixties I had made so many jokes, and tried so hard to entertain and scandalise, that the critic's abuse felt like an accolade. Alone, uncommercial and unadmired, owing neither synopsis nor explanation to anyone, I was again the writer I always wanted, and want, to be.